Jurji Zaidan

Contributions to Modern Arab Thought and Literature

Jurji Zaidan

Contributions to Modern Arab Thought and Literature

Proceedings of a Symposium
The Library of Congress
(June 5, 2012)

Edited by

George C Zaidan

and

Thomas Philipp

Published by The Zaidan Foundation, Inc.

ISBN: 098484354X
ISBN 13: 9780984843541
Library of Congress Control Number: 2013919038

The Zaidan Foundation
For Enhancing Intercultural Understanding, Inc

7007 Longwood Drive
Bethesda, MD 20817
Email: george@zaidanfoundation.org
Website www.zaidanfoundation.org
Tel/Fax: (301) 469-7231

For Hada

my wife, and our son

George Shukri

Contents

Preface

The essays comprising this volume were commissioned by the Zaidan Foundation for a Symposium on ***Jurji Zaidan's Contributions to Modern Arab Thought and Literature.*** The Symposium was sponsored by the Library of Congress, the Kluge Center and the Zaidan Foundation and held at the Library of Congress on June 5th, 2012 in Washington DC.[1] The essays were prepared by a group of eminent scholars in literature, history and other disciplines in leading universities in the US, Canada, France and the Middle East working on the Nahda or Arab awakening[2] of the late nineteenth and early twentieth centuries and, in particular, on Jurji Zaidan's leading role in this movement.

The Zaidan Foundation was established in 2009 to enhance inter-cultural understanding. The publication of the Proceedings of the Symposium is part of its efforts to bring the thought and literary treasures of Jurji Zaidan to English-speaking readers. Jurji Zaidan was a well-known leader of the Nahda. His leadership derived from the many roles he played in that movement—as historian, linguist, novelist, journalist, educator, political scientist, social reformer and much more. The Foundation is promoting his contributions in many of these areas through various initiatives.

---

1 The Library of Congress webcast of the Symposium is in two Parts. Part (1) covers the morning session at: http://www.loc.gov/today/cyberlc/feature_wdesc.php?rec=5576 Part (2) follows at: http://www.loc.gov/today/cyberlc/feature_wdesc.php?rec=5575 Press and TV coverage of the Symposium and many other details of this event are posted on the Zaidan Foundation's website at www.zaidanfoundation.org

2 For more on the significance of this term see the last section of Thomas Philipps' Overview.

First, the Foundation has so far sponsored the translation of five of his twenty one historical novels into English. In the hundred years since they were written almost all these novels were translated into one or more languages—there were more than one hundred translations but surprisingly none into English. Of the five novels, two are set in Spain, two others are set during the 'Abbasid period and the fifth novel deals with Saladin.[3] All the essays in this volume reviewing Zaidan's contributions as a historical novelist were prepared by several of the translators of these novels—all eminent literary scholars in their own right.

Second, the Foundation is supporting a new evaluation of how Jurji Zaidan's approach to history and the Arabic language shaped Arab nationalism. The author is Professor Thomas Philipp, a leading expert on the thought of Zaidan. His book is entitled ***Jurji Zaidan and the Foundations of Arab Nationalism.***[4] It is the first to analyze Zaidan's thought on history, language and nationalism as an integrated whole.

The above initiatives leave several "gaps" so to speak in covering some of the areas that Zaidan influenced in important ways—in particular his role as journalist, political scientist, educator and social reformer. The essays commissioned for the Symposium on Jurji Zaidan and published in this volume cover some of these areas from a variety of different angles. Indeed, the aim of the Symposium was to bring together scholars with an interest in the intellectual and literary legacy of Jurji

---

3 The five novels were all published by the Zaidan Foundation, Inc. in 2011 and 2012. They are available at www.amazon.com and are in historical chronological order:

1. *The Conquest of Andalusia* translated by Roger Allen, October 2011.
2. *The Battle of Poitiers* subtitled *Charles Martel and 'Abd al-Rahman* translated by William Granara, March 2012.
3. *The Caliph's Sister* subtitled *Harun al-Rashid and the Fall of the Persians* translated by Issa J. Boullata, March 2012.
4. *The Caliph's Heirs* subtitled *Brothers at War: The Fall of Baghdad* translated by Michael Cooperson, March 2012.
5. *Saladin and the Assassins* translated by Paul Starkey, March 2012.

4 Philipp, Thomas (New-York, Syracuse University Press, 2014).

Zaidan and in his role in the Nahda. A second goal was to let this collection reflect the state of scholarship on Zaidan's works and thought in the various academic disciplines. Until recently the tomes of A.L. Dupont and T. Philipp were the only scholarly monographs[5] on Zaidan. The response by scholars interested in the subject was most encouraging and revealed an unexpected new interest in Zaidan and the Nahda. I was both surprised and delighted to realize how much research and study on the Nahda and Zaidan was being done in leading Western universities. "Jurji Zaidan" is no household name in the West the way it is in the Arab world where his novels are still published every few years. But the serious research that is being done in the West on the Nahda is no less—and some would say more—than the research that is occurring in the Arab-speaking world. The contributors to this volume have demonstrated how rich Zaidan's works are and how much they still have to tell us almost a century after his death. By applying the analytic tools of different academic disciplines and by putting Zaidan's work in the wider context of the Nahda, the Symposium shed much new light and opened perspectives on his scholarly, journalistic and literary works. It is hoped that it will stimulate more scholarship on Zaidan and the Nahda movement—a cultural and historical phenomenon that deserves our full and renewed attention. This research is encouraging not only in its own right but also because it is especially relevant and timely with the tumultous events unleashed by what is being dubbed as the Arab Spring.

In all these ways the Foundation plans to support as broad an area as possible of Zaidan's contributions. It is particularly fitting that both the Proceedings of the Symposium and the aforementioned book by Thomas Philipp are being published on the occasion of the hundredth anniversary of Jurji Zaidan's death in 1914.

---

5 Dupont, Anne-Laure. *Ǧurǧī Zaydān 1861-1914: Écrivain réformiste et témoin de la Renaissance arabe* (Damas, Institut Français du Proche-Orient, 2006) and Philipp, Thomas. Ǧurǧī *Zaidān: His Life and Thought*. Beiruter Texte und Studien, vol. 3 (Beirut, Franz Steiner Verlag, 1979).

The activities sponsored by the Foundation could not have come to fruition without the support and dedication of so many people too numerous to mention. But let me single out a few who were instrumental in making the Symposium possible and as successful as it turned out to be: at the Library of Congress Dr. James Billington, the Librarian of Congress and Mary-Jane Deeb, Chief of the African and Middle Eastern Division and her staff, in particular Christopher Murphy and Muhannad Salhi, for their sponsorship and support of the Symposium; Dr Isma'il Serageldin, the Director of the Library of Alexandria, for documenting Jurji Zaidan's legacy in the Memory of Modern Egypt Series he spearheaded in that Library as well as his keynote address at the Symposium; and all the other contributors to the Symposium for their enriching perspectives of Zaidan as well as their collegiality, patience and help in putting this volume together. Finally, special thanks are due to Professor Thomas Philipp for helping me in the design of the Symposium and editing this volume; and to all the members of the Foundation's Advisory Council and, in particular, Ambassador Hussein Hassouna, for promoting, tirelessly and effectively, the work of the Foundation in so many ways. Last but not least I owe a special debt of gratitude to my wife, Hada, who had the original idea for several of the works sponsored by the Foundation. She and our son George Shukri worked tirelessly in helping me to transform so many ideas into the products supported by the Foundation and described above.

George C. Zaidan
President
The Zaidan Foundation
November, 2013

A Note on Transliteration

To make the reading less cumbersome, Arabic book and Journal titles, proper nouns and names as well as other Arabic words have generally been rendered in the text of this volume in a simplified form of transliteration. They all appear in full transliteration in the footnotes and the Bibliography. The transliteration follows the rules suggested by the International Journal of Middle Eastern Studies with one exception: the silent alif in the article al- is shown by a straight single quotation mark thus ['] and not by a dash.

The Editors

Jurji Zaidan in His Forties (*Courtesy of Fedorof*)

Jurji Zaidan
(1861-1914)

Jurji Zaidan with his family circa 1908. From left to right are wife Maryam, daughter Asma, son Emile and Jurji holding in his lap youngest son, Choucri (Shukri).

Jurji Zaidan at his desk.

Overview

Thomas Philipp

Jurji Zaidan's Life and Times

Jurji Zaidan (1861-1914), son of an illiterate restaurateur (*qahwaji*), was an autodidact par excellence and a self-made-man. Apart from two years in his youth with a cane-beating and bigoted priest, learning incomprehensible psalms by heart, and in his teens spending one year in the medical school of the Syrian Protestant College (SPC), all of Zaidan's learning was self-taught. In 1882, he left Beirut for Cairo following a prohibition on the teaching of evolutionary theory by overzealous missionaries in the SPC and his participation in a student strike protesting these limits to free speech. When he arrived in Cairo he gave up the idea of continuing his medical studies and worked for a while in the newspaper business. In 1884, he joined the Wolseley expedition as an interpreter, together with his close friend Jabr Dumit. The expedition, sent to save Gordon in Khartoum came too late. After returning to Cairo from the Sudan, Zaidan and his friend continued on to Beirut, where he met all his old friends and teachers. He immersed himself in the study of ancient languages and participated in the ongoing debates about contemporary issues—not the least being the theory of evolution. This must have been a very intensive intellectual experience for him. He probably settled then on a career as a writer. His first book, on the philosophy of language, was published when he was twenty-five. In 1886, again with his friend Jabr Dumit, he traveled to England, where they spent a whole month reading in the British Museum. There, Zaidan read systematically for the first time European Orientalist writings.[1] But by the winter Zaidan was back in Cairo. He worked first as an administrative manager for the journal *al-Muqtataf*, gave Arabic lessons and wrote books on history[2] and in 1891 published his first historical novel, *The Fugitive Mamluk,*[3] which was very successful. Encouraged by this success and by his experience with *al-Muqtataf* he launched in 1892 his largest project, the magazine *al-Hilal.* Together with *al-Muqtataf* launched by Ya'qub Sarruf and Faris Nimr and *al-Manar* by Rashid Rida, these magazines provided the most important intellectual forum of the Arab Nahda. They introduced new ideas, translated essays from Western journals, popularized modern sciences and technologies, discussed Arabic literature, reformed the language, offered new interpretations of Arab history, and debated needed reforms of society. Zaidan was now definitely settled in Cairo. He had become a well established writer, living a bourgeois life and gathering a wide circle of friends around him, which included Muslims and Christians, Syrians and Egyptians and the occasional Orientalist visitor from Europe. He remained an extremely private man—participation in organizations and public activities, especially of the political kind were alien to him—until his popularity and fame as a writer gave him a public role. For the last twenty-two years of his life he managed an enormous workload: he continued editing the monthly *al-Hilal* to which he was also the main contributor; he wrote multi-volume scholarly works on Arab history and literature and some twenty one[4] historical novels which popularized his scholarly findings. With that output he became, in spite of being a somewhat shy person, a very public person, which made him a typical representative of the Nahda. The

1 See A.L. Dupont's essay in this volume.

2 For a complete listing of all his works see the bibliography at the end of this volume.

3 *Al-Mamlūk al-Shārid.*

4 The bibliography of Zaidan lists twenty two novels but one of these, Lovers' Struggle, is not a historical novel.

Nahdawis' major activity was writing and debating a wide range of topics. Their public forum was the evolving press, in which they all participated in one way or another. The essay, more than the novel or the scholarly work, were their preferred means of communication and debate.

The Nahda, often described as a literary revival, was much more than that. It referred to, reproduced and analyzed in the widest sense all aspects of modernity as it was developing in Europe and America—in contrast to the European Renaissance, which harked back to a classical period of the past. But it would be wrong to reduce the Nahda to a mere "translation movement" and the copying of the concepts and ideas of modernity. In the process of translating, summarizing or adapting texts into Arabic they were analyzed, criticized and put into a relevant Arab societal context. The interests pursued and topics debated covered everything from the thought of the Enlightenment to modern sciences; from ancient Arab history to modern nationalism; from the natural rights of men and women to evolutionary theory. Opinions about these issues and their analytical interpretation varied widely. Radical secularists, Muslim reformers, Arab nationalists, Ottoman constitutionalists and others participated in this discourse, which lasted from the 1830s until World War I and was carried out mainly in journals published in Beirut and Cairo. Together they formed a secular intellectual elite, promoting a secular liberalism in Arab society. They considered themselves the guides to a better future of society and opposed and replaced to a large degree the traditional educated elite trained in religious studies. In their discourse over the movement's aims and the means to reach them, the Nahdawis tackled several issues successfully—however much they may have differed in social background and educational experience. The most important and lasting was certainly the reform of the classical Arabic language and the creation of a modern standard Arabic as the print language serving all readers of Arabic. Similarly, the construction of a secular narrative of Arab history—distinct from that of Islamic history—preoccupied many Nahdawis. Their ideas on how best to enlighten and educate the individual were closely connected to their faith in the progress of society. The debates over all these questions were accompanied by the continuous inquiry into the meaning of the modern natural sciences, evolutionary theory, the thoughts of the Enlightenment, the program of the French Revolution and with the ideas of nationalism, liberalism and constitutionalism. Zaidan was as much a product of this movement as one of its leaders.

Contributions to this Volume

The contributions to this volume were not intended to cover all possible angles and aspects of Zaidan's monumental work. But we can recognize certain clusters of themes. The first would be the attempt to locate Zaidan in his general intellectual and also moral and ethical environment and the general impact of his work to this day. A further thematic cluster concerns his scholarly works on history and his essays on society and politics, mainly written in his later years. A third cluster is the analysis of the role of his historical novels in the history of modern Arab literature as well as how they reflect his own ideas and times. He deliberately used the novels as a pedagogical tool to familiarize the readers with their history and to encourage and prepare them to read more scholarly works. In a way, the novels are today perhaps the most alive and tangible testimony of the impact of Zaidan's work. Their most recent translations into English and Uighur and the regularly reprinted Arabic editions are evidence of this, as are the frequently heard statements by educated Arabs of how his novels initiated their interest in and knowledge of Arab history— as attested by Isma'il Serageldin and Georges Corm in their essays.

The papers of Isma'il Serageldin, Georges Corm and Jens Hanssen belong to the first cluster. Isma'il Serageldin, in a broad brush survey touches on all the important aspects of Zaidan's work and life. He puts an emphasis on Zaidan's role in founding the mass media, i.e. the press, and lauds his efforts to find the right balance between the emulation of the

West by popularizing the European natural sciences and thought while reviving the traditional cultural roots of the East. Serageldin recognizes him as the first to have written a major historical study of Islamic culture. He also mentions the influence of European Orientalism on Zaidan, an issue that Anne-Laure Dupont discusses extensively in her contribution to this volume. For Serageldin Zaidan is a "prismatic" author which seems to be an accurate description of Zaidan's intellectual activities. In the process of reading and absorbing materials on history or literature, for instance, he analysed and studied them and did not just simplify the information to popularize it but shed new light and interpretations on the material he passed on.

Georges Corm's paper describes how Jurji Zaidan's contributions as a historian, novelist, linguist, publisher and journalist played a central role in developing a secular Arab identity and consciousness. Zaidan's work was close to that of many prominent reformist Muslim scholars who sought to modernize Islam and make it more relevant to the modern world. This made for a tolerant relationship between Muslim and Christian Arab intellectuals that characterized the "secular liberal age" of the Nahda. The secular military dictatorships that came to many Arab states, starting in the 1950s and the extreme, narrow and rigid forms of Islamism, supported by powerful oil-exporting Arab countries, displaced the Nahda heritage. For the author, the present lack of awareness of the intellectual achievements of the Nahda constitutes in fact a dangerous breakdown of the modern Arab collective memory. This stifles efforts to build on its accumulated knowledge and intellectual heritage, inhibiting efforts to continue to extricate Arab societies from all their social, political and economic ills and their total dependence on regional and international powers. The author makes an impassionate plea to rediscover Jurji Zaidan's intellectual achievements, which should be complemented by simultaneous efforts to reinstate the very rich patrimony of the Arab Nahda, especially in the context of the present Arab fluid political transformations.

Jens Hanssen approaches Zaidan and the Nahda from a very different angle. He begins by pointing out how easy it is to this day to suppress or obliterate the existence of the Nahda—not only as Georges Corm observes in the Middle East but even more so in Western scholarship. Hanssen takes this as a challenge to critically analyse the Nahda and uncover its many layers and origins. This entails the dissolution of a monolithic image of the Nahda but also promises to provide a much richer picture of heterogeneous and contrasting elements, arranged and rearranged in a constant analysis about the meaning of the Nahda. He recognizes Hourani's model of organising various groups of Nahdawis by generation, but replaces its "methodological constant of interacting with the West" with "shifts in urbanisation, political events and socio-economic processes in Bilad al-Sham". This leads him to associate Zaidan with the generation which eye-witnessed the massacres of 1860 in Damascus and Mt. Lebanon. Under the impact of these events this generation pleaded for a more harmonious and civilized society. Central to this demand was a new morality of social responsibility and cohesiveness. Zaidan's autobiography, in particular, testifies to his role as a public moralist.

In the second cluster we find four essays all concerned with Zaidan's works in the social sciences concerning history, society, and politics. Anne-Laure Dupont follows the influences of European Orientalists on Zaidan's historical writings. She traces the persons, travels and extensive readings of Zaidan that led him to the Orientalists—and, eventually, the Orientalists to him. There is no doubt that Zaidan admired the achievements of many Orientalists and was influenced by their thinking and methodology. Alfred von Kremer's concept of "Culturgeschichte"[5] is only one example. But he also could be very critical of Orientalism and in the quintessential Occident-versus-Orient dispute between Renan and al-Afghani[6] he sided with the latter. As a "colonial citizen" and

5 "The History of Culture."

6 See Anne-Laure Dupont's essay in this volume.

national thinker he operated in an intellectual field of tension, admiring the achievements of the Orientalists but wanting to develop an authentic Arab narrative of history. Dupont puts it well, when she observes that he felt gratitude for the Orientalists' work but felt at the same time that the Arabs should take over their own historiography. He himself, according to Dupont, tried this by constructing a new periodization of Arab history, which gave him the opportunity to integrate Arabo-Muslim history with World history. Arabo-Muslim history provided the link and mediation between Antiquity and the Modern Age. Also as an actor of history, it incorporated heretofore unknown peoples into world history through the expansion of Islam. Zaidan also set out to expand Arab history to link it through Babylonia and Hamurabi to Antiquity. Among Eastern scholars he was bitterly attacked. They did not perceive this intellectual tension in him. As Dupont tells it, they disqualified him either as depending too much on Orientalism (Muslim scholars) or not having understood Orientalism sufficiently (Christian scholars). Both were united, it seems, in their opposition to his secular interpretations of history. As Dupont observes, the Nahda was not a fixed frame of reference within which Zaidan worked, but a fluid "intellectual construction, in which he vigorously participated".[7]

Marwa Elshakry analyzes Zaidan's studies of the Arabic language and demonstrates how its sacred origin in the community of the believers was replaced with an evolutionary linguistic explanation centered around the community of the language. This secularization of the history of language is part and parcel of a secular interpretation of Arab history. Elshakry follows the development of Zaidan's attempts to organize and periodize Arab history from an extended pre-Islamic time to a Modern Age, which is based on the sciences. Central for her discussion is the introduction by Zaidan of several "Golden Ages"; one in Antiquity, or what he called the First *Jahiliyya*, a second in the *Jahiliyya* just before Islam in combination with the early rise of Islam and, a third one in the

7 Ibid.

early 'Abbasid period. She observes astutely that *every* golden age is by definition followed by a decline. Zaidan constructs here a cyclical alternation between golden ages and decline and is thereby able to place the Nahda of his own time at the beginning of a new "Golden Age" for the Arabs. This was preceded, as Cooperson says by a long period of decline which began with "the advent of the Ottomans, or the Mongols, or even the Buyids". This construction gives Zaidan an alternative to the Orientalists' constructions of Arabo-Islamic history that allows him to define the role of the Nahda of his time and legitimize the responsibilities that the new class of educated secular intellectuals claimed for itself.

Thomas Philipp's essay makes a foray into the rather unknown territory of Zaidan's political and social thought. The victory of the Japanese over the Russians in 1905—a victory of a constitutional political system over a notoriously autocratic European power—is the source of Zaidan's interest not only as political history but in terms of a contest between political systems. Philipp traces the development of Zaidan's analysis which became predominant in his thought with the Ottoman revolution. Constitutionalism and the belief in social progress—products of the Enlightenment—made of Zaidan an enthusiastic supporter of the Ottoman Empire after the Young Turk revolution. Here, too, as discussed in other essays, we can observe the admiration for European ideas or models even as he used them to counter the threat of European imperialism. However, what remains puzzling is his enthusiastic support for the Ottoman Empire after he had dedicated his life to construct an Arab history and an Arab identity. In the end, a multiplicity of possible reasons are given to explain his views.

At first sight it may appear that Zaïneb Ben Lagha's essay belongs to the third cluster of "historical novels" because it is exclusively concerned with novels. However, it does not cover their literary history or their impact on readers and the mass media. Neither does the essay analyze the historical information in the novels. Instead Ben Lagha uses the novels to ascertain Zaidan's views on women. Interestingly enough it is the anachronisms in his historical novels that draw her interest—something she shares with Michael Cooperson, writing on how the novels affect historical representation in television series today. When she analyzes the anachronistic dialogues between women about their rights and demands for freedom, these historical novels leave the category, which Roger Allen calls "The way it was" and shifts to the one called "The way it will be" or, perhaps, to what he calls the "Distant Mirror".[8] Ben Lagha pursues the discussion of the emancipation of women in Egypt, brought to the attention of the public by the books of Qasim Amin at the turn of the twentieth century. She is able with a careful reading of the novels to tease out a great amount of information about Zaidan's precise position in this debate and the ideas he disseminated in his novels about this topic. But it has to be pointed out that this is not a fundamentalist case[9] of using an idealized past to build a utopian future. The Nahdawis were interested in building their own society in their own life time. They did not need to construct a utopia, because they knew what they were aiming at: the European culture and society of their time. Their unshakable faith in progress demanded only that they should initiate certain changes through education, which would then lead to a modern society according to their own laws.

The third cluster on the historical novel consists of three essays by Roger Allen, Michael Cooperson and William Granara. Taking a broad view of things, Allen tries to locate Zaidan's novels in the development of the European historical novel as well as in modern Arab literature, where the novel as a literary category was a new phenomenon. The English term "novel", as he points out, does not aim so much at the newness of the literary genre but at the times the novels describe, "history and

---

8 See Roger Allen's essay in this volume.

9 In the sense of going back to sources, mainly written, with the expectation that a literal understanding of the text, directly applied to society's morals and behaviour will lead to an ideal society, regardless of the changed historical circumstances.

society in motion". Allen's quote of Daiches[10] fits precisely Zaidan's historical novels and the Nahda movement as a whole. Providing several categories for the historical novel, Allen places Zaidan's in the category of "The way it was". This is certainly an accurate description as Zaidan often buttresses the novels' verisimilitude with scholarly quotations. Yet, if we look at Ben Lagha's analysis we find also examples of "The way it will be". Wisely, Allen refrains from determining "firstness" or a "single strand of development" of a literary genre. Whole complexities in European as well as Arab literary developments have to be considered as well as whole groups of authors. Only in such a context, he proposes, can it be stated that Zaidan played a significant and central role in the development of the Arab novel.

Michael Cooperson's essay moves into a different time zone, asking what impact these novels have today on historical series produced for television. He elaborates on a dispute between members of the Nahda about the "Golden Age" of Islamic history. A new tendency arose rehabilitating the Umayyad period because of its strong emphasis on its Arab character, considering that the "foreign" elements entering Islam in later periods were causes for its decline. The early 'Abbasid period was already idealized in the tenth century. This trend became even stronger in the nineteenth century and the Nahda movement, with Zaidan actively promoting this idealization by calling it the "First Nahda". Looking at the television episodes coinciding with Zaidan's novels, Cooperson observes that the premises of historical representation established by Zaidan are alive and well. The television productions are full of anachronisms just as the analysis by Ben Lagha had established for some of the novels. Scenes of debates over religion in the ninth century, using the terminologies of today have, according to Cooperson, a remarkable result: "the historicization" of religion, i.e. the undermining of the idea of religion as a once-revealed set of teachings and doctrines, whose truth is self-evident and unchangeable,

10 See Roger Allen's essay in this volume.

which is reminiscent of Protestant biblical research in the nineteenth century and later. To Cooperson's discussion of another series, shown on Iranian television, one can add that already by the 1930s all but one of Zaidan's novels had been translated into Persian. After the Islamic revolution of Iran in 1978/79 all have been reprinted or retranslated and they seem as popular today as ever.

Summarizing a long tradition of non-religious Arab literature to adapt to change, to innovate literary genres and to revise the Arabs' position in history, William Granara argues for the resilience of Arab literature. He sees the challenges to literature in the time of the Nahda in the particular fields of intellectual tensions Zaidan and his contemporaries had to face. One was the "conscious decision to embrace the *foreign* modern *European* novel as a literary site to launch a modern *Arabic national* literature" and the second was "the acceptance of western culture while at the same time rejecting western colonial rule". It was also a time of tremendous change in the Ottoman Empire and Arab society. Zaidan adopted the genre of the historical novel wholeheartedly, according to Granara, to create a pan-Arab identity to counter European expansionism. Zaidan chose to write three historical novels set in Arab Andalusia—the major point of contact and confrontation with Western Europe in the Middle Ages. Granara sees as historical cycles "the age of Gods, the age of heroes, and the age of men". He sees this sequential order in Zaidan's three Andalusian novels reflecting the growth of Zaidan's historical consciousness "from the epic to the romantic to the realistic".

The three clusters discussed above reviewed Jurji Zaidan's professional contributions. But beyond his professional life is the kind of man that Jurji Zaidan was and that enabled him to be so successful in so many different areas. This aspect is dealt with by his grandson, George C. Zaidan. His essay assesses the personal values and qualities that made his grandfather such an effective "cultural entrepreneur". Basing himself on the influence of Samuel Smiles' book *Self-help* had on the young Jurji, he convincingly describes his value system and qualities as that of the Victorian middle classes. Using articles that Jurji Zaidan wrote in *al-Hilal* he demonstrates how he sought to communicate to his readers his values of self-discipline, honesty, self-reliance, time-management, entrepreneurship and modesty. We also have the good fortune that Jurji Zaidan provided us with the first modern autobiography in Arab literature, which is a rich source for understanding how his formative years shaped his world view and ethics. But George Zaidan goes beyond using all these written sources. He also uses his unique access to family lore about Jurji Zaidan and his close interactions with his father and uncle to gauge the value system and qualities imparted by their father. This makes his analysis especially valuable. It also helps to explain their success in building Dar-al-Hilal into what became one of the biggest publishing house for periodicals in the Middle East. George Zaidan's essay is followed by five translated articles of Jurji Zaidan that illustrate many of the aspects he discusses in his paper.

Conclusions

Zaidan was a product of the Nahda, a major contributor to it, and one of its first historians. Looking at all the essays in this volume, some common issues debated therein emerge. Some have to do with what I would call "fields of intellectual tension", with which Zaidan had to deal: the tension between his great appreciation for Europe as the origin of modern science and knowledge, Enlightenment, Constitutionalism etc. on the one hand and the fear of Europe's expansionism, leading to the loss of one's own roots and identity and hence authenticity, on the other. Another example of these tensions is the tension between Enlightenment thought, relating the progress of society closely to a humanistic education, and the doctrine of social Darwinism or the survival of the fittest providing an alternative way of reaching the same goal of progress in society. Many of the essays also deal with the issue of defining the role of the Nahda and its fluid and evolving character, how it led to a secular construct of Arab history and Zaidan's contributions to and interpretations of the role of the Nahda.

*****

A postscript on the use of the term "*al-Nahda*" is appropriate. It comes from the Arabic root *n-h-ḍ,* and means "a single act of rising, a motion or movement ... also power, ability, strength".[11] In 1870 the term lacked any particular abstract meaning or connotation of a specific historical event.[12] When in 1868 al-Yaziji addressed his famous ode to the Arabs "Arise ye Arabs and awake" he did not use that term.[13] During the following twenty years, however, the term with that specific connotation must have become accepted. In 1888 *al-Muqtataf* used the term in connection with the contemporary development of Arab medicine.[14] In 1892 an article by Zaidan about the "latest Egyptian Nahda" appeared in the first volume of his magazine *al-Hilal*.[15] Neither in 1888 nor in 1892 is the term explained which implies that readers were by then familiar with it.

The term "*al-Nahda*" is most often translated as Renaissance or "Arab Renaissance", just as the European Renaissance is translated in Arabic as "*al-Nahda al-Urubbiyya*". To speak of the Nahda as a "Renaissance" suggests a European frame of history as a reference and as a normative standard of historical development. This, ironically, has always implied a European denial of historical development to Arab society or—for that matter—to the entire non-European world. It was not possible

11 Lane, E. W. *Arabic Language Dictionary* in 2 vols. (London, Williams & Norgate, 1863).

12 Al-Bustānī, Buṭrus. *Muḥīṭ al-Muḥīṭ* in 4 vols. (Beirut, s. n., 1867-1870) vol. 2, entry 2137.

13 "Tanabbahū wa-stafiqū ayyuha al-'Arab!" quoted below, the title of Antonius' *The Arab Awakening.*

14 "Nahḍat al-Ṭibb fī Miṣr," *al-Muqtaṭaf* 12 (Sept. 1888) pp. 735-9, p.753.

15 *Al-Hilāl* 1 (Nov. 1892) p.123.

to recognize the "normative" sequence of Renaissance, Humanism, Reformation, Revolution etc. in non-European histories; therefore Europeans considered only their own history as valid. This denial led in the worst case to a racist sense of European superiority and in its most benign version to the claim that these historical phases had taken centuries to develop in Europe and would take as long in the non-European world. The observed normative character of European historical development was conceived as a development each culture had to go through. Since that European experience was not one that was available to them, the historical "maturity" of these cultures is pushed into a utopian future.

Following all these observations, the term "*al-Nahda*" is consistently used in this volume in its anglicized form, in order to emphasize its unique and specific character. This seems a better solution than trying to describe it with inadequate or even misleading English expressions.

Part I

Jurji Zaidan and the Nahda

Jurji Zaidan's[1] Contributions to Modern Arab Thought and Literature

Ismail Serageldin

I. Introduction: Providing the Context

I am honored to have been invited to join in celebrating the legacy of a remarkable man, who in the short span of half a century, had a profound impact on the culture of his people, the history of his region, and the literature of his language. He helped forge the modern identity of the Arabs, founded the modern mass media there and brought culture to the broad public as he pioneered the use of the novel in Arabic. He was a man of letters who understood and publicized science; a man of the Christian faith who had a profound knowledge of Islam and the history of the Muslim peoples, and helped bring that history to life for generations of Muslims, including myself.

It is a remarkable legacy, and it is most appropriate that we should be celebrating this one hundred and fiftieth anniversary of his birth, and the one hundred and twentieth anniversary of the founding of his publishing enterprise (Dar al-Hilal) and his cultural magazine *al-Hilal*, which is the longest-lived and still functional cultural journal in the Arab World.

Let me start with a brief overview of Zaidan and his times. It was a remarkable period of change and transformation—called the period of

---

1 The spelling of the name varies from one text to another. Therefore, in direct quotes, the paper will retain the original transcription of the quote. However, the author of this paper will be using the agreed-upon spelling of the conference organizers for this work.

the Nahda or the "Arab Renaissance" or the "Arab Awakening", to use the title coined by George Antonius in his 1938 book.[2] Zaidan, I submit, was one of the artisans of that societal *prise de conscience.*

Like an unchecked cancer, bad governance had turned the once mighty Ottoman Empire into the "sick man of Europe". Ottoman ossification had brought the Arab and Muslim worlds to a new low. The jolt of reawakening was to come in the form of the French invasion of Egypt in 1798. After the French defeat and withdrawal, chaos reigned under the nominal suzerainty of the Ottomans until Muhammad 'Ali took the reins of power in Egypt and started his ambitious development and modernization programs. The momentum of reform was to continue, and by the second half of the nineteenth century, a true movement to modernize Egypt was underway.

It was in that world of transformation and transition that Zaidan would flourish. He was to make a signal contribution to this Arab Renaissance, the Nahda. Indeed he is considered by some like Philipp to have been "the archetypal member of the Arab Nahda (Awakening) at the end of the nineteenth century".[3]

Two strands come together in this Nahda, this transformation: One is admiration for European achievements that promotes emulation of the West; and the other, an insistence on reviving the roots of the culture of the East. Each of these, in turn, has two identifiable strands:

In looking to the West, there is the desire to fully emulate it in terms of technology, modernity and much more; but a resistance to full westernization in terms of refusing to promote values that would undermine our own cultural roots and nascent national identity.

---

2 Antonius, George. *The Arab Awakening: The Story of the Arab National Movement* (London, H. Hamilton, 1938).

3 Philipp, Thomas. "Jurji Zaydan's Role in the Syro Arab Nahda: A Re-evaluation," in *The Origins of Syrian Nationhood* edited by Adel Beshara (New York, Routledge, 2011) p.79.

And again, when it comes to reviving the eastern identity and cultural roots, two strands can be identified: those who wanted a pan-Islamic revival as championed by Afghani, and those who wanted an Arab revival as championed by al-Kawakibi.[4]

It was part of the genius of Jurji Zaidan that he epitomized the weaving together of these four strands, as few have been able to do before or since. In so doing, he responded to a deep latent desire among Arab and Muslim intellectuals and reformers.

But Zaidan was much more than a contributor to the intellectual debates of his time. He transformed society by helping build the Arab media, the key instrument to educate the public in those days, and was an important literary figure, a pioneer of the novel and a historian of Islamic civilization.

So let's discuss several facets of Jurji Zaidan:

- Zaidan the builder of the Arab Press
- Zaidan the intellectual
- Zaidan the activist reformer of the Nahda
- Zaidan the literary author
- Zaidan the man

Then, I would like to conclude with a few comments about why I think that Zaidan and his thinking are both pertinent and relevant for our times, the times of the "Arab Spring".

---

4 Al-Kawākibī, 'Abd al-Raḥmān. *Ṭabā'i'al-Istibdād wa Maṣāri'al-Isti'bād* (*The Nature of Despotism and the Struggle Against Enslavement*) in *Al-Fikr al-Nahḍāwī al-Islāmī* (*Islamic Awakening Thought*). Introduction by Majdī Sa'īd (Cairo, Dār al-Kitāb al-Maṣrī; Alexandria, Bibliotheca Alexandrina; Beirut, Dār al-Kitāb al-Lubnānī, 2011).

II. Zaidan, Builder of the Arab Press

It is difficult for people today to imagine a world without the internet and without cell phones and television. And even for those who, like myself, grew up without these modern wonders which we take for granted, it is almost impossible to imagine a world without newspapers, magazines and books. Yet up to the early part of the nineteenth century, that was the situation in Egypt, and except for a few lucky readers in Lebanon, it was so for the rest of the Arab World. A handful of men were to change all that, and Jurji Zaidan was one of them.

Following the introduction of the printing press in Egypt in 1820, and the official journal in 1828, the printed word began to spread throughout Egypt and much of the Arab world. Albert Hourani paints the picture vividly:

> There grew up a new generation accustomed to reading... For those who had been educated to a high level in Arabic, a new literature was being produced. Printing in Arabic had scarcely existed before the nineteenth century, but it spread during the century, particularly in Cairo and Beirut, which were to remain the principal centers of publishing: government schools in Cairo and mission schools in Beirut had produced a comparatively large reading public. Apart from school texts, books were less important in this period than newspapers and periodicals, which began to play a large part in the 1860s and 1870s. Among the periodicals of ideas, opening windows on to the culture, science and technology of the West, were two produced by Lebanese Christians in Cairo: *al-Muqtataf* by Ya'qub Sarruf (1852-1927) and Faris Nimr (1855-1951) and *al-Hilal* by Jurji Zaydan (1861-1914).[5]

5 Hourani, Albert. *A History of the Arab Peoples* (Cambridge MA, Harvard Univ. Press, 1991) pp. 303-4.

It was these same people who would promote public education and public debate; they were to be the primary artisans of the Nahda. We all now recognize that the printing press, and especially the journal and the newspaper, were the major instruments for public debates in the Nahda. Every single member of the Nahda was a writer, a publisher, an editor, and/or owner of newspapers and journals. *Al-Hilal* with *al-Muqtataf* and *al-Manar* became the highest intellectual authorities within the Nahda movement. But Zaidan, the self-made man, achieved what none of his contemporaries was able to do: he created a lasting institution. This was the unique strength of Zaidan, that far from simply creating something that he dominated—and dominate it he did—he successfully institutionalized *al-Hilal* so that it survived him by a century and is today the oldest continuously publishing cultural journal in the Arab World. He is rightly considered to have been one of a handful of individuals who created modern Arab journalism.

Zaidan's commitment was to educate the public, not just to produce a literary magazine primarily for entertainment. Indeed, his foreword to the first issue of *al-Hilal* crystallizes his commitment to educating society in a liberal, pluralistic fashion, which he considers a duty: [6]

> Our plan is to be true to our objective, honest in our tone, and to endeavor to do our best for the task we have set out to perform. To achieve this, we must necessarily support all contemporary writers and intellectuals from every realm and corner. What we aim at is to elicit the interest of the majority to read what we write, approve of it and forgive us our mistakes. If we accomplish this, we will have achieved satisfaction and will thus endeavor harder to attain what we consider our duty.[7]

6 All translations from Arabic in this paper are by the author.

7 *Dār al-Hilāl: Madrasat al-Tanwīr* (*Dār al-Hilāl: School of Enlightenment*), edited by Maḥmūd 'Ezzat (Alexandria, Bibliotheca Alexandrina, 2010) p.15.

Jurji Zaidan was the founder, writer, editor-in-chief, manager and printer of *al-Hilal* magazine. His dedication to making *al-Hilal* a successful, popular periodical that would, inevitably, influence public opinion and help educate the people, made him exert great effort to maintain its excellence, high circulation rate and quality.[8]

He turned it into a platform for the works of distinguished authors, pioneers of Arabic literature, including giants like Husayn Haykal, Taha Husayn,[9] Muhammad Farid Wajdi,[10] 'Ali al-Jarim, 'Abbas Mahmud al-'Akkad, Mustafa Lutfi al-Manfaluti and Ahmad Amin.[11] And because of that, *al-Hilal* achieved great fame and survived his death, and became a towering institution of journalism.

But to achieve that popularity and continuity, Zaidan had noted from the beginning, that while he had to educate the public in what it did not know, he had to respect the taste, traditions, and moral values of the readers, even while trying to change them. Al-Tamawi cites him as

8 Ibid.

9 Ḥusayn, Ṭāha. *Mustaqbal al-Thaqāfa fī Miṣr* (*The Future of Culture in Egypt*) in *Al-Fikr al-Nahḍāwī al-Islāmī.* Introduction by 'Imād Ḥusayn (Cairo, Dār al-Kitāb al-Maṣrī; Alexandria, Bibliotheca Alexandrina; Beirut, Dār al-Kitāb al-Lubnānī, 2012).

10 Wajdī, Muḥammad Farīd. *Al-Madaniyya wa'l-Islām* (*Civilization and Islam*) in *Al-Fikr al-Nahḍāwī al-Islāmī.* Introduction by Mu'tazz Shukrī (Cairo, Dār al-Kitāb al-Maṣrī; Alexandria, Bibliotheca Alexandrina; Beirut, Dār al-Kitāb al-Lubnānī, 2012).

11 The main purpose of this new magazine was to educate the public and help writers reach the readers and express their ideas no matter how diverse their intellectual schools were. See 'Ezzat. p.13. These authors had great loyalty to the Journal and it is thanks to them that the magazine achieved great fame and carried on after his death to become a towering institution of journalism. See 'Imāra al-Zākī, 'Alī. "Jūrjī Zaydān." http://wadelhilew.ahlamontada.com/t94-topic, Sat 20 Feb, 2010.

saying: "the writer writes for the citizens of a country, and he relies on them to read what he has written." [12]

Another major point of strength that Zaidan brought to *al-Hilal*, was the fact that he expanded the cultural scene to include more than just literature, and starting with Science,[13] he made sure to offer his readers a variety of interesting, informative and intellectually stimulating areas of knowledge as 'Ezzat observes: "At the time *al-Hilal* was first issued, culture in Egypt was limited to literature. The new periodical gave it a wider and more comprehensive meaning. It included history, philosophy, science, sociology, politics and economics, thus merging intellectual thought with art, and science with philosophy."[14] Zaidan believed in the importance of education for all of society, in the broadest sense of education.[15] While it could be argued that this was out of self-interest,[16] I personally do not share that view and rather believe that Zaidan, like several of his reformer colleagues, all artisans of the Nahda, believed that education was the best means of achieving

12 Al-Tamāwī, Aḥmad, H. *Jūrjī Zaydān: Naqd al- Adāb* (Cairo, National Book Organization, 1992) p. 125.

13 Al-Tamāwī observed that "... he created a special column in the magazine for scientific news, and was known to carefully note poets' references about scientific issues as is seen in his article on Abī 'l-'Alā' and his knowledge of stars and astronomy and his book on Abū Nuwās in which he describes him as a man well versed in astrology." p.11.

14 'Ezzat, p.13.

15 Al-Tamāwī remarks: "His competence in the English, French and German languages helped him a great deal to follow Western culture and journalism closely. His readings in these languages helped him to provide *al-Hilāl* all the new scientific, social, historical, political and literary topics on a bi-weekly basis." p.14.

16 Philipp comments: "He and many of his colleagues in the Arab Nahda fit perfectly Benedict Anderson's concept of 'print capitalism'. The art of printing was the world's introduction to mechanical mass production. As Anderson argued, a larger market for printed items meant lower costs per unit and higher profits for the print entrepreneur. This market could be widened by increasing literacy in the population and by the creation of a written language accessible to more sections of society than just the learned class." See "Jurji Zaydan's Role in the Syro-Arab Nahd," op.cit. p 86.

societal progress. To stay in circulation also required navigating the shoals of political censorship of his day. Confronting western occupation in the Middle East and North Africa was no easy feat, but Zaidan managed it with a delicate balance between cultural and political activism.[17]

III. Zaidan, the Intellectual

But beyond Zaidan the journalist, the media mogul and the editor, is Zaidan the intellectual. While many would consider him to be primarily a historian, or novelist or journalist, the sum total of his contributions represented an enormously distinctive, effective and coherent body of work that made an enormous difference to the entire Arab World. His views on many topics were influential with his contemporaries and for subsequent generations.

What can we say about the thinking of this self-made man? While it was undoubtedly multi-faceted, I will try to limit my remarks to a few of the many areas where he made important contributions. Specifically let me address his attitudes towards, science, culture, and women.

On Science and Rationality

First, he had a profound belief in rationality and science. Indeed, he had defended the right to teach Evolution when Darwin was still unacceptable to the Christian Church. Brugman notes that:

> Zaidan supported avant garde ideas, and believed in the value of science to the extent that he had to pay a price for that. When in 1882 as a young medical student at the American College

17 'Ezzat observes: "Many of the magazines that were issued at the time such as *al-Ahrām* (founded in 1876), *al-Muqtaṭaf* (founded in 1876 in Lebanon—transferred to Cairo in 1885), *al-Muqaṭṭam* (1889), *al-Mu'ayyid* (1889), *al-Nīl* (1891), *al-Bustān* (1892), *al-Ustāz* (1892) and others could not adapt to the challenges facing Egyptian society during that period. Several magazines could not continue due to the clash with the ruling (British) authorities or because they could no longer appeal to the public." pp.13-14.

> of Beirut he supported a certain Dr. Lewis who had given lectures on Darwin's theory of evolution, Zaidan, among others, was refused admittance into the then still Christian Protestant university.[18]

He believed that the scientific approach was the key to education more generally. This carried over into his work as a journalist, where we note that Zaidan, who had been exposed to an education in medicine, chemistry, mathematics and pharmacology, wrote about many scientific issues such as radium, Roentgen's X-rays, tuberculosis and limestone.

Zaidan saw science as an important dimension of culture, and in his view, culture also included history, philosophy, science, sociology, politics and economics, thus merging intellectual thought with art, and science with philosophy. His commitment to science and getting the facts right, noted by al-Tamawi and Philipp among many, meant that he also wanted to apply this approach to understanding one's culture.

On Culture

So how did that "scientific" approach reflect itself in his writings on Culture? As I said at the outset, he was able to weave together the four strands of westernization and cultural authenticity as well as Arabism and Islam. These last two strands, involved important and distinct political projects, to which I will devote the next section of this paper. Allow me here to focus on Westernization and cultural authenticity.

---

18 Brugman, J. *An Introduction to the History of Modern Arabic Literature in Egypt* (Leiden, E.J Brill, 1984) p. 219. Although this is a verbatim quote from that source in fact Zaidan was a student at the Syrian Protestant College and neither the American College of Beirut nor the Christian Protestant university. Zaidan was admitted to the Syrian Protestant College, but a year later, after a junior teacher had been censured by the faculty for lecturing somewhat sympathetically about Darwin's theory, Zaidan participated in a student protest and eventually did not return to the College. The Syrian Protestant College subsequently became the American University of Beirut.

Zaidan was certainly open to the ideas of the West, though he was not uncritical of some of the aspects of what he saw there. In fact, El-Enany cites Zaidan's list of Do's and Don'ts in cultural borrowing from the West:

> In the civilization of France and that of other European parts, there are many virtues that we should borrow and benefit from, but it has also vices that should be avoided. The virtues that we will do well to borrow are:
>
> 1. Recognition of duty;
> 2. Punctuality and not wasting time;
> 3. Refinement of the manners of the commonalty through true education;
> 4. The education and edification of women;
> 5. The promotion of education and expansion of the [study of] letters;
> 6. Hard work.
>
> As for the faults of that civilization, the most important to remember of those are:
>
> 1. Excess of freedom and using it wrongly;
> 2. Whatever contradicts oriental decency, notwithstanding the adoption of a measure of knowledge and education that is suitable for our customs;
> 3. Indifference to religion...for that is the cornerstone of ruin.[19]

Cultural authenticity meant that he had to define what constituted the oriental roots that he felt needed to be affirmed in the face of westernization in order to be able to develop our own renaissance, our Nahda.

Zaidan was able to make a profound commitment to the notion of Arabism, as distinct from relating exclusively to Egyptians or Phoenicians, even

19 El-Enany, Rasheed. *Arab Representations of the Occident: East-West Encounters in Arabic Fiction: Culture & Civilization in the Middle East* (New York, Routledge, 2006) p. 39.

though he recognized the contributions of these cultural strands. It was the common language of Arabic that established a true bond between Arabs. But with Arab culture he saw the influence of Islamic civilization as a major factor giving Arab culture a content and depth beyond its own linguistic reach, and contributing to the formation of the Arab identity. Though he shunned political activism, "he was nonetheless concerned with Arab history and wrote openly of an Arab nation".[20]

On Women

Political reform brings into focus the issue of the status of women. While Zaidan undoubtedly believed in the education of women[21] and says: "No two intelligent people differ in the matter of the education of women,"[22] he still shows a certain wariness towards the full emancipation of women. Indeed, he writes with wistfulness about the more timid and tame oriental women of his time compared to the brazenness which he was witnessing in Paris.[23]

---

20 Matthews, Weldon C. *Confronting an Empire, Constructing a Nation: Arab Nationalists and Popular Politics and Mandate Palestine* (London, I.B. Tauris & Co, 2006) p.12.

21 Mūsā, Nabawiyya. *Al-Mar'a wa'l-'Amal* (Women and Work). Introduction by Mona Abū-Zayd in *Al-Fikr al-Nahḍāwī al-Islāmī* (Cairo, Dār al-Kitāb al-Maṣrī; Alexandria, Bibliotheca Alexandrina; Beirut, Dār al-Kitāb al-Lubnānī, 2011) pp.13-14. Nabawiyya Mūsā's book is a seminal text on the education and work of women.

22 Philipp, Thomas. *Jurji Zaidan and the Foundations of Arab Nationalism* (New York, Syracuse Univ. Press, 2014).

23 Quoted by El-Enany as follows: "Jurji Zaydan's conservatism shows at its most extreme, as is common among modernizers of his and indeed later generations, when the issue is that of female emancipation and sexual mores. After describing the emancipation of the European woman and the parity she has achieved with men, he goes on to comment wistfully, 'We used to protest at the ignorance and veiling of the oriental woman, and envy the European woman for her education and freedom. Now that we have seen the latter in Paris, one has almost reverted to being content with the ignorance and the veil; they [the Europeans] have harmed that gentle creature with excessive freedom'." p.38.

His views on the status of women were more conservative than those of some of his contemporaries such as Qasim Amin.[24] El-Enany further notes: "As conservatism regarding female emancipation tends to be habitually associated with Islam, we will do well to remember that Jurji Zaydan was a Christian." [25] So, where does all this leave us?

On the whole, this prismatic author and publisher, historian and public educator made a major contribution to the culture of the Arab Renaissance, the Nahda, as one of his successors, Muhammad Farid Wajdy, said: "If I were to count the unique personalities that have appeared in the Middle East in the last fifty years—those who have enriched it with their writings and ideas—I find myself obliged to put Jurji Zaidan at the forefront." [26]

IV. The Arab Nahda as a Cultural and Political Project

On Being an Arab

The cultural and political project of the Pan-Arab Nahda did not only have to cope with the issues of westernization and cultural authenticity, it had also to cope with the rival project of the Pan-Islamic Revival. It had to answer what constituted an Arab identity that would transcend the identities of Egyptians, Phoenicians, Iraqis, Syrians, etc.

> Egypt detached itself from the Arab movement and evolved a nationalist policy of her own. The change had begun in

24 Amīn, Qāṣim. *Taḥrīr al-Mar'a* (*The Emancipation of Women*); and Ḥarb, Muḥammad Tal'at. *Tarbiyat al-Mar'a wa'l- Ḥijāb* (*Women's Education and the Veil*) in *Al-Fikr al-Nahḍāwī al-Islāmī.* Introduction by Amina al-Bandari (Cairo, Dār al-Kitāb al-Maṣrī; Alexandria, Bibliotheca Alexandrina; Beirut, Dār al-Kitāb al-Lubnānī, 2012).

25 El-Enany, p. 38.

26 Quoted in Imāra al-Zākī. "Jūrjī Zaydān", op.cit.

> the seventies of the nineteenth century, during the reign of the Khedive Isma'il, when that ruler's extravagance and his entanglements with European finance had brought about a wave of popular discontent. Hitherto, the movement of ideas in Egypt, so far as the Arabic cultural revival and the birth of the Arab national consciousness went, had marched hand in hand with the same process in Syria; and the lead given by one country evoked a ready response in the other.[27]

This is further emphasized by Antonius again when he remarks that:

> It is in the nature of the Arab temperament to conceive action in spasms rather than on a plan of sustained effort, and the history of the national movement is in a sense a chronicle of vivid outbursts with periods of recovery and preparation between them. It unfolds itself in a pattern of flames shooting upwards from a dull fire of smoldering feeling.[28]

Zaidan, who straddled the Levant and Egypt was firmly committed to the Arab identity, and for him, the Arabic language was the key. "For Zaidan the existence of the Arabic language...as a functioning means of communication and information for society was proof that an Arab bond existed." [29]

In his ability to transcend geographic affinities as well as religious ones, and to emphasize language as the cornerstone for defining his cultural worldview, Zaidan was not only progressive, but he also rejected the racial or ethnic basis on which other intellectuals in Europe and elsewhere were building their view of society and politics. Zaidan is considered to have been an architect of the modern Arab identity and, as Philipp rightly says: "Zaidan is considered to have laid the foundation

27 Antonius, pp. 99-100.

28 Ibid, p. 89.

29 Philipp. "Jurji Zaydan's Role in the Syro-Arab Nahda," p. 85.

for a pan-Arab national identity."[30] Here it is important to note that his Arabism is not of the extreme and chauvinistic kind supported by people like Mustafa Sadiq El-Rafa'i,[31] a judgment held by no less eminent a person than Muhammad Husayn Haykal Pasha.[32]

On Islamic Civilization

Zaidan was a distinguished historian of Islamic civilization. He undoubtedly read western sources and admired the precision and method that European Orientalism brought to the task of interpreting history. But while, like other Arab intellectuals in the nineteenth and early twentieth century, he was profoundly influenced by the methods of European research, he also had enormous mastery of Arab and Muslim history and his historical knowledge came often from Arab writers, whom he also criticized severely.

The balance of these various influences is best seen in his writing, and it is amazing that this largely self-taught man should have produced the first modern historiography of Islamic civilization. That enormous multi-volume work would open the door to successors, most notably Ahmed Amin. In fact, no less a figure than Salama Musa notes:

> Jurji Zaydan was a self-made man, culturally as well as in matters of finance. He was the first who, in our modern age, devoted his life to studying Islamic history; he wrote a great many historical novels, in addition to his major work *The History of Islamic Civilization.* Writing the latter was a pioneer's task, by which he opened the way for all the historical

30 Ibid.

31 Egyptian poet, intellectual, critic and writer. Born in 1880 and died in 1937.

32 Haykal, Muḥammad, Ḥusayn. "Jūrjī Zaydān kama 'araftuhu," *al-Hilāl* 47, p. 964.

> studies that have after him, in the past twenty or thirty years, appeared in ever increasing numbers.[33]

Others were seeking to revive a pan-Islamic project. But Zaidan remained true to his Arab cultural project, even though he did more than any other to link it with the content of Islamic civilization. Beyond his master work on Islamic Civilization it would be as novelist that he would introduce Islamic and Arab History to a very wide public (see below).

While many thinkers, both Muslims and Christians, shaped the Arab nationalism that emerged with the Nahda, Zaidan was truly a founding figure. Al-Tamawi goes further and says: "Jurji Zaidan is considered one of the greatest guides of Arab culture in its modern renaissance (Nahda)."[34]

Zaidan and the Pan-Islamic Revival

The Ottoman Empire could no longer provide a viable model for those who saw power and modernity embodied in the West with its nationalism and imperialist tendencies. Yet that old Muslim empire had been capable of accommodating a plethora of local identities, precisely because the Muslim faith was embracing so vast a territory with so many cultures and subcultures, and so many ethnicities and religious minorities. The national parliament, the Ottoman *majlis al-milli* provided some sort of recognition and even some channels of communication to the Sublime Porte and to the centralized decision-making structure when there was a need for it. Local affairs were largely dealt with locally.

Some were intent on reforming the Ottoman Pan-Islamic project, and intellectuals from Afghani to Muhammad 'Abduh to Rashid Rida provided the intellectual framework for such political endeavors. If Zaidan differed with these and others on the pan-Islamic versus the Arab

---

33 Mūsā, Salama. *The Education of Salama Mūsā*, translated by L.O. Schuman (Leiden, E.J. Brill, 1961) p. 153.

34 Al-Tamāwī, p.16.

dimension of his cultural project, he shared with many his belief that education of the public would be the key to modernizing the backward eastern societies. As Musawi aptly puts it: "Jurji Zaydan's contributions are in line with a sense of national commitment and an intellectual moral responsibility to participate in the education of the public."[35]

But the political dimensions of the Pan-Islamic project were to continue for quite a while, and even until today, echoes and variations are found in the works and actions of intellectuals and politicians from Iran to Morocco and from Pakistan to Turkey, while Egypt remains at the heart of that debate, even as the debate remains at the heart of Egypt. However, I believe that the polarization that we now witness between liberal secularist reformers and pan-Islamic revivalists denies a meeting ground that has a long and distinguished intellectual tradition, which my colleagues and I, at the Library of Alexandria, are trying to revive by "reissuing the classics" of the last two hundred years.[36] However, even though I will allude to this in my concluding comments about the "Arab Spring", this important discussion is beyond this paper focusing on Zaidan and his work.

The twentieth-century was to bring many transformations. To list but a few: the changes within the Ottoman Empire before the First World War; the war itself and the famous Arab revolt against the Ottomans, supported by Lawrence and aborted by Sykes-Picot; the

35 Mūsawī, Muḥsin Jāsim. *Islam on the Street: Religion in Modern Arabic Literature* (Maryland, Rowman & Littlefield, 2009) p. 29.

36 The Bibliotheca Alexandrina, the New Library of Alexandria, is re-issuing the classics of Muslim humanist and reformist thinking in the last two centuries, in an authoritative edition, each with an introduction by a specialist about the author and the work in question. Since the series is about the masterworks of many Muslim intellectuals who were the predecessors, contemporaries and successors of Jurji Zaidan, the reader may wish to consult some of the works issued by the Bibliotheca Alexandrina in that series entitled *Al-Fikr al-Nahḍāwī al-Islāmī* (Cairo, Dār al-Kitāb al-Maṣrī; Alexandria, Bibliotheca Alexandrina; Beirut, Dār al-Kitāb al-Lubnānī).

1919 revolution in Egypt, and the subsequent emergence of a liberal regime with the 1923 constitution; the destruction of the Ottoman Empire and the emergence of modern Turkey under Mustafa Kemal Ataturk; and the abolition of the Caliphate; then Palestine and the military coups that came after the Second World War and the autocratic regimes that ruled the Arab World till the current waves of revolutionary movements we refer to as "The Arab Spring". All of that was to have a profound impact on the subsequent evolution of the ideas championed by Zaidan during his brief lifetime. But discussion of these issues is, again, beyond the scope of this paper. However, two observations are worth making here:

First, since there was competition between the Pan-Islamic and the Arab cultural projects, the changes in the Ottoman Empire before its final collapse and the impact of these changes on the Nahda are worth noting. In fact reformers in both camps were encouraged, showing that they had a substantial common ground. Here are Anne-Laure Dupont's observations on the impact of the 1908 Ottoman Constitution:

> The return of the Ottoman constitution in 1908 was immediately perceived as a revolution (*inqilab*), and was widely commented in the Arabic press—not only in newspapers but also in cultural and educational reviews such as *al-Hilal* and *al-Manar*, both edited in Cairo by Syrian Ottoman subjects, Jurji Zaydan and Mohamed Rashid Rida. Until then, Zaydan and Rida had not been directly involved in political matters but, as advocates of the reform (*islah*) and progress (*taqaddum*) of society, they felt encouraged in their mission by the advent of a constitutional regime in Istanbul and the granting of new rights. They actually saw in these the triumph of their ideas and ideals. Both were very typical of the modernist or reformist movement in Egypt, and the Arab provinces of the Ottoman Empire, of its shared values as well as its various

trends. Zaydan and Rida claimed to educate individuals and society.[37]

On Political Reform vs. Revolution

It was not a call for violent revolution or political upheaval that these enlightened men sought. Indeed "both Zaydan and Rida believed in education but feared social change. They wanted a 'revolution without a revolution'."[38] To them, Liberty was a state of mind.

Zaidan remained committed to educating the public very broadly, not just on political issues. In furthering this cause of educating the public more generally, he saw clearly the importance of bringing valuable, affordable knowledge to the general reader. Thus in 1894, Zaidan issued the series "*al-Hilal* Historical Novels" which were mainly translated works meant for the general public, and sold at a low price by his own Dar al-Hilal. With these novels he aimed to compete with other works that he viewed were not in line with the general habits and traditions of the culture he was defending and the cause he was advancing.[39]

Toward the end of his life, Zaidan added to his interests as he reflected on what made a society distinctive and what made power legitimate. But he remained overall committed to his great cultural project and did not succumb to the siren song of participating in political power.

---

37 Dupont, Anne-Laure, "The Ottoman Revolution of 1908 as seen by *al-Hilāl* and *al-Manār*: The Triumph and Diversification of the Reformist Spirit" in *Liberal Thought in the Eastern Mediterranean: Late 19th Century Until the 1960s,* edited by Christoph Schumann (Leiden, E.J.Brill, 2008) pp.122-146, p.123.

38 Ibid. Dupont's complete quote is: "both Zaydan and Rida believed in education but feared social change. They wanted a 'revolution without a revolution,' one which would give power to the newly educated elites and let them achieve their reformist program." p.134.

39 'Ezzat, p.15.

V. The Literary Work of Zaidan

Jurji Zaidan's instrument was the pen. He was a writer. He pioneered the use of the historical novel—and, indirectly, the novel in general—as a genre of Arab literature. His twenty-two novels were popular and enjoy until today an unbroken fame. "Despite his short literary life, which did not exceed twenty-two years Zaidan carved for himself a distinguished place among Arab writers, and his name has been forever recognized by everyone." [40]

If he was not of a literary stature comparable to later figures like Taha Husayn, 'Abbas al-'Akkad or Naguib Mahfouz, he was the precursor and pioneer who revolutionized the Arab novel and paved the way for them.[41] And, as Albert Hourani noted:

> Jurji Zaydan did more than any other [writer of the Nahda] to create a consciousness of the Arab past by his histories and still more by his series of historical novels, modeled on those of Scott and creating a romantic image of the past as Scott's had done.[42]

But beyond the societal impact of Zaidan's novels, his literary work in these novels had certain characteristics that set them apart, as the attention to historical context is pronounced, much more so than the treatment of character and plot, usually a love story with a happy ending. Walid Hamarneh comments on his literary style, saying:

> Many critics have observed that his novels are composed of two basic elements. The first element consists of the historical

---

40 'Imāra, al-Zākī. "Jūrjī Zaydān." op.cit.

41 "Though Zaydan may not be considered a great novelist in some world sense, he revolutionized the Arab novel and paved the way for future novelists, whether they were inspired by historical themes or not." See Moosa, Matti. *The Origins of Modern Arabic Fiction,* 2nd edition (Colorado, Lynne Rienner, 1997) p. 213.

42 Quoted in *Literature and Nation in the Middle East*, edited by Yāsir Suleimān and Ibrāhīm Muhāwi (Edinburgh, Edinburgh Univ. Press, 2006) p.12.

> background, which can be subdivided into two types—historical time, usually composed of long passages (sometimes with footnotes and references to historical works) that provide the reader with an elaborate temporal context; and a second type associated with space, where Zaydan provides elaborate and detailed descriptions of cities or areas in which the action takes place. The second element in Zaydan's novels is the love story. This typically involves a man and a woman who fall in love, then are separated by circumstances, only to meet again and in most cases come together in a happy ending. The plot structure can thus be considered closed and dominated by historical facts.[43]

These distinctive characteristics of his approach, as contrasted to western novelists of the time as well as those that followed him in the Arab world, enable us to appreciate his political and cultural purpose, not just his literary achievement.

The Zaidan project was a great success. He succeeded in promoting historical knowledge among the non-intellectual elite and thus provided a broad grounding for a common Arab identity. As noted earlier, no less an authority than Albert Hourani remarks that "perhaps it was Jurji Zaydan who did more than any other to create a consciousness of the Arab past by his histories and still more by his series of historical novels."[44]

Zaidan wrote in clear and simple prose. It was a distinctive style, that no less a stylist than Manfaluti admired his pellucid prose.[45] But beyond

43 Hamarneh, Walīd. "Jurji Zaydan," in *Essays in Arabic Literary Biography: 1850-1950*, edited by Roger Allen (Wiesbaden, Otto Harrassowitz, 2010) p. 385.

44 Hourani, Albert. *Arabic Thought in the Liberal Age* (Cambridge, Cambridge Univ. Press, 1986) p. 277.

45 "As I read Jūrjī Zaydān written style, I always imagined it to be like a clean, perspicuous mirror." Manfaluṭi quoted in ʻImāra. "Jūrjī Zaydān," op.cit.

style, as Philipp notes: "His writings contributed massively to the development of Modern Standard Arabic, a simplified written language which is today understood by all literate Arabs."[46]

Zaidan remains a towering figure in the history of modern Arab Literature. His legacy endures. It has stood the test of time. More importantly, Zaidan the novelist, has had a major impact on Arab letters and on global literature, for it is through his work that the novel was introduced into Arabic literature. Moosa confirms this by saying that: "It was with the appearance of the eminent writer Jurji Zaydan that the Arab novel, and in particular the historical novel, was brought to fruition."[47]

Zaidan's impact on the development of the genre in Arabic cannot be overestimated. Philipp notes that he was a true pioneer.[48] He paved the way for his successors, who in the last hundred years produced phenomenal developments culminating with Naguib Mahfouz being awarded the first Nobel Prize for an Arab novelist. Zaidan with his serialized novels encompassing Arab-Islamic history was the major pioneer of the Arabic novel. His novels were popular and enjoy until today an unbroken popularity. Roger Allen, in his classic historical and critical introduction to the Arabic novel observes that:

> The novels of Zaydan and other contributors to the historical-romantic and philosophical novel certainly fulfilled the important function of bringing fictional genres into the public awareness and at the same time using episodes from

---

46 Philipp. *Jurji Zaidan and the Foundations of Arab Nationalism*, op.cit.

47 Moosa. op.cit. p.195.

48 Philipp. In "Jurji Zaydan's Role" op.cit. he says: "Zaydān was a true literary pioneer, establishing the historical novel—and, indirectly, the novel in general—as a genre of Arab literature." p. 83.

> Middle Eastern history as a means of rousing and fostering an emerging Arab Nationalist consciousness.[49]

Zaidan himself recognized that there were many types of novels, thereby emphasizing that the genre he had selected was to suit his own purpose. He says: "Today, novels have diverse types that differ according to the mode and purpose of their creation; there are didactic, historical, scientific, literary and other forms." [50]

There is no doubt that he selected the historical novel as a means of promoting—nay, creating—a new Arab consciousness. He was, of course, a specialist in Arab and Muslim history, but that is not the sole reason he chose that genre. After all, he had broad knowledge of many aspects of literature.[51] In fact Moosa underlines that, in his view, where "writers like Scott and Dumas only used historical settings for their characters, Zaidan used the novel and its characters as a means of teaching history to the public." [52]

To emphasize that point, Moosa observed that the challenge for Zaidan was not how to integrate historical knowledge into the novel's narrative as much as how to spice up the historical narrative by using the fictional characters almost as props. The novel was not a means of exploring the human frailties and sensibilities of the characters the

---

49 Allen, Roger, M. A. *The Arabic Novel: An Historical and Critical Introduction* (New York, Syracuse University Press, 1995) p. 62.

50 Quoted in al-Tamāwī, p. 218.

51 Some specialists have noted that "Zaydān's view of literature as a living entity facilitated his knowledge of its development and his ability to delineate all the novel images and meanings across different ages." See al-Tamāwī, p. 97.

52 "While Scott and Dumas used historical events only as a frame for the novel and took liberty in relating these events to achieve their novelistic ends, Zaydān, on the contrary, stuck to actual historical events because his main objective was to teach history to the public." Moosa, p.199.

author created, rather the unfolding historical events were the story, and thus:

> In his historical novels Zaydan did not follow strict canons of historiographical practice in his attempt to reproduce the past. His intention was to recall some of its more salient and entertaining aspects to reach a popular audience and inform them of their unknown past. This is why Zaydan's novels invoke historical events rather than minutely reconstruct and profoundly analyze them. Thus, Zaydan portrayed most of his fictitious characters as simple and fixed—being almost passive instruments for the unfolding for an already determined general historical sequence. Often, he was compelled to create fictitious characters and tie them in somehow with the real ones to lend the novel necessary excitement and adventure. He could not do this with authentic historical characters.[53]

So, in the end, what did those historic novels amount to? They certainly pioneered the use of the novel in the Arab World, and they certainly were a marvelous tool that introduced generations of Arabs and Muslims to their history, and created the Arab public's consciousness of a collective past, and hence a common bond, if not an outright commitment to a common future.

V. Zaidan—the Man

Born on the 14th of December, 1861 in Beirut to an Orthodox Christian family of limited means, Zaidan was forced to drop out of school after two years of elementary education to help his father run his restaurant business. Yet, his enthusiasm for education and his keenness on improving himself finally got him into the Syrian Protestant College as a medical student, which he eventually left after supporting his professor's right to academic freedom against the administration. He then went to

53 Moosa, p. 213.

Cairo to study medicine but finally opted for a career in writing which created the legend that he became.

In 1891 he married Maryam, a girl he loved, and they had three children: Emile, Asma and Choucri born in 1893, 1895 and 1900 respectively. He was devoted to his family and to his work. He died in July 1914, at his desk, completing the last tome of his work on the history of Arab Literature. He was only fifty two years old.

Jurji Zaidan: A man of dedication and rectitude, a self-made man and largely a self-taught intellectual of encyclopedic breadth, he was a man whom everybody loved. There are many great testimonials by his contemporaries and his successors. Ahmed Amin described him as "A self-made man, who built himself, bore the burden and outlined an example he believed in, drew careful plans and did not rest until he reached what he aimed for. He wanted to learn but had no money and so he bent time to his will, and balanced between his desire to learn and to make money."[54] Similarly, the renowned 'Akkad saw him as:

> A man whose intellect is not characterized by bias, fault finding or disturbance but rather mostly distinguished by gentle and subtle guidance. And has this reduced his sense of direction? No, in fact it has increased it. But he did not benefit from the attention and limelight he could have received had he been a man of prejudice and extremism.[55]

With regard to his contribution to the revival of Arabic literature, Haykal told us that Zaidan was "the first to tackle this history (of Arabic literature) in a way that resembles modern research in its absence from bias

54 Quoted in al-Jindī, Muḥammad. "Jūrjī Zaydān, Mu'assis al-Hilāl," *al- Hilāl* Special Issue (Jan. 2012) p. 324.

55 Quoted in al-Bīsī, Sanā'. "Jurī Zaydān: Lā Yaṣiḥḥ illa al-ṣaḥīḥ." May 10, 2012. http://www.ahram.org.eg/90/2010/02/27/10/9358.aspx

and its seeking of truth for its own sake".[56] Indeed, Zaidan's integrity and achievements have won him the admiration of many as Bishara Takla's comment after his death clearly demonstrates: "In truth, if historians measured his age to his legacy, they will realize that the owner of *al-Hilal* was one hundred years old when he was only in his fifties when he departed." [57] But perhaps it is Emile Amin who captures it best in this brief summary statement:

> We can summarize his life by saying that this man, Christian by religion and Islamic by culture, who succeeded through his fiction to introduce Islamic history with ease and lucidity, highlighting its aspects of tolerance and rationalism represented a bridge for positive connection between East and West.[58]

VI. Jurji Zaidan and the "Arab Spring" of Today

Zaidan died before the 1919 revolution and the liberal age between the wars (up to 1952 in Egypt). His thinking and contributions had a profound impact on that period. Today, following the totalitarian systems that ruled the Arab world for the second half of the twentieth century, we are witnessing the "Arab Spring". Is Zaidan's thinking still relevant for a democratic Arab society today? Or is it only of historical interest for a few scholars?

Can the Nahda as the liberal and national base for Arab thought and politics serve as an inspiration for the unfolding events set in motion by the revolutionary waves of the "Arab Spring"? Is it a viable alternative to fundamentalist tendencies?

---

56 Haykal, p. 964.

57 Quoted by al-Bīsī, Sanā'. "Jurjī Zaydān: Lā Yaṣiḥḥ illa al-ṣaḥīḥ."

58 Amīn, Emile. "Jūrjī Zaydān: al-Mufakkir al-Masīḥī al-'Arabī wa-Ru'yatihi li'l-Islām wa-Ḥaḍāratihi," April 21, 2012 http://www.terezia.org/section.php?id=2300

Today, the polarization in our countries, the Arab and Muslim worlds, generally is between those who seek the revival of Muslim culture while others choose to follow the path of western style political liberalism and pluralistic democracy. Both parties imagine that there is no meeting ground possible, but that is not true. From its antecedents in the modernization efforts of Muhammad 'Ali and Rifa'at al-Tahtawi [59] to the Nahda of Jurji Zaidan and others, the meeting ground of the two currents is indeed a Nahda for the twenty first century, a new renaissance of the Arab world and through it a broader renaissance of the Muslim world. Thus Zaidan's legacy has a major relevance today. He was a Christian scholar of Islam, and Arab nationalist who saw the importance of the Islamic component of Arab culture and identity; he revived the understanding of the Muslim tradition, while championing modernity, science and westernization. He saw educating the wide public as primarily the elite's responsibility. He recognized the importance of an open exchange of ideas and practiced it by creating the best intellectual forum for such exchanges, *al-Hilal*, the longest-lived and still surviving cultural journal in Arabic.

VII. Conclusions

This is but a very brief overview of some of Jurji Zaidan's accomplishments. It was a remarkably productive professional life of some three decades. So it is most fitting that we should celebrate the one hundred and fiftieth anniversary of his birth to honor the life of a man who with deceptive ease went from striving to success, from ambition to achievement and from humble beginnings to the heights of recognition. Throughout the Arab World he is remembered for his glorious contribution to the modernization of values and the values of modernization. A man of many facets, he was an artisan of the Nahda, the renaissance of

59 Al-Ṭahṭawi, Rifā'at. *Manāhij al-Albāb al-Miṣriyya fi Mabāhij al-Ādāb al-'aṣriyya* (*Paths for Egyptian Minds in the Joys of Contemporary Culture*) in *Al-Fikr al-Nahḍāwī al-Islāmī.* Introduction by Abdu Ibrahim Aly (Cairo, Dār al-Kitāb al-Maṣrī; Alexandria, Bibliotheca Alexandrina; Beirut, Dār al-Kitāb al-Lubnānī, 2011).

the Arab World. He championed all the right causes, from the rationality of science to the romance of history, from the importance of knowing the cultural heritage of the past, to the value of creating the cultural heritage of the future... Jurji Zaidan was a giant among his contemporaries, and successive generations of Arab readers rediscover him with joy. Such is the legacy he gave his people and the world.

Jurji Zaidan as a Promoter of Modern Arab Identity

Georges Corm

Jurji Zaidan has played an extraordinary role in raising the Arabs' collective consciousness of their identity. Most of his remarkable intellectual efforts were devoted to making Arab and Islamic civilization accessible and known to the ordinary Arab man with no prior specialized knowledge of his historical patrimony, ancestry, achievements and glorious past. In fact, his various and diverse writings all converged towards one main goal, i.e. the pride of being an Arab. Through his writings, Zaidan popularized the two main reasons for this pride: the beauty of the Arab classical language on the one hand and the Arab central role in the development of Islamic civilization with all its cultural, artistic and scientific achievements on the other. As we will see, Zaidan's work and writings are a central element of the Arab Nahda that began with Rifaʿat Tahtawi, an Egyptian Azharist, trying to understand the social and political dynamics behind the economic development and military might of France when he visited France between 1826 and 1830.

This Nahda would last until the seventies in the twentieth century. It produced many eminent thinkers, poets, novelists, historians and religious reformers that belonged to diverse Muslim as well as Christian Arab religious communities. For over a century and a half the Arab cultural and intellectual environment was tremendously enriched by all these actors in the Nahda to a degree that was inconceivable at the end of the eighteenth century when Napoleon Bonaparte invaded Egypt. It was a time of increased intellectual activity in all Arab societies that analyzed and sought to understand the causes of Arab and Islamic decline during the previous centuries, at a time when Europe was undergoing social and economic change at an ever increasing pace that began in the fifteenth century.

In these efforts, the merits of Zaidan's work has probably not been recognized enough compared to other more prestigious thinkers who were part of the local academic world or who studied abroad or who belonged to prominent social families. It is true, however, that all the splendid intellectual efforts that took place during the period of the Arab Nahda have now been questioned and subtly pushed aside to be replaced by a debilitating pseudo-political literature focused on a narrow conception of Islam that encapsulates all the complexities of Arab identity and Arab political and social needs and aspirations. A position that most Arab secular or religious reformists of the Nahda period had contested with an enlightened broad-mindedness and tolerance but without abandoning their religious faith.

The reasons for this dramatic change are numerous and need not be described here in detail. But there is no doubt that the succession of military coups in the Arab world that began at the end of the 1940s, contributed to the promotion, in an authoritarian way, of various brands of this ideology even though they advocated Arab nationalist aspirations. The military dictatorships thus suppressed political liberties which contributed to checking the creativity of the Nahda's intellectual dynamism. The crushing Arab defeat in the war launched by Israel in 1967 against Arab armies was another factor discrediting the Arab collective consciousness that came to be called negatively as "pan-Arabism". This opened the door to an increased influence of the Kingdom of Saudi Arabia, a kingdom practicing an extreme form of Islam (Wahhabism) as well as to increased local activism by various brands of the "Muslim Brotherhood". Members of the Brotherhood had previously been repressed in Egypt under Nasser and in other Arab dictatorships, as were the activities of Arab communist parties. This Muslim "fundamentalist" influence is still increasing nowadays due to the financial wealth accumulated by the kingdom and other oil exporting emirates in the Arabian Peninsula.

In this present context, it is extremely important to remember the Arab Nahda and to honor Jurji Zaidan's central position in this Nahda. This is the more so because the present state of Arab culture ignores the contributions of so many great Arab thinkers during a century and a half—contributions that promoted the reform of Arab societies and the inflexible and dogmatic way in which Islam was being interpreted and practiced. This lack of awareness of the intellectual achievements of the Nahda constitutes in fact a dangerous breakdown of the Arab collective memory. It is stifling efforts to build on its accumulated knowledge and intellectual heritage, inhibiting efforts to continue to extricate Arab societies from all their social, political and economic ills and their total dependence on regional and international powers.

In my view, Zaidan's most important contribution to the spirit of the Nahda was his attempt to build a proud Arab identity and consciousness based on heroic episodes and outstanding personalities of the glorious past. He successfully managed to promote a very harmonious identity in which an Islamic civilization introduced by Arab conquerors was a source of pride due to its great scientific achievements, to its famous philosophers, jurists, and well known travelers, like Ibn Batuta or Ibn Jubayr. But the glory of the past would not imprison a modern Arab identity nor would it become a corset that prevents the Arabs from reinventing themselves after centuries of backwardness.

Thus, his twenty two novels written in a very simple and clear Arabic language constituted a kind of historical encyclopedia of the most interesting Arab and Islamic heroic figures, both masculine and feminine. These twenty two novels made these figures familiar to the reader who could easily acquire some basic knowledge of the complexities of Arab and Islamic history. At the same time, the reader was able to reconstitute through the various novels the most important episodes of this history. The quality and importance of his novels has been studied in depth by specialists of the Nahda period, so I need not describe them here. But what is particularly striking is the prominence given by Zaidan to heroic women in so many of his novels. Most of his novels include assertive and strong-willed women and no less than one third of his novels have these heroines in their title: *Armanusa the Egyptian; The Ghassanid Damsel; The Virgin of Quraysh; The Caliph's Sister; The Bride of Farghana; The Damsel of Kairouan, The Young Lady of Karbala* and *The Tree of Pearls* (or *Shajarat al-Durr* in Arabic which is a woman's name). While the role of men was emphasized in traditional Arab and/or Islamic history, here was a modern novelist who singled out at that time several Muslim women to show their importance and their many qualities as part of the glorious history of the Arabs.

Thus, Zaidan played a doubly innovative role through his novels, as he not only introduced historical novels in Arab culture but also emphasized through many of them the eminent role of women in Arab history. Given the rigidly structured forms of education in schools—then and today in many parts of the Arab world— young men and women were provided by Zaidan with pleasant and easy readings that would allow them to acquire some basics about Arab and Islamic history.

In addition, at a time when written Arabic was still rigid and complex, the simple style of Zaidan's writings allowed any young man or woman who had only a rudimentary knowledge of Arab history and the Arabic language to understand easily what he or she was reading and to be made to feel they were the descendants of all those—men and women— who shaped the heroic acts of this history. Today some Arabic TV series present certain episodes of Arab history that aim at replicating what Zaidan sought to do, although most of those efforts do not have the impact of Zaidan's novels.

As for the many young Arabs studying in French or British schools where they acquired a very deep knowledge of European history, but only a very limited knowledge of their own history and complex language, reading the Zaidan novels opened a whole new world. Arab and Islamic history then appeared as attractive and interesting as European history or the history of Western Christianity. Zaidan thus offered them an easy and accessible way of becoming as familiar with Arab and Islamic history as with European history including the history of Western Christianity that they were acquiring through European educational institutions. I can myself attest to how much my discovery and readings of Zaidan's novels was a key factor in making me eager to develop my knowledge of Arab history and Islamic civilization so that I would become at least as knowledgeable about it as I was with French and European as well as Ancient Greek and Roman history that I acquired during all my school years at the Cairo Jesuit College.

In this respect, one may regret that Zaidan did not touch through his novels the history of Eastern Christianity that dominated the region before the advent of Islam in the seventh century. But I believe that his main preoccupation at that time was to show that an Arab Christian writer and novelist could identify himself with the great achievements of Arab and Islamic civilization, of which Eastern Christianity was a part, through interaction between the Syrian Aramaic culture and the new emerging Arab Islamic civilization. More recently, an Arab Islamic scholar, Yusif Zaidan, having the same family name as our great novelist (what a coincidence!) produced a splendid novel, *Azazil,* in an attempt to restitute to us the intricacies of early Christian Eastern history and its theological debates.[1] But one could in this respect also refer to the writings of the famous Lebanese historian and theologian Maronite priest, Yoakim Moubarac (1924-1995)[2] who belonged to another generation

1 The novel published in Cairo 2008 by Dar al-Shurūq was greatly praised. It received the prestigious prize of the best Arab novel in 2009. Yūsif Zaydān wrote also a very challenging book, *Al-Lahūt al-'Arabī wa Uṣūl al-'Unf al-Dīnī (The Arab Theology and the Sources of Religious Violence)*, (Madinat al-Nasr, Cairo, Dār al-Shurūq, 2009) in which he attempts to show all the common elements of the three monotheistic faiths (Judaism, Christianity and Islam) which leads him to identify it as the Arab Theology—the three faiths having appeared and developed in what is the Arab region today.

2 See *Yoakim Moubarac, Un homme d'exception. Textes réunis et présentés par Georges Corm* (Beyrouth, Librairie orientale, 2004). See also Moubarac,Yoakim. *Pentalogie Antiochienne. Domaine maronite* (Beyrouth, Editions du Cénacle Libanais, 1984).

than Jurji Zaidan and wrote in another context, less harmonious than the one that prevailed at the time of the Nahda.

As many of his Christian contemporaries, Zaidan was more preoccupied in asserting their capacity to be part of an Arab Nahda alongside their Muslim brethren than in asserting a specific and separate Christian culture and identity. Let us not forget that European domination of the Arab East was viewed by many Muslims as being a Christian domination. This might explain why the numerous Arab Christian scholars that participated so actively in the Arab Nahda beginning in the nineteenth century did not devote their attention to the very rich history of Eastern Christian churches. They rather preferred to show how deeply and strongly they were identifying themselves with Arab history and Islamic civilization. Neither Zaidan nor any of his Christian contemporaries were keen to show Arab Christian communities as having a separate cultural or ethnic identity. Instead they were keen to show how attached they were to the Arabic language and Arabic history of which they were part. Zaidan's novels in this respect would depict the role of Christians in Arab and Islamic history through creating in his novels Christian protagonists working, collaborating and supporting the Muslim heroes of his novels.

These were times when great tolerance and mutual respect existed between Muslim and Christian scholars, as has been so well described by Albert Hourani in his classic and well-known book *Arabic Thought in the Liberal Age*. Specific ethnic, religious or sectarian identities were not cultivated or promoted as opposed to what today would be called an "Arab-Muslim personality" described by the Tunisian intellectual Hichem Djaït.[3] The intellectual political scene was in fact dominated during that period by a secular Arab nationalist ideology or secular local nationalism in countries like the ones that developed in Egypt or Lebanon, Syria and Iraq. Even those attracted to some kind of Muslim

3 Djaït, Hichem. *La personnalité et le devenir arabo-musulman* (Paris, Le Seuil, 1974).

ideology, such as pan-Islamism, were advocating a renovated Islam adapted to modern technical and scientific progress and to modern democratic values. Such an ideology was designed to allow greater resistance to European colonialism, but without rejecting all that European civilization could offer to the Arabs and Muslims to build their own brand of "Nahda". Wahhabism and the Egyptian Muslim Brotherhood had not yet emerged as a political force rejecting the new brand of enlightened Islam that renowned Azharists such as Muhammed 'Abduh, Ahmad Amin, 'Ali 'Abd al-Raziq, Taha Husayn and others were successfully promoting.

Zaidan's efforts to shape an Arab collective identity are also to be found in his prominent role in the development of Arab periodicals. The famous magazine he founded in 1892, *al-Hilal,* became one of the most important sources of information on all aspects of the cultural life in Egypt and other Arab countries, including arts, literature and poetry. *Al-Hilal* survived his death in 1914 and remains a very popular magazine in the entire Arab world after more than a century. In this sense, he was a remarkable "cultural entrepreneur", as he would be described today.

A quick survey of his other works and writings indicate how deeply Zaidan was committed to developing an Arab modern identity and giving a sense of pride for being Arab. As with many other fellow Lebanese Christians, he devoted so much energy to promoting classical Arabic as a sophisticated and rich language and a magnificent tool of expression. This represents another side of Zaidan's intellectual efforts to strengthen an Arab identity. These efforts were devoted to studying the history of the Arabic language and that of the Arab culture.

Zaidan also wrote extensively on the history of Islamic civilization and all its great achievements. Here again, he was showing that an Arab Christian could be proud of having been part of these achievements. In this way, he was asserting that the Islamic content of the Arab collective identity did not constitute a barrier to Arab Christians. This specific Zaidan legacy is what distinguishes his intellectual work from that of most other Christian intellectuals of his time. As previously mentioned, his whole work tended to have one main goal, i.e. to construct an Arab modern identity whereby Arabism and Islamism would coexist in a harmonious way and, far from excluding Arab Christians, would make of them a pillar of this identity.

Unfortunately, this harmonious integration has been shattered during the last decades by ferocious debates about the relations between an Islamic identity and an Arab identity. The changes brought in 2011 by Arab revolutions, far from appeasing tensions and controversies about the content of the Arab identity (religious and political) have increased them without any consensus on how to resolve these tensions.

This is why I believe that we need to go back to the fundamentals of Zaidan's approach to the Arab collective identity and its relation with Islamic civilization. This should be part of an effort to rehabilitate all of the Nahda patrimony. In fact it is sad and counterproductive for the development of Arab societies to see Arab writings and attitudes about *'uruba* (Arabism) and "Islam" being trapped in a vicious circle since the end of secular pan-Arabism in the late twentieth century and the resurgence of a new brand of exclusive and closed pan-Islamism, very different from the one that existed at the end of the nineteenth century and the beginning of the twentieth century.

As mentioned earlier, this earlier brand of pan-Islamism was open to new values adapted to scientific and technical progress and democratic values, while the present one is rather closed and defensive, encapsulating the complexities of Arab identity in a rigid and authoritarian approach to Islamic values as embodied in a dogmatic and simplistic approach to the *Shari'a*. It views the outside world as hostile and "pagan" and has developed a very narrow understanding of the "Spirit of Islam" and its patrimony.

This was never the case with the different brands of *'uruba* ideologies that were all characterized by a strong sense of the positive values of secularism. The fact that many Arab dictatorships tried to legitimize their suppression of political liberties by adopting pan-Arabism should not discredit all the valuable writings of those who advocated a secular Arab identity tied to a liberal and open approach to the role of Islamic civilization in shaping the Arab historical identity. This identity cannot and should not be viewed as exclusively structured by religion in a closed and formalistic way, thus becoming totalitarian and excluding all the other elements that a human being needs in order to feel he can be an intrinsic part of this identity.

This is why it is worthwhile to study in greater depth how the first generation of Arab reformists to which Zaidan belongs were able to develop an Arab collective sense of identity in a harmonious way without contradicting the Islamic patrimony. It is my belief that reconsidering Zaidan's works along this *problématique* could be of great value. In this respect, a study of the interaction between Zaidan and his fellow enlightened Muslim clerics like Muhammad 'Abduh, Ahmad Amin, 'Ali 'Abd al-Razik and so many others could provide a key contribution to changing the path of the present sterile debates between those advocating a secular identity for the Arabs and those insisting on keeping Arab identity as part of a closed and exclusive Islamic identity. Did Zaidan's work on Islamic civilization inspire Ahmad Amin's remarkable history of this civilization? Or was Zaidan influenced by the teachings of Muhammad 'Abduh? In my view there are many intellectual efforts that could be devoted in the future to promoting the magnificent works of all these scholars, Muslims and Christians, in which the figure of Zaidan remains central in raising Arab consciousness of their identity at a time when the Ottoman Empire was crumbling and Arabs were becoming "orphans" in the new world order that would emerge from the First World War.

Jurji Zaidan and the Meaning of the Nahda

Jens Hanssen

A historical period can be judged by its way of looking at the period that preceded it. A generation that devalues the previous generation and is incapable of recognizing its great achievements and its essential significance is bound to be mean and lacking in self-confidence, even if it displays gladiatorial postures and a craving for greatness.

A.Gramsci, 8th Notebook

Jurji Zaidan was born into the Arabic revival and reform movement that emerged in the cosmopolitan centres of Arab provinces of the Ottoman Empire and in North Africa a generation or so before his birth in 1861. In this paper I argue that *al-Nahda al-'Arabiyya* is much more than merely a historical process with a distinct origin and a set of legacies for the future but rather a kind of Archimedian point on which Arab modernity rests precariously. In other words what we know about the long unfolding of the Arab past today is refracted through the "Age of the Nahda" of the nineteenth century. In this process of refraction, Jurji Zaidan became one of the most important producers of Arab modernity and canonizers of Arab history. This article does not share the hagiographic liberal accounts of Jurji Zaidan as a genius who synthesized Arab desire to emulate the technology and modernity of the West with the passion of reviving Oriental identity and cultural roots.

Arabs continue to invoke and elaborate on the Nahda's master narrative on Arab civilization: the veneration of the 'Abbasids, the vilification of the Ottomans and the idiom of modern awakening. But these are interpretations passed down from the nineteenth century not historical facts. They are borne out of a certain cultural milieu and at a political conjuncture in history. As a historical process, the Nahda is a dynamic and contradictory generational phenomenon embedded in political and socio-economic transformations in the Mediterranean provinces of the Ottoman Empire. This essay elucidates the complex entwinement between historical process and giving meaning to Arab intellectual production in the shadow of colonial conquest. It does so in the mold of A. Gramsci, R.G. Collingwood and Quentin Skinner, David Scott and others where, like them, they share a form of historical criticism sensitive to the particular "problem-spaces" that generations of thinkers address.[1] In this perspective, Jurji Zaidan's life and work crystallizes larger questions about modern Arab culture. In order to get a comprehensive sense of the wider popular currency of Zaidan and his fellow Nahdawis, however, more research on the culture of reading and a systematic engagement with reception theory is required; not least because the Nahda writers themselves, much more than their predecessors whom they accused of self-aggrandizing verbosity, spoke in the name of their readers.[2]

On the Malice of Ignorance

The Nahda's tremendous intellectual, literary and educational transformations are totally absent from the bigoted works published

1 Fiori, Giuseppe. *Antonio Gramsci: Life of a Revolutionary* (London, Verso, 1970); Collingwood, R.G. *An Autobiography* (Oxford, Oxford Univ. Press, 1939); Tully, James. *Meaning and Context, Quentin Skinner and his Critics* (London, Polity, 1988); Scott, David. *Refashioning Futures; Criticism and Postcoloniality* (Princeton, Princeton Univ. Press, 1999).

2 Recent scholarship has made steps in this direction: Al-Baghdadi, Nadia. *Vorgestellte Öffentlichkeit: zur Genese moderner Prosa in Ägypten, 1860-1908* (Wiesbaden, Reichert, 2010); Holt, Elizabeth. "Narrative and the Reading Public in 1870s Beirut," *Journal of Arabic Literature* 40 (2009) pp. 37-70; Ayalon, Ami. *Reading Palestine: Printing and Literacy, 1900-1948* (Austin, Univ. of Texas Press, 2004).

on modern Arab culture during the War on Terror. Dan Diner's *Versiegelte Zeit: Über den Stillstand in der islamischen Welt*[3] is one such ignoble book. Cultural historians of the Arab world have largely neglected this text, with the exception of a serious and devastating review by Thomas Philipp.[4] Yet, it was deemed profitable enough for Princeton University Press to invest in a translation and make its even less ambiguous title available to the chattering classes and policy-makers in Washington. The "native fig leaf" that gave Diner's screed the appearance of legitimacy was Shakib Arslan's famous series of newspaper responses to an Indonesian cleric's question *Li-madha Ta'akhkhar al-Muslimun wa li-madha Taqaddam Ghayruhum?*[5] as well as the Arab Human Development Report of 2002.[6] To Diner, these public interventions break what all Muslims and Arabs know but are too ashamed to admit: that they have to take responsibility for their own backwardness. And to Diner falls the unpopular but noble task of breaking the Arab and Muslim consensus that blames others and offers a way out of the malaise. He combines this evidence of Arab and Muslim lack of self-criticism—itself a common trope of Orientalism—with a little-known, similarly policy-oriented study by an Iranian anthropologist who advocates abandoning literary Arabic and the Arabic script in favor of the Egyptian dialect on the grounds that classical Arabic blocked modern expression.

---

3 Diner, Dan. *Lost in the Sacred: Why the Muslim World Stood Still* (Princeton, Princeton Univ. Press, 2009). The beginning of the German title means literally "Sealed Time".

4 Philipp, Thomas. "Creating the Enemy," *Die Welt des Islams* 48 (2008) pp.50-7.

5 "Why did the Muslims lag behind and why did others advance?"

6 For Arslan's text, see Cleveland, William. *Islam against the West: Shakib Arslan and the Campaign for Islamic Nationalism* (Austin, Texas Univ. Press, 1985) ch. 6. For a deconstruction of the UN's AHDR, see Hasso, Frances; Adely, Fida; Jad, Islah; and Abu-Lughod, Lila. "Engaging the Arab Human Development Report 2005 on Women," *International Journal of Middle Eastern Studies* 41 (2009) pp. 59-122.

Criticism of Arabic grammar dates back to al-Sibawayhi and is alive and well in the twenty first century.[7] But taking a pedagogical tract from 1929, a UN report for neo-liberal consumption and an anthropologist's pamphlet—whose interests, we may assume, are more in the spoken than in the written language—Diner, at face-value as well as out of context, deftly draws his own conclusions: Arabs have failed to secularize and modernize, i.e. become like the West, *because their language was sacred.* But even if Arabic had still been of Koranic quality and Arabs had still considered their language as sacred and unchangeable, by the time European armies and commodities flooded the Ottoman empire, this would hardly have made for a historically-grounded argument. This book is based on the assumption that a religious community is inferior because of its linguistic culture and the only way to shed its backwardness is to abandon the Arabic script and grammar.[8] In ordinary times, *Versiegelte Zeit* would have been consigned to the trash heap of Western pontifications about Islam and Arabs. But studies like Diner's, along with Bernard Lewis' and Rafael Patai's more notorious works, have had a way to surface and resurface during the Bush years in the aftermath of September 11, 2001.[9]

The only way Diner's argument could possibly appear plausible to anyone receptive to Orientalist logic is by its erasure of an entire century of modern Arab intellectual history and the activities of the Arab reform and revival movement during the Nahda. Eminent Nahda scholars like Thomas Philipp are right to point out that Diner is totally ignorant of the profound impact of

---

7 Suleimān, Yāsir. "Arabic Language Reforms, Language Ideology and the Criminalization of Sibawayhi," in *Grammar as a Window onto Arabic Humanism,* edited by L.Edzard, and J.Watson (Wiesbaden, Harrassowitz, 2006) pp. 66-83.

8 If today cultural aetiology has replaced biological racism, as many postcolonial scholars claim, then this book contains elements of cultural racism.

9 Lewis, Bernard. *What is Wrong? The Clash Between Islam and Modernity* (New York, Perennial, 2003); Patai, Rafael. *The Arab Mind* (New York, Scribner, 1973) has been reissued in 2002 by the Hatherleigh Foundation and made required reading for American soldiers preparing for the occupation of Iraq.

the Nahda on Arab language and culture.[10] However, as scholars of the Nahda we can afford neither to disregard this ignorance nor to embrace uncritically the Nahda as evidence of all the attributes Islamo- and Arabophobes are denying. To limit our task to affirm defiantly the existence of the Nahda and merely to document its positive influences on Arab modernity would be to "stand still" intellectually and to validate *a posteriori* Diner's malicious logic. The study of the Nahda needs to be free of nostalgia, overcome monolithic understandings, and be critical of its many limitations and blind spots if it is to inform the Arab future, as I believe it should.

Diner takes the trope of *al-ta'akhkhur* and translates it into cultural backwardness but it could also mean underdevelopment or simply delay. This fateful verbal noun entered the Arab political vocabulary during and throughout the Nahda. Salim al-Bustani may have been the first in hundreds, if not thousands, of Arabic newspaper editorials to ask the question "Why are we in a state of delay?" [11] Like Shakib Arslan, Constantine Zurayq and many others after them, the answers have been a hodgepodge of economic and military reasons, social conditions, as well as political practices and religious attitudes.[12] As we shall see below, from our contemporary perspective some of these responses are easy prey to the charges of self-Orientalization. A translation that is more historically attuned to the shifting meanings of *al-ta'akhkhur* and more sensitive to the historical moments in which this idea gets expressed complicates the matter further.

Diner has translated the verb *ta'akhkhara* as "zurückbleiben" in German and "to fall behind" in the English edition. As Manfred Sing has recently argued, the shift of the meaning of *al-ta'akhkhur* from economic to cultural dimensions was not self-evident but a response to political developments in the Middle East after the Arab military

10 Philipp. "Creating the Enemy."

11 Al-Bustānī, Salīm. "Li-madha naḥnu fi al-Ta'akhkhur?" *al-Jinān* 1 (1870) pp. 162-164.

12 Zurayq, Constantine. *The Meaning of Disaster* (Beirut, Khayyat, 1956).

defeat in 1967.[13] While early twentieth-century thinkers like Arslan or Zurayq built in faint critiques of European capitalism and militarism into their understanding of the term, Nahda thinkers like al-Bustani had conceded Arab *al-ta'akhkhur* and sought the white man's recognition on nineteenth-century liberalism's terms. At the time, the idea of gaining cultural and economic ground merely by trying harder was rooted in a particular optimism about the future and a perception of comparative advantage with countries further to the east.[14] Nahda thinkers tended to believe in the Ottoman state's unassailability and longevity and invoked *al-ta'akhkhur* not as a historical law but as a "wake-up" call in order to incite people into action. In this light, the term *al-Nahda* formed something of an antonymic unit with *al-ta'akhkur* long before *al-inhitat*—"decline"—entered in the Nahda's vocabulary.[15]

There is a hagiographic tradition of the Nahda as a golden liberal age of tolerance. As the example of Bustani's cultural one-upmanship over India suggests, the Nahda's tolerance is a slippery concept in a world dominated by competitive ideas about free trade, self-help and progress. It is understandable that in the long decades of colonial oppression and authoritarian rule which may finally come to some kind of end after the Arab revolts would tempt us to glorify the era before colonial occupation and state-organized sectarianism. But there are also many more

13 Sing, Manfred. "The Leftist Critique of *takhalluf*: Revisiting Cultural and Psychological Approaches to Arab Societies," paper delivered at "Intellectual History of the Arab Left," *Workshop held at the American University of Beirut,* Beirut, 6-7 July 2012.

14 In another editorial, Salīm al- Bustānī makes the Orientalist argument that Arab civilization may lag behind Europe's but it was much more advanced than India's where "they still burn their brides". In "Markazuna," *al-Jinān* 3 (1872) p.145.

15 J. Brugman dates the first use of the verb form *nahaḍa* to an article by Adib Ishaq written in 1878, i. e. eight years after Salīm al-Bustānī invoked *al-ta'akhkhur* but some twenty years before the appearance of *al-inḥiṭāṭ* which Zaidan adopted at the end of his life. Brugman, J. *An Introduction to the History of Modern Arabic Literature in Egypt* (Leiden, E.J.Brill, 1984) pp. 8-10.

nuanced critiques of the Nahda in Arabic that would have deserved Princeton University Press' translation much more than Diner's attempt to deny Arabs contemporaneity.[16]

Metanarratives of Enlightenment

In the history of the reception and mobilization of the Nahda there have been two broad interpretative schemes. The first scheme on the Nahda was in a Voltairean-Habermasian mode: the Nahda represents the pivotal moment of a still incomplete historical process in which "classical" Arab science and reason were rediscovered to triumph over ignorance and imitation in an ever-expanding realm of liberty and liberation. 'Abd al-'Aziz al-Duri's *Al-Takwin al-Tarikhi lil-Umma al-'Arabiyya* (1960) was in this optimistic mode; so was Ibrahim Abu-Lughod's *Arab Rediscovery of Europe: A Study in Cultural Encounters* of the same year. Two years later, Albert Hourani's classic *Arabic Thought in the Liberal Age* lamented the passing of the liberal age but also embraced Arab nationalist currents that led to independence.

Pessimists in this scheme see the noble spirit of the Nahda betrayed by the spread of radical ideologies, nativism and Islamism since the 1940s and then, after 1967 by what came to be known as the "Arab malaise". In English-language scholarship, the most prominent representative of this scheme is Fouad Ajami's work, particularly *The Arab Predicament* (1981) and *The Dream Palace of the Arabs* (1998).[17]

16 Most notably 'Azmī Bishāra's highly popular and sophisticated *Ṭarūḥāt 'an al-Nahḍa al-Mu'āqa* (London, Riad el-Rayyes Books, 2003). See also Mahdī, Āmīl. *Azmat al-Ḥadāra al-'Arabiyya am Azmat al-Burjuwaziyya al-'Arabiyya?* (Beirut, Dar al-Farabi, 1974).

17 Ajami, Fouad. *Dream Palace of the Arabs: A Generation's Odyssey* (New York, Random House, 1998) and *The Arab Predicament: Arab Political Thought and Practice since 1967* (UK, Cambridge University Press, 1992). The first edition of this book was published in 1981.

The second interpretive scheme of the Nahda echoes the critical approaches to modernity associated with Rousseau, Weber or Foucault. This scheme views enlightenment and modernity as inherently alienating, disenchanting and constricting.[18] If the first scheme celebrates the Nahda's original intellectual curiosity and cultural openness—even as its representatives have differed on the longevity—the second laments that the Nahda paved the way for Arab dependency and derivative modernity. In their search for cultural innovation and a revival of the past, the *Nahdawi*s have merely aped the standards of the West. As a pejorative, Westernization signified a loss of authenticity and intellectual naivité or direct complicity in European cultural imperialism. These trends have been particularly pronounced in the aftermath of the 1967 defeat. More recently, Islamist critics of the Nahda have rediscovered the late nineteenth century anti-European polemicist Yusuf al-Nabhani (1849/50-1932) and other conservatives of the late Ottoman period who, they argued, were deliberately obscured by liberal scholarship.[19]

By contrast, for the Moroccan epistemologist Muhammad 'Abid al-Jabiri, the Nahda was a valiant but ultimately futile attempt to combine the revival of the Arabo-Islamic heritage with a political and intellectual reform project because the remedies that the nineteenth-century intellectuals invoked were based on superficial philosophical understandings of critical thought. Like Zaidan before him, al-Jabiri has spoken of multiple renaissances of which the Nahda was only the last. But while Zaidan confidently saw the nineteenth century as a cultural culmination al-Jabiri viewed that century as less inspiring than the age of recording back in the eighth and ninth centuries.

---

18 Kramer, Lloyd."Habermas, Foucault, and the Legacy of the Enlightenment Intellectuals," in *Intellectuals and Public Life; Between Radicalism and Reform* edited by Leon Fink, Stephen T. Leonard and Donald M. Reid (Ithaca, London, Cornell Univ. Press, 1996) pp. 30-50.

19 Nabhānī's defence of the caliphate has made him a grandfather to *salafī* groups like Ḥizb al-Taḥrīr which was founded by his daughter's son.

Laroui and other Marxist Arab intellectuals have spoken of a "second true Nahda which is sometimes described as a dynamization (*tathwir*) of Arab thought" in the 1960s. In the 1980s, as the West grew intolerant of Third World liberation struggles and the Reagan-Thatcher tandem policed the world, enthusiasm for the second Nahda waned and gave way to epistemological critiques of the West, most influentially by Edward Said. In a long-forgotten study, the former leader of the Syrian opposition, professor of political science in Paris, Burhan Ghalioun, has combined the epistemological and political-economic critiques of the Nahda in his *Le Malaise Arabe: état contre nation* and *Ightiyal al-'aql.* In it he affirms the liberal-secular project of the Nahda but laments how the Arab rationalists of all political stripes have been on the side of the exploitative classes since the Nahda:

> Western rationalism was a culmination of a long-standing suspicion in all the traditional systems of thought, and was an affirmation of the freedom of man, individual, community, and nation. However, Arab rationalism has affirmed and justified the existing system … of modernity and dependency, either in the name of progress or the logic of history, but always against the freedom of the individual.[20]

The Place of Zaidan in the Anglo-Arab Tradition

The public reception of the Nahda in English started with George Antonius' magisterial *The Arab Awakening* whose narrative performance of becoming modern and worthy of independence has defined academic and non-academic discourse of the Arabs' political desire for recognition and European betrayal ever since. After "a false start" in Muhammad 'Ali Pasha's Egypt in the first half

20 Ghalyūn, Burḥān. *Ightiyāl al-'Aql: Mihnat al-Thaqāfa al-'Arabiyya bayna 'l-Salafiyya wa'l-Ṭabī'iyya* (Cairo, Madbouli, 1990) quoted in Abu Rabi', Ibrahim. *Contemporary Thought: Studies in post-1967 Arab Intellectual History* (London, Pluto Press, 2009) p.122.

of the nineteenth century, the Nahda emerged as a missionary-educated, intellectual circle in Beirut in mid-century before Sultan 'Abdulhamid II's autocracy politicized and then exiled the leading Syrian intellectuals to Egypt where they became Arab nationalists under British occupation.

Even though, as we shall see presently, Jurji Zaidan's itinerary exemplified these shifts, Antonius mentions neither him nor his works. And he should have. The first volume of Zaidan's epochal *Biographies of Renowed Men from The East in the Nineteenth Century*[21] contained biographies of—and these are his categories—"the Egyptian ruling family", "kings and princes", "leaders", "administrators and politicians" and "men of affairs". The second volume was dedicated to eight "pillars of the scientific revival", nine "publishers and journalists," thirty one "other men of science and culture" and fourteen "poets".[22]

Antonius used almost no nineteenth-century Arabic sources and relied largely on the memories of his octogenarian father-in-law, Faris Nimr. But the main purpose of *The Arab Awakening* was to prove to its audience

21 *Tarājim Mashāhir al-Sharq fī'l-Qarn al-tāsi' 'ashar* was first published in 1907.

22 The eight were Dr. Clot Bey, Shaykh Naṣīf al-Yāzijī, Rifā'at Bey al-Ṭaḥṭāwī, Buṭrus al-Bustānī, 'Alī Pasha Mubārak, Dr. Cornelius van Dyk, Sayyid Jamāl al-Dīn al-Afghānī, Sayyid Aḥmad Khān; the nine publishers and journalists were Adīb Isḥāq, Aḥmad Fāris al-Shidyāq, Muḥammad Nāmiq Kamāl, Salīm Taqlā and his brother Bishāra, Sayyid 'Abdallah Nadīm, Ibrāhīm Bey al-Muwayliḥī, Shaykh Ibrāhīm al-Yāzijī, Khalīl Khūrī, and Rizqallah Ḥasūn; the poets were Shaykh Amīn al-Jundī, Mu'allim Buṭrus Karāma, 'Abd al-Bāqī al-'Umarī, Fransis Marrāsh, Sayyid 'Abd al-Ghaffār al-Akhras, Ḥajj 'Umar al-Unsī, Shaykh Khalīl al-Yāzijī, 'Abdallah Pasha Fikrī, As'ad ṭirād, Mu'allim Nājī, Ilyās Ṣāliḥ, Shaykh Najīb Ḥaddād, Maḥmūd Pasha Sāmī al-Bārūdī, 'Abduh al-Ḥamūlī (musician); others included Salīm Buṭrus, Muḥammad Pasha Falakī, Nawfal Nawfal, Dr. Mikhā'īl Mishāqa, Shaykh 'Abd al-Hādī Najjār al-Abyārī, Shafīq Bey Manṣūr, Shaykh Yūsuf al-Asīr, Shaykh Ibrāhīm al-Aḥdab, Aḥmad Cevdet Pasha, Maḥmūd Ḥamza al-Ḥusaynī, Amīn al-Shumayyil, Marūn Naqqāsh, Naṣīf Ma'lūf, Salīm dī Nawfal, Muḥammad Bayram, Niqūlā Tūmā, Ḥasan Pasha Maḥmūd, Jamīl Mudawwar, Bishop Yūsif Dibs, Salīm Mikhā'īl Shiḥāta, Drs. Wortabet and Post.

of diplomats and public opinion shapers that Britain owed the Arabs an independent Palestine and the right to self-determination elsewhere for their contributions to defeating the Ottoman empire and winning World War I. The Nahda was instrumentalized to convince the reader that Arab nationalism derived from the principles of the Enlightenment transmitted by Protestant missionaries.

While Antonius' book failed to have the intended effect and Britain abandoned Palestine to the Zionists, *The Arab Awakening* remains the scholarly keystone for Arab nationalism. In a retrospective, Albert Hourani concluded that Antonius' book should be judged not merely as a scholarly enterprise but also as a political manifesto. Hourani himself set out to write a book that would illuminate the part he deemed was missing in Antonius and his critics, that of the emergence of Arabism, the culture of modern social and political ideas in Antonius' epoch, the Arabic liberal age. Where Zaidan's *Tarajim* identified comprehensive but static social categories and Antonius merely lined up Nahda thinkers in terms of their contribution to the formation of an emerging nationalism, Hourani's methodological innovation over Zaidan and Antonius was to introduce the concept of generational change.[23]

In Hourani's dialectic progression, the Nahda becomes the work of three generations. The pioneers around al-Tahtawi, Khayr al-Din al-Tunisi, Butrus al-Bustani and, in supporting roles, Nasif al-Yaziji and Faris al-Shidyaq, were born between the 1800s and 1820s.[24] The middle generation was born between 1839 (al-Afghani) and 1874 (Farah Antun) and included 'Abd al-Rahman al-Kawakibi, 'Abdallah Nadim, Muhammad 'Abduh and his disciples Qasim Amin, Husayn Jisr, Tahir al-Jaza'iri, 'Abd al-Qadir Maghribi, Kurd 'Ali, Shakib Arslan, and, most prominently, Rashid Rida. This generation also comprised two 'cohorts' of

23 Albert Hourani does not explicitly engage with the sociology of knowledge, e.g. Karl Mannheim's influential overview "The Problem of Generations," in his *Essays on the Sociology of Knowledge* (London, Routledge & Kegan Paul, 1952) pp. 276-322.

24 They were also awarded biographical information.

Christian secularists represented by Shibli Shumayyil, Adib Ishaq, Farah Antun and Jurji Zaidan.[25] Hourani's third and final generation of the Nahda was epitomized by the towering figure of Taha Husayn who was born in 1889 and died in 1973.[26] They stood for the final Hegelian synthesis of the entire Arab renaissance project for they felt culturally at home in—and combined the best of—both worlds: a superior knowledge of the West owing to long years of studying in Europe and a deep-rooted sense of belonging and contributing to Arab and Islamic culture.

One of the critical responses Hourani received for *Arabic Thought* was by 'Abdulatif Tibawi.[27] He shared Hourani's interest in the effects of Protestant missionaries on the production of knowledge in Beirut.[28] However, the Palestine-born Muslim-education specialist Tibawi heavily criticized Antonius, Hourani and other anglophile scholars on a number of grounds. The Arab revival did not start "in Lebanon, spreading to Egypt and thence to other parts of the world".[29] Neither was it the result of missionary schooling or publishing, nor carried "more by the Christian element than the Islamic".[30] Too many western scholars,

---

25 Abū 'l-Hūdā al-Sayyādī, Muḥammad Bayrām and Aḥmad Khān get a brief mention in a chapter dominated by Afghānī's famous debate with Renan. Rashīd Riḍā got his own chapter in which Ḥusayn Jisr, Tāhir al-Jazā'irī, 'Abd al-Qādir Maghribī, Kurd 'Alī and Shakīb Arslān are mentioned as his cohort.

26 Husayn (d. 1973), al-Sayyid (d. 1963) and Rāziq (d. 1963) were the only ones still alive at the time of writing his book and for whom he used the present tense.

27 Tibawi, 'Abdulatif. "Some Misconceptions about the Nahda," in his *Arabic and Islamic Themes; Historical, Educational and Literary Studies* (London, Luzac, 1976) pp. 304-314.

28 Tibawi, 'Abdulatif. *American Interests in Syria, 1800-1901* (Oxford, Oxford Univ. Press, 1966).

29 Beeston, A. F. L. *The Arabic Language Today* (London, Hutchinson, 1970) p.15; quoted in Tibawi, "Misconceptions." p. 304.

30 Tibawi. "Misconceptions." p. 305.

Tibawi argues, have been blinded by the light of the Syrian Protestant College (later the American University of Beirut).

Tibawi had little time for Beirut-centrism and relocated the cradle-debate to Egypt where state schools and the Bulaq publishing press churned out printed editions of classical Arabic texts and European translations a decade before schools and presses started operating in Beirut. Islam, not contacts with Western missionaries provided the anti-colonial impetus for the great historical force of Arab nationalism. Rejecting the conventional historiographical starting point that Napoleon's invasion signaled the arrival of the modern era in the Middle East, Tibawi calls for an Islamic hermeneutics to trace modern texts to early modern Arab and Muslim writers.

Hisham Sharabi is the third Arab scholar of intellectual history whose work is important to understanding Beirut's position in the intellectual revival and its successor movements of Arab nationalism. The Acre-born Marxist political scientist whose academic home became Georgetown University, in Washington D.C, has identified the period from 1875 to 1914 as the "formative years" in modern Arab thought in which a host of intellectual strands vied with each other over the nature of Arab relations with the West. Whether Islamic Reformist, Christian Westernizer or—Sharabi's most cherished category—Muslim Secularist, all Arab intellectuals of the turn of the century were forward-looking and therefore modern: "the Golden Age lay not in the past but in the future".[31] With Sharabi's work, the focus of Arab intellectual history shifted to the Syrian, Iraqi and Egyptian cities of the interior where educated Muslims were motivated by alternative modernist thought. Their upper middle class origins "exposed [them] to more or less the same process of socialization: they experienced similar patterns of upbringing; they had the same value system; and they received the same type of education".[32]

31 Sharabī, Hishām. *Arab Intellectuals and the West: the Formative Years, 1875-1914* (Baltimore, John Hopkins Press, 1970) p. 7.

32 Ibid. p.19.

The Place

I have followed Hourani's still innovative model to disaggregate the Nahda into distinct phases carried by the generational forging of a modern Arab intellectual tradition. But rather than measure the generational dialectic against the methodological constant of interaction with the West as Hourani has done, I propose to relate intellectual shifts to urbanization, political events and socio-economic processes in Bilad al-Sham. In my past work I have inverted the search for wider circulation of Nahda networks and ideas by reducing the scale of inquiry to the level of *intra* urban intellectual dynamics within the Nahda. I have considered whether in a city like Beirut there were distinct *milieux* or schools of thought that emerged in parallel or in competition with each other.

In his biography of the Arab luminary Ibrahim al-Yaziji (1847-1907), the Lebanese intellectual historian Paul Soueid divides the geography of mid-nineteenth century Beirut into three distinct cultural spheres. Chronologically, the first intellectual hub was centred in Zokak el-Blat where the Bustanis and Yazijis lived, taught and published an enormous range of literature from the 1840s to the 1880s, and where they founded the Syrian Society for Arts and Sciences.[33] The second cultural centre—"no less important"—was in the Saifi area on the other side of what became the Beirut-Damascus road in 1863. The Jesuit missionaries settled there in 1831 and set up the Oriental Society in 1850 to compete with Zokak el-Blat's Syrian Society for the Arts and Sciences founded three years earlier. The third wellspring of the Beirut-based renaissance was in Hayy Mar Marun, east of the city's main square, Sahat al-Burj. It was created and maintained, insists Soueid, by a sole person, Marun al-Naqqash (1817-1855).[34] The first Arab theatre circle formed around

33 Al-Bustānī, Buṭrus. *Al-Jam'iyya al-Sūriyya li'l-'Ulūm wa'l-Funūn, 1838-1852*, edited by Yūsuf Quzma Khūrī (Beirut, s. n., 1990).

34 Soueid, Paul. *Ibrahim al-Yaziji, l'homme et son Œuvre* (Beirut, Université, 1969) p. ix.

this famous playwright and his brothers, before it moved to Egypt after Naqqash's death.

Why excavate this rare introductory passage from a long-forgotten book? How is our knowledge and understanding of such a broad and contested phenomenon as the Arab intellectual revival furthered by zooming in on the cultural geography of a single city, let alone by focusing on a heterogeneous quarter that has never received any systematic scholarly attention? Even though long-forgotten Zokak el-Blat was the initial engine of Beirut's contribution to the Nahda, Ashrafiyyah where the University of St. Joseph received the papal seal of recognition in 1881 and Jumayze, where wealthy minority merchants attended Naqqash's performances, have assumed paradigmatic status in Beirut's historiography. These two Christian quarters in East Beirut lent themselves to historical inquiry largely because of their relative confessional and social homogeneity: most of the newly prosperous families of nineteenth-century Beirut, who were Christian merchants and entrepreneurs, lived there.[35]

I have come to consider Zokak el-Blat an urban microcosm that represents Beirut's syncretistic intellectual atmosphere during the Nahda. In the second half of the nineteenth century, the quarter—no larger than two square miles—was a place where leading Arab intellectuals converged and developed the main trends of Arab thought in the twentieth century: Arabism and Arab nationalism.

The Event

The most significant event for the transformation of the Nahda occurred in the summer of 1860 when 12,000 people were killed and many more maimed and displaced in Mt. Lebanon and Damascus. This gruesome event represents a deep caesura for Arab thought, literature and

35 Fawaz, Leila. *Merchants and Migrants in nineteenth Century Beirut* (Cambridge, MA., Harvard Univ. Press, 1983).

culture.[36] More or less up until that point the Nahda had predominantly been a philological revival movement. It drew its strength and popular appeal from the rediscovery and adaptation of diwans of classical Arabic poetry. The climax was Nasif al-Yaziji's 1856 diwan *Majm'a al-bahrayn.*

The neo-classical mode of the Nahda continued well into the twentieth century.[37] However, the civil war generated a new approach to writing, a new urgency to address "the compatriots" in written speech, and new genres of literature. The most prominent of these were the political pamphlet and the didactic and often historical novel.[38] Butrus al-Bustani's *Nafir Suriyya* appeared first in Beirut only weeks after the end of the civil war and ran eleven issues. In these pamphlets Bustani made passionate appeals to his fellow countrymen to overcome their sectarian differences, individual and communal self-interest and work together for a better and more dignified common future. In developing the ideal foundations of a harmonious society in these pamphlets, Bustani developed an affective new discourse of public morality that was to become a central motif in Arabic thought in the next generation.

Beiruti public moralists displayed an acute awareness of the interactive relation between society and the urban *milieu*. They increasingly turned the social life of Beirut into a new object of analysis and intervention. Social thought in Beirut after 1860 was not dissimilar to that of the British public moralists of the time,[39] who identified London's poor as a

36 See Hanssen, Jens. *Fin de Siècle Beirut; The Making of an Ottoman Provincial Capital* (Oxford, Clarendon Press, 2005); Khury-Makdisi, Ilham. *The Eastern Mediterranean and the Making of Global Radicalism, 1860-1914* (Los Angeles, Univ. of California Press, 2010).

37 Noorani, Yaseen. "The Rebellious Subject," *Journal of Arabic Literature* 29 (1998) pp. 1-30.

38 Sheehi, Stephen. *Foundations of Modern Arab Identity* (Gainesville, Univ. of Florida, 2004).

39 The terms "public morality" and "public moralists" are borrowed from Collini, Stefan. *Public Moralists, Political Thought and Intellectual Life in Britain, 1830-1930* (Oxford, Clarendon Press, 1991).

root problem of society, and were one in the belief that there were "savage tribes lurking at the bottom of our civilization, which if not tamed and disciplined would ultimately overthrow it".[40] The 1867 Ottoman police law had stipulated that beggars were to be apprehended on sight and incarcerated.

The Public Moralist

Jurji Zaidan was one such public moralist whose autobiography—written in 1909—represents a pertinent commentary on the perceived social dangers in Beirut. Born in downtown Beirut in 1861 and attending the Syrian Protestant College for barely over a year, he left Beirut for Egypt in 1882 to pursue a distinguished career as a journalist, publisher, historian and literary critic. Constant fear of local knaves was a recurrent theme in his memoirs. His criticism was all the more severe as he was born into a poor family and came in close contact with the roughs and toughs of Beirut while working in his father's restaurant off Sahat al-Burj, Beirut's main public square. Subsequently he raised himself from his social background through "hard work", "perseverance", "awareness of time" and "discipline".[41] Reminiscing about his youth as a restaurant boy, Zaidan complained:

> There remained for company only the idle people who had no work that they enjoyed. These people would gather in my place; some would spend their leisure time during work between morning and evening here. Their talk differed from the talk of crooks only in form and expression: one would boast how he committed adultery taking possession of so-and-so, the wife of the honourable such-and-such...Another would show off

40 Harris, Jose. *Private Lives, Public Spirit: Britain, 1870-1914* (London, Oxford Univ. Press, 1993) p. 242.

41 Philipp, Thomas. *Ǧurǧi Zaidān: His Life and Thought*. Beiruter Texte und Studien vol. 3 (Beirut, Franz Steiner Verlag, 1979) p. 11.

> with his abilities in fornication. Amongst them was a young hunchback whom I heard saying that his hunch was the result of immoderation. ...Such were the *mores* of the masses of Beirut.[42]

The roughs and toughs of Beirut (the *qabaday* and *rijal al-futuwwa wa abna' al-hawa*) elicited the young Zaidan's fear and admiration. They were infamous in Beirut for their drinking bouts which "would be attended by the wise man and the ignorant, because the Beirutis have for a long time believed the alcoholic anis drink *'araq* to be of benefit before the meal and wine with the meal". Decent people would turn boisterous in the taverns.

> Usually three or four would sit together to get drunk. One of them would order a *khamsiniyya*. It would be poured for him and his friends until it was empty. Then another one would order a second, and so on until none owed the others anything... When the wine went to their heads, one would start singing a Baghdadi *mawwal*. They would listen well to his song and would interpret from it something that he wanted from them, be it by way of praise and laudation or criticism and negative comments. It would then behove him or one of his friends or his companions to answer to the *mawwal*. Provided the singing was done with good humour, the party would take a turn for the better. But if it consisted of criticism and insinuations, it would lead to quarrelling and eventually to the drawing of knives and unsheathing of sticks.[43]

Zaidan divided Beirut society into two classes (*tabaqatan*): the commoners, *al-'amma*—"riff raff, artisans, all the other people with menial occupations, and the small merchants"— on the one hand and the elites,

42 Philipp. *Zaidān*, p.145.

43 Philipp. *Zaidān*, pp.146-47.

al-khassa—"people of the government and the rich"—on the other. The Beirut lower class, *al-'amma*, was uneducated because of the few schools available to it. "Obscene expressions and indecent talk prevailed in their speech." [44] Zaidan concluded his brief analysis of Beirut's class structure by stating that there developed after the 1860 civil war a third class amongst the Beirutis, the intellectuals, educated in the European missionary schools. They began to dress in western clothes and were considered effeminate and seen to be breaching traditions. Yet Zaidan felt most at ease in this circle, partly because they, like him, abstained from alcohol and other urban "vices".[45] "This social group was determined to change the social norms from what they were to what they became, so that the contemporary morals of Beirut became comparable with the most advanced habits and customs of the Europeans." [46] Like Bustani, Zaidan's life work was to consist of educating society and attune individuals to the spirit of the age through history books and his Cairene journal *al-Hilal*.

Zaidan employed abstract values of contemporary European civilization as pedagogical ideal-types which he viewed through what his American contemporary Charles Horten Cooley called "the looking-glass self". However, foreigners in Beirut were themselves associated with many of the vices that surrounded young Zaidan:

> The term 'English language' was strange for the Beirutis to hear because the only characteristic of the English they knew was contained in the expression 'English drunkenness'. Frequently they would observe drunken members of the English navy in the streets of the city.... They would roam

44 Philipp. *Zaidān*, pp.147-48.

45 Significanly, Zaidan distanced himself from his drunkard associates only after his attempts to blend in with the drinking groups ended with him throwing up heavily. Ibid. p.151.

46 Ibid. pp. 148-9.

> around in the city, eat, drink and most would be overpowered by drunkenness. When they were drunk they would quarrel boisterously in a language nobody understood. So the expression 'English drunkenness' was on everybody's lips in Beirut, implying excessive drinking.[47]

As outspoken public moralists, Butrus al-Bustani and Jurji Zaidan urged citizens to embrace new opportunities of learning, productivity and the public good. Bustani admonished those who wasted their time "in coffeehouses which are filled with youths and grown-ups who frequently visit them in order to kill time during the day and during the night they kill time at home playing dominoes and cards".[48] Jurji Zaidan was even more explicit in an answer to a letter to the editor which complained that "in some of your articles on leisure time you consider sitting in a café an ugly habit. We don't understand what is so bad about this activity and those places. What breaches manners and culture?" Zaidan answered:

> We are not saying that coffeehouses and their surroundings in public places are a breach of manners. What we have said and are saying is that staying in cafés for days on end is idleness and that this is particularly bad for the young given how difficult it has become to find work these days. After thirty five you won't find a job and the chances for the youth are little after fifteen. Between twenty and twenty five is the best time of life, so why waste it sitting in coffeehouses drinking beer and playing backgammon? It is then that we determine our

47 Ibid. p. 151.

48 Al-Bustānī, Buṭrus. "Al-Ḥayāt al-ijtimā'iyya fī Bayrūt," in *A'māl al-Jām'iyya al-'ilmiyya al-Sūriyya, 1868-1869,* edited by Y. Al-Khūrī (Beirut, 1990) p. 207. For a less scathing and more analytical article on the problem of unemployment, see al-Shidyāq, Aḥmad Fāris. "Fī'l-'Amal wa'l-Bāṭala." in his *Kanz al-Gharā'ib fī Muntakhabāt al-Jawā'ib* in 5 vols. (Istanbul, Maṭba'at al-Jawā'ib, 1878) vol.1 pp. 151-153.

> future and the rest of our life depends on it. You lose time and money if you gamble.[49]

These innocuous social vices disturbed the Nahdawis profoundly. Not only did such practices seem to confirm the Western stereotypes about the indolent East they worked so hard to dispel. They also made them nervous because in their worldview, time had become money and Arabs could ill-afford to waste this precious commodity. The cure-all against these dangers and the path to a more prosperous future lay in schools. In late Ottoman Beirut, the place I know best, and elsewhere in the Arab provinces hundreds of primary and secondary schools opened after 1860. Many were missionary schools, many more were Ottoman state schools and some were founded at the initiative of local philanthropic societies and wealthy families.[50] In contradistinction to colonial and many missionary schools which were meant to provide practical education, Ottoman imperial and local Arabic curricula included advanced sciences, language and literature. But exposure to the Arabic canon posed a new problem for the Nahda pedagogues: how to deal with those free-minded authors and works that indulge in behavior they deemed inappropriate; what to do with Abu Nuwwas' depictions of drinking bouts or sexual references in *ghazal* poetry more generally, for example?

In a recent study, Joseph Massad has offered a fundamental re-reading of the Nahda based on these questions.[51] *Desiring Arabs* argues in the section which introduces Jurji Zaidan that "[t]he implication of these questions was civilizational in scale, as what was included in the archive

---

49 *Al-Hilāl* 7 (Oct.1897) pp.137-138.

50 Hanssen. *Fin de Siècle Beirut*; and also "The Birth of an Education Quarter: Zokak el-Blat as a Cradle of Cultural Revival in the Arab World," in *History, Space and Social Conflict in Beirut; The Quarter of Zokak el-Blat* edited by R. Bodenstein et.al. (Beirut, Orient Institut, 2005) pp. 143-174.

51 Massad, Joseph. *Desiring Arabs* (Chicago, Chicago Univ. Press, 2007).

of Arab heritage would reflect immediately on the stature of Arab civilization".[52]

One of the main themes of the early Nahda's novels—when they were still serialized—was the pursuit of desire and the struggle of love over social conventions. Allegories of the modern Arab national subject, these stories validated the Nahda's and the Ottoman state's overlapping reform projects rather than tolerate social transgression or destabilize patriarchy and hetero-normativity.[53] Massad goes one step further than Sheehi and argues that the more anxious Zaidan grew about the image of the Arab in the West the more he censured *ghazal* poetry. His canonization of Arabic literature was as much about recovering and making accessible certain texts as it was about burying and stigmatizing others.

Massad does not hold Zaidan's generation responsible for self-Orientalization. They "did not dictate subsequent discussions of sex in modern Arab intellectual history". Indeed, the doyen of the next generation, Taha Husayn, "reveled in the sexual history of the medieval Arabs under Islam".[54] But the abiding critique and original insight of *Desiring Arabs* is that—contrary to the perception of heroic knowledge expansion—the Nahda has, in its desire to emulate and find acceptance in the West, inaugurated a collective disavowal of the ideas and practices that had characterized Arab life before the Western cultural conquest of the Arab world.[55]

The Linguist

Having elucidated critically the living legacy of the Nahda and Zaidan's key role in it, let us return to the refutation of the argument

52 Ibid. p.57.

53 Sheehi. *Foundations*, ch.3.

54 Massad. *Desiring Arabs*, p. 225.

55 Ibid. *passim*.

that the Arabic language is still enthralled by classical Islamic precepts. Like most nineteenth century scholars, Jurji Zaidan's linguistic work was projecting modern ideas about the "intrinsic nationality of languages" back into a past where no nations in the modern sense had existed. But for our purposes, his philological speculations are a testament to the blindness of Dan Diner's insights. In late nineteenth century Egypt there were two linguistic schools, the advocates of what came to be known as modern standard Arabic, spearheaded by Rifa'at Rafi' al-Tahtawi on the one hand, and the Egyptianists around Muhammad 'Uthman Jalal and Muhammad Taymur who wanted to make the Egyptian dialect the mode of literary expression, on the other.[56] The question of literary, *fusha,* versus vernacular, *'ammiyya,* Arabic dominated discussion among Arab intellectuals in Cairo and the Arab provincial capitals of the late Ottoman empire. In these cities, the expansion of print capitalism and the mechanical reproduction of information brought about changes to the Arabic language itself. Not every Nahdawi welcomed the triumph of content over form and the ensuing depoeticization of Arabic. In Beirut, Butrus al-Bustani, Ahmad Faris al-Shidyaq and Ibrahim al-Yaziji led a protracted philological battle.[57] Later in Cairo Ibrahim al-Yaziji, the son of the great reviver and innovator of the classical *maqamat* lyricism Nasif al-Yaziji, launched a general critique of what he called the simplicity of "newspaper Arabic" and upheld the virtues of the rhymed prose of *saj'.* [58]

But in Egypt, this linguistic struggle acquired political urgency after the British invasion in 1882 and subsequent colonial attempts to eliminate

56 Sa'īd, Nafūsa Zakārīyā. *Tārīkh al-Da'wa ilā 'l-'ammiyya wa-athāruhā fi Miṣr* (Alexandria, Dār Nashr al-Thaqāfa, 1964). See also Bardenstein, Carol. *Translation and Transformation in Modern Arabic Literature: The Indigenous Assertions of Muḥammad 'Uthman Jalāl* (Wiesbaden, Harrassowitz, 2005).

57 Chibli, Antoine. *Al-Shidyāq wa'l-Yāzijī: Munāqasha 'ilmiyya adabiyya, sana 1871* (Beirut, s.n., 1950).

58 Al-Yāzijī, Ibrāhīm. *Lugha al Jarā'id* (Cairo, s.n., 1900).

literary (*fusha*) Arabic.[59] Precursors to Diner's ill-conceived linguistic logic, British officials worked hard to institutionalize English as the official language of Egypt while promoting Cairene dialect as the national language.[60]

Here Zaidan's business prerogatives coincided with his ideological commitment to his native tongue. An Arabic print language that was not inflected by Egyptian or Levantine dialects would travel better to the far corners of the Arabic-reading public. A little-known correspondence between Jurji Zaidan and the 'Ibadi sultan in Zanzibar reveals both the intellectual and business connections between the Nahda and the Indian Ocean. His *al-Hilal* was well-subscribed among the Zanzibari elite and his *History of Islamic Literature* was a popular textbook. The Zanzibari court subsidized other members of his generation, like Ibrahim al-Yaziji.[61]

Zaidan had quite distinctive ideas about the evolution of Arabic for his time. In his first foray into philology, *al-Falsafa al-Lughawiyya* (1886), he relied on the fall of Babel narrative in the Hebrew Bible but gave geo-historical as well as anthropological explanations for the dispersion of humanity into distinct language communities of solidarity.[62] Of all

59 Dupont, Anne Laure. *Ǧurǧī Zaydān 1861-1914: Écrivain réformiste et témoin de la Renaissance arabe* (Damas, Institut Français du Proche Orient, 2006) pp. 365-74.

60 Diem, Werner. *Hochsprache und Dialekt im Arabischen. Abhandlungen der Kunde des Morgenlandes* (Wiesbaden, Franz Steiner, 1974) pp.130-32. See also Dupont, Anne-Laure. "What is the *katib 'amm*? The Status of Men of Letters and the Conception of Language According to Jurji Zaydan," *Middle Eastern Literatures* 13 (2010) pp. 171-181.

61 Ghazal, Amal. *Islamic Reform and Arab Nationalism: Expanding the Crescent from the Mediterranean to the Indian Ocean, 1880s-1930s* (London, Routledge, 2010) pp. 62-4.

62 Zaydān, Jurjī. *Al-Alfāz al-'Arabiyya wa'l-Falsafa al-Lughawiyya* (Beirut, Maṭba'at al-Qidīs Jāwrjiyūs, 1886). For translated parts of this book, see Philipp, Thomas. *Jurji Zaidan and the Foundations of Arab Nationalism* (New York, Syracuse Univ. Press, 2014). See also Philipp, Thomas. "Language, History and Arab National Consciousness in the Thought of Jurji Zaidan," *International Journal of Middle East Studies* 4 (1973) pp. 3-22.

the Semitic languages, Arabic proved to be the strongest. Zaidan credited the Koran and Islam's linguistic codification with the steadfastness and sophistication of Arabic.[63]

Zaidan was influenced by the tenth-century grammarian Ibn Jinni.[64] Ibn Jinni's phonetic theories of Arabic bore some resemblance to the Leipzig School which emerged in the late nineteenth century to challenge the single-origin orthodoxy of Indo-Germanic linguistics.[65] While Leipzig's *Junggrammatiker* were primarily concerned with the infallibility of their theory, Zaidan's investment in linguistics was more existential.[66] In 1904 he returned to the question of language in a programmatic book entitled *The Arabic Language as a Living Organism, Subject to the Laws of Evolution.* In it he charts the eight overlapping trajectories that constituted the evolving Arabic language. The pre-Islamic period contained an abundance of Ethiopian, Persian, Sanskrit and Greek terms, the early Islamic period gave Arabic first a new religious and philosophical lexicon, then, under the Umayyads the political vocabulary of state-building. The 'Abbasids enriched the language with scientific terms and concepts. Wherever and whenever non-Muslims started to adopt Arabic, words and constructions from Aramaic, Hebrew and other languages entered Arabic. After the Crusades and Mongolian invasions, Arabic acquired words from non-Arab Muslims. Finally, the great achievement of the Nahda, according to Zaidan, was

---

63 Philipp. *Jurji Zaidan and the Foundations of Arab Nationalism.*

64 Sawaie, Moḥammed. "Jurji Zaydan: A Modernist in Arabic Linguistics," *Historiographica Linguistica* 14 (1987) pp. 287-8.

65 Olender, Maurice. *The Languages of Paradise: Race, Religion, and Philology in the Nineteenth Century* (Cambridge MA, Harvard Univ. Press, 2008).

66 Osthoff, Herman; Brugman, Karl. Preface to *Morphologische Untersuchungen auf dem Gebiet der indogermanischen Sprachen I* (Leipzig, Hirzel, 1878) in *A Reader in Nineteenth Century Historical Indo-European Linguistics* (Bloomington, Indiana University Press, 1967) pp. 199-202.

to "contemporize" Arabic.[67] His mission and that of his fellow scholars and teachers was to imbue the Arabic-speaking people with the sense that their language is their most essential identity. [68] The idea that language has any essence at all has received a devastating blow from Saussurian semiology but Zaidan's cohort and the generation preceding his were working on a political project against the perceived threat of cultural conquest and sectarian fragmentation.

The Nahdawis' promotion of a modern literary Arabic was not so much a Manzonian project to impose one dialect as a national language over the rest of the linguistic community.[69] Rather, they believed they were reviving an organic language to which all religious and ethnic communities who spoke it contributed at one time or another. Zaidan's cumulative account of the evolution of Arabic and the valorization of its ability to incorporate multiple sources was not only a call for political unification but also a level-headed refutation of the Orientalist consensus of his day. Ernest Renan considered Arabic a sterile outgrowth of other Semitic languages and notoriously reduced any intellectual achievements of and in Arabic to non-Muslims and Persians in his famous lecture on "Islamism and Science" at the Sorbonne on March 29, 1883.[70] Ignaz Goldziher, whom Diner invokes effectively to authorize his allegations of Muslim aversion to writing,[71] was one of the Orientalists most sympathetic to contemporary Arabs and was

67 Zaydān, Jurjī. *Al-Lugha al-'Arabiyya bi-'itibārihā Kā'in ḥayy, khāḍī li-Nāmūs al-Irtiqā'* (Cairo, Maṭba'at al-Hilāl, 1904).

68 Bou 'Ali, Nadia. "Collecting the Nation: Lexicography and National Pedagogy," in *al-Nahḍa al-'Arabiyya*. Manuscript under review kindly shared with the author.

69 For a critique of Alessandro Manzoni's top-down, artificial nationalization of the Tuscan dialect in nineteenth century Italy, see Gramsci, Antonio. *Il Grido del Popolo* (Feb. 16, 1918) quoted in Ives, Peter. *Gramsci's Politics of Language: Engaging the Bakhtin Circle and the Frankfurt School* (Toronto, Univ.of Toronto Press, 2004) p. 31.

70 On Renan's dispute with al-Afghani see Dupont's essay in this volume.

71 Diner. *Versiegelte Zeit*, p. 113.

an admirer of Shidyaq's witty etymological method of lexicography.[72] Even he did not look much beyond the fifteenth century grammarian Jalal al-Din al-Suyuti who, Goldziher exclaimed "belongs to the most illustrious names of Muslim scientific literature and whose productivity has hardly been surpassed in Arabic literature, which [*pace* Diner] was never lacking for prolific writers".[73]

As a consequence of the Nahda's educational and literary interventions, Arabs from Morocco to Zanzibar can communicate in a modern and standarized form of Arabic. Moreover, the language has become the one unifying symbol across the otherwise fractured Arab world. But the much-vaunted dichotomy between 'high' and 'low' Arabic is rhetorical at best. Arabic boasts at least five levels of Arabic ranging from *fusha al-turath*—the vehicle of the Islamic and classical Arabic legacy—to *'ammiyya al-ummiyyin*—the Arabic of the illiterate. As Sa'id Muhammad Badawi's study on Arabic in Egypt has illustrated, both levels contain the least European terms or influence. In between, *fusha al-'asr* has come to constitute the written and oratory modern standard Arabic of the highly educated, while *'ammiyya al-muthaqqafin* is the level of Arabic this social group uses in professional contexts. Finally,*'ammiyya al-mutanawwarin* represents the everyday Arabic of Egyptians with grammatical schooling.[74]

Conclusions

As Gramsci reminds us in his prison writings, the way a generation treats its forebears reflects back on them. Before we dehumanize the Nahdawis into icons or villains and distort their lives and works to fit

72 Goldziher, Ignaz. *On the History of Grammar among the Arabs* (Amsterdam and Philadelphia, John Benjamins, 1994).

73 Ibid. pp. 51-2. Like most scholars Goldziher missed the lexicographical work of the seventeenth and eighteenth century scholars 'Abd al-Ghanī al-Nābulsī and Murṭaḍa al-Zabīdī and their vast intellectual networks.

74 Badawī, Muḥammad. *Mustawayāt al-'Arabiyya al-Mu'āṣira fī Miṣr: Baḥth fī 'Alaqāt al-Lugha bi'l-Ḥadāra* (Cairo, Dār al Ma'arif, 1973).

our present exigencies, we would do well to take the time to understand the complexities and constraints of their own times. They were both anxious and optimistic, both elitist and marginal, few fully understood European imperialism and most were Ottomanist to the core. The civilizational scale on which they sketched their identity facilitated as much as hindered critical self-reflection. They invoked a discourse of religious tolerance but were intolerant of their less fortunate compatriots. Fearful of the very people in whose name they claimed to speak, their politics was reformist and rarely emancipatory.

Whether the perception of cultural threats emanating from transgressive classical literature or contemporary lower classes was exaggerated or justified is not for later generations to castigate or celebrate. Fear is never a good guide for judgment. Over the course of the twentieth century some Arab intellectuals have embraced the working class and the wretched of the earth while others have embraced the colonizers and the neo-liberals. If their work is to inform the Arab future in a meaningful way, such choices are hardly the responsibility of the Nahdawis who deserve to be judged on the (in)consistencies of their own priorities and against the pressures of their own contemporary moment.

There is indeed a great need for a better understanding of the Nahda as Georges Corm's contribution advocates.[75] In fact, if this current revolutionary moment in the Middle East has any lasting emancipatory intellectual effect, it is that we can revisit the Nahda with renewed rigor. The Nahdawis cannot provide the answers to current problems. They were answering different questions without the benefit of hindsight. Rather than repeating nineteenth-century thought, the point is to continue cultivating problem-spaces where the second Nahda left off. ʻAbdallah Laroui and other Arab Marxist thinkers of the twentieth century have demanded a historical sensitivity that is conscious of hegemonic constraints to Arab independence and prosperity on the one hand and at same time exercises constructive criticism of previous intellectual traditions.

75 See Georges Corm's essay in this volume.

Part II

Jurji Zaidan's Social, Political and Historical Thought

How Should the History of the Arabs be Written? The Impact of European Orientalism on Jurji Zaidan's Work

Anne-Laure Dupont

Jurji Zaidan is known for having made extensive use of European Orientalists' works in his major books: *History of Islamic Civilization*, *History of the Arabs before Islam* and *History of Arab Literature*.[1] These books provide good illustrations of the way an Arab scholar could appropriate concepts and knowledge involving his own culture and reshape them as the basis for a national history in spite of their foreign inspiration. Zaidan appears here as a mediator. His works exemplify the indirect participation of Orientalists in the emergence of Arab nationalism,[2] and that is their primary historical import. Nevertheless the influence of Orientalism in the making of an Arab national history was (and still is)

1 Zaydān, Jurjī. *Tārīkh al-Tamaddun al-Islāmī* in 5 vols. (Cairo, Maṭba'at al-Hilāl, 1902-6); *Al-'Arab qabl al-Islām* (Cairo, Maṭba'at al-Hilāl, 1908); *Tārīkh Ādāb al-Lugha al-'Arabiyya* in 4 vols. (Cairo, Maṭba'at al-Hilāl, 1911-4). Edition used here *Tārīkh Ādāb al-Lugha al-'Arabiyya* edited by Shawqī Ḍaif (Cairo, Dār al-Hilāl, 1957).

2 A source of inspiration for me has been an article by Kramer, Martin. "Arabistik and Arabism: the Passions of Martin Hartmann," *Middle Eastern Studies* 25 (July 1989) pp. 283-300. Online:
www.martinkramer.org/sandbox/reader/archives/arabistik-and-arabism-the-passions-of-martin-hartmann
The first page sums up Kramer's main concerns: he not only points out "the similarity between many of the nineteenth-century theories propounded by European scholars and the twentieth-century theories propounded by Arab nationalists", but also examines, through the case of German Orientalist Martin Hartmann, how "a handful of the European scholars became so enamored of their theories that they themselves embraced a sort of Arab nationalism".

a focus of polemics. Zaidan was at one and the same time an actor and a victim in a debate that arose as early as the 1860s, or even earlier, about the validity of academic Orientalism: is a non-specialist in the religious sciences (*'ulum al-din*) qualified to write on Islamic issues?

To trace this debate, we must first examine how Zaidan made himself familiar with Orientalist works, what he read and with which of contemporary European scholars he was acquainted. Then we will study his position in the debate about Orientalism and assess how he made use of European knowledge about Islam and the Arabs in his own works. Finally we will pose the question as to the extent to which his position was accepted by his readers, focusing on attacks leveled at his *History of Islamic Civilization* and his portrayal of the Arab Umayyad dynasty as being chauvinistic. The actors in this polemic, his compatriot Muhammad Rashid Rida and the Indian scholar Shibli Nu'mani, combined religious considerations and political discourse in their criticisms. What was at stake was the role of Islam in the emerging Arab identity, and that in a period when the Islamic community and Ottoman solidarity were being challenged by nationalisms.

Readings and sociability

It seems that Zaidan's interest in Orientalism developed alongside his conversion to literary activities between 1883 and 1886. In this period, which coincided with his migration to Egypt, he abandoned the study of medicine that he had started at the Syrian Protestant College of Beirut, turned to journalism and dragomanry, studied Hebrew and Syriac, and published his first book *Arabic Expressions and the Philosophy of Language*.[3] He became interested both in the writings of European scholars about the Arab and Islamic East and in their attempts to preserve the Arabic heritage through the collection of manuscripts as well as the printing of old texts.

---

3 Zaydān, Jurjī. *Al-Alfāẓ al-'Arabiyya wa'l-Falsafa al-Lughawiyya,* 1st edition (Beirūt, Maṭba'at al-Qiddīs Jāwrjiyūs, 1886).

In Zaidan's initiation to Orientalism, the support of the Syrian Protestant College of Beirut was doubtlessly decisive. Even though he had interrupted his medical studies, he retained strong connections with his fellow-students and teachers, and remained a member of various cultural and educational societies affiliated with the College: a branch of the YMCA;[4] the Oriental Scientific Academy;[5] and Free Masonry.[6] Zaidan was greatly influenced by Cornelius Van Dyck (1818-1895), the most "easternized" of his American teachers and the only man whom he ever acknowledged as his "master" (*ustadh*). A parish minister, medical doctor and translator of the Bible into Arabic, Van Dyck had an encyclopedic cultural knowledge, one which his students came to regard as a model to be emulated.[7] He was the one who made Zaidan familiar with ancient languages such as Hebrew and Syriac and encouraged him to write on Arabic lexicography.

Another person who probably contributed to Zaidan's turn towards European scientific production about the East and the Arabs was his friend, Jabr Dumit (1859-1930). The latter was also a former student at the Syrian Protestant College; where, in 1889, he became employed as a teacher of Arabic language and literature.[8] He and Zaidan had met in Egypt and the

---

4 *Jām'iyyat Shams al-Birr* (The Society of the Sun of Charity).

5 *Al-Majma' al-'ilmī al-Sharqī.*

6 Dupont, Anne-Laure. "Usages et acculturations de la Franc-maçonnerie dans les milieux intellectuels arabes à la fin du XIXe siècle à travers l'exemple de Jurjī Zaydān (1861-1914)" in *Cahiers de la Méditerranée. La Franc-maçonnerie en Méditerranée (XVIIIème-XXème siècles): Modèles - Circulations – Transferts* 72 (June 2006) pp. 331-52. Online: http://cdlm.revues.org/document1175.html

7 Khūrī, Yūsuf Kuzma. *Al-Duktūr Kurnilyūs Fān Dīk wa-Nahḍat al-Diyār al-Shāmiyya al-'ilmiyya fī'l-Qarn al-tasi' 'ashar* (London, Dār Sūrāqiyā, 1990). Ya'qub Ṣarrūf, another student of Van Dyck, inserted a biography of him in his translation of the famous *Self-Help* by Samuel Smiles (1st edition 1859). See Smiles, Samuel. *Sirr al-Najāḥ,* 2nd edition. Translated by Ya'qub Ṣarrūf (Cairo, Maṭba'at al-Muqtaṭaf, 1886) pp. 215-26.

8 On Jabr Ḍūmiṭ, see Dāghir, Yūsuf. *Maṣādir al-Dirāsa al-adabiyya* (Beirut, Maktabat Lubnan Nāshirūn, 2000) pp. 448-50. Sulaymān, Suhayl. *Athār al-Banna'īn*

Sudan where they had been recruited as dragomans for the British army in 1884. In early summer 1886, they traveled together to England, spending a whole month in London, from June 8th to July 8th. They may have planned to stay longer, but Dumit's health could not tolerate the weather, and they decided to return.[9] This short journey is generally considered to have been decisive in Zaidan's exposure to Orientalism. His recently published diary indicates that the aim of the journey was to visit the British Museum where he and Dumit went several times.[10] What did they do there? We don't know exactly. They probably spent their days in the Museum's reading rooms and libraries. Zaidan's diary is much more eloquent about the circumstances of the journey, the conditions of life onboard and his acquaintances in London: expatriate Syrians and English missionaries. It seems that the YMCA and its Beirut branch, Shams al-Birr, helped with the organization of the trip and perhaps also provided funding.

After these formative years and the journey to England, Zaidan regularly read Orientalist works which he was to use later to compose his books about Islamic civilization, the Arabs before Islam, and Arab literature. A few of these Orientalist works had been translated into Arabic: there existed for instance a translation, or at least a short adaptation, of the *Histoire générale des Arabes* by Louis Amélie Sédillot (1808-1875),[11]

al-Aḥrār fī'l-Adab al-Lubnānī 1860-1950 (Beirut, Nawfal, 1993) pp. 123-4. In the same group of young scholars who were educated by the American missionaries in Beirut and to whom Zaidan was close, was also Na'ūm Shuqayr (1863-1922), a future historian attached to the government of the Sudan during the period of Anglo-Egyptian Condominium.

9 This information is given in Zaidan's journey diary (see footnote 10 below). There is a mistake in my book on Jurjī Zaydān where I wrote that he stayed in England until February 1887. Dupont, Anne-Laure. *Ǧurǧī Zaydān 1861-1914, Écrivain réformiste et témoin de la Renaissance arabe* (Damas, Institut Français du Proche-Orient, 2006) p. 258.

10 Zaydān, Jurjī. *Yawmiyyat Riḥla baḥriyya* edited by Jean Daye (Damascus, Fajr al-Nahḍa, 2010) pp. 39, 42.

11 Sédillot, Louis Amélie. *Histoire générale des Arabes: leur empire, leur civilisation, leurs écoles philosophiques, scientifiques et littéraires* in 2 vols. (Paris,

published in Cairo in 1309/1891-2.[12] But Zaidan was able to dispense with translations thanks to his knowledge of foreign languages: English first of all, but also French, and even German, a language that he could at least read. It is said that he learnt German in a few months in 1904, after realizing the importance of the contribution of German scholars to research on Arab archeology and Arabic literature.[13] This was the period for instance when Carl Brockelmann's fundamental work, *Geschichte der Arabischen Literatur*, was first published (1898-1904).[14] But Zaidan may have been able to read some German even before that, while he was preparing his *History of Islamic Civilization*, the first volume of which, published in 1902, refers to German scholars such as Alfred von Kremer and August Müller.[15] Where did Zaidan read, and where did he find copies of the books in which he was interested? We know that he used to visit public or private libraries such as *Dar al-Kutub*—the Khedivial Library in Cairo—and the library of Ahmad Taymur (1871-1930), but his primary focus in such places was rare manuscripts.[16] It can also be presumed that he bought books for his own use and received free copies of new publications for review in *al-Hilal*. It is impossible here to provide an extensive list of what Zaidan read. He knew enough about European Orientalist

---

Maisonneuve et Cie, 1877). Like his father Jean Sédillot, Louis Amélie Sédillot was a historian of Arab astronomy. His *Histoire générale des Arabes* was a popular text first published in 1854 and a second edition in 1877. See Messaoudi, Alain. "Sédillot, Louis Amélie," in *Dictionnaire des orientalistes de langue française,* edited by François Pouillon (Paris, IISMM-Karthala, 2008) pp. 884-885.

12 The translator was the Egyptian engineer, scholar and minister, 'Ali Mubārak (1824-1893). See Zaydān. *Tārīkh Ādāb,* vol. 4 p. 149.

13 *Jurjī Zaydān 1861-1914* (Cairo, Maṭba'at al-Hilāl, 1915) p. 12.

14 Carl Brockelmann (1868-1956).

15 See below.

16 Zaydān. *Tārīkh Ādāb,* vol. 3 p. 5. About Aḥmad Taymūr's library, see ibid., vol. 4 pp. 111-113; and Hafez, Sabri. *The Genesis of Arabic Narrative Discourse* (London, Saqi Books, 1993) p. 55.

scholars from the end of the eighteenth century to his own time to make a chronological presentation of them in the fourth volume of his *History of Arab Literature,*[17] with brief mentions of their nationalities, professions and main scientific contributions. This, of course, does not mean that he had read them all.[18] It appears that he made extensive use of the resources provided by the network of Asiatic and Oriental societies that had been founded in Europe in the first part of the nineteenth century in order to institutionalize Orientalism: publications such as the French *Journal asiatique*, the *Journal of the Royal Asiatic Society* in London, or the *Zeitschrift der Deutschen Morgenländischen Gesellschaft* (Journal of the German Oriental Society) in Leipzig were thus a major source of information for him.[19] A glance at the books which inspired the methodology of his *History of Islamic Civilization* gives us an idea of his interests. Zaidan referred to them in the introduction to volume 1, namely the *Histoire du Bas-Empire* by Charles Le Beau (1701-1778), a French specialist on the Byzantine Empire, and *The History of the Decline and Fall of the Roman Empire* by Edward Gibbon (1737-1794).[20] Such works were paragons

17 Zaydān. *Tārīkh Ādāb,* vol 4 pp. 144-63.

18 In any case his survey may have been inspired by Dugat, Gustave. *Histoire des orientalistes de l'Europe du XII*[e] *au XIX*[e] *siècle précédée d'une esquisse historique des études orientales* in 2 vols. (Paris, Maisonneuve et Cie, 1868-70).

19 These periodicals are mentioned in Zaidan's notebooks now held by the Jafet Library at the American University of Beirut. There are also many references to them in the pages of *Tārīkh Ādāb*, vol. 4, which deals with orientalists (see references in footnotes 14 and 50). The *Journal asiatique* was (and still is) a publication of the Société asiatique founded in Paris in 1822; the Royal Asiatic Society was founded in the same period, 1823, and launched its journal in 1834; in 1845, some German orientalists and members of the Asiatic societies of Paris, London and Calcutta created the Deutschen Morgenländischen Gesellschaft in Leipzig. The publication of the *Zeitschrift der Deutschen Morgenländischen Gesellschaft* started two years later in 1847. See websites of these societies: www.aibl.fr/societe-asiatique and www.royalasiaticsociety.org and www.dmg-web.de

20 Le Beau, Charles. *Histoire du Bas-Empire en commençant à Constantin le Grand* in 29 vols. (Paris, Desaint et Saillant, 1757-1817); Gibbon, Edward. *The History of*

of what at the time was termed "philosophy of history" because they attempted to explain the course of history through the dialectic of rise and fall. They answered the question as to why some empires and civilizations rose while others declined. Zaidan made particular use of these works to analyze how, in the seventh century of the Christian era, the Arabs, despite their comparative numerical and military weakness, were able to conquer both the Byzantine and Sassanid Empires. Zaidan also referred to more recent works by specialists on Islam: Stanley Lane-Poole (1854-1931) and his chronological and genealogical tables,[21] for example; August Müller (1848-1892) and *Der Islam im Morgen und Abendland;*[22] and Alfred von Kremer and his *Culturgeschichte des Orients unter den Chalifen.*[23] *Culturgeschichte* is the German equivalent of the concept of "history of civilization", a discipline that aims to go beyond the chronicles of war and political change. Like Zaidan at a later stage, Kremer had divided his book into thematic chapters, each one dealing with a particular aspect of Eastern life under the Umayyads and 'Abbasids: political institutions, finances, justice, religion, commerce and industry, arts and sciences, etc.

Among the references listed on the first pages of *History of Islamic Civilization,* one is a popular work that illustrates Zaidan's eclecticism: *La civilisation des Arabes* by the French publicist Gustave Le Bon (1841-1931).[24] Le Bon was not a specialist in oriental studies, but he had

---

the Decline and Fall of the Roman Empire in 6 vols. (London, W. & A. Strahan, T. Cadell, 1776-1788).

21 Lane-Poole, Stanley. *The Moḥammadan Dynasties: Chronological and Genealogical Tables with Historical Introductions* (London, Constable, 1893).

22 Müller, August. *Der Islam im Morgen und Abendland* (Berlin, Grote, 1885-1887).

23 Kremer, Alfred von. *Culturgeschichte des Orients unter den Chalifen* in 2 vols. (Wien, Wilhelm Braumüller, 1875-1877). Translated into English by S. Kuda Bukhsh as *The Orient under the Caliphs* (Calcutta, Univ. of Calcutta, 1920; reprint Delhi, 1983).

24 Le Bon, Gustave. *La civilisation des Arabes* (Paris, Firmin-Didot, 1884). For a biography of Le Bon, see Marpeau, Benoit. *Gustave Le Bon. Parcours d'un intellectuel. 1841-1931* (Paris, CNRS éditions, 2000).

traveled in the East. As he considered the Arabs to be a "superior race" (*race supérieure*) and viewed Islamic civilization as a model of tolerance and scientific development, his book *La civilisation des Arabes* was especially admired in the Arab and Islamic worlds where for a long time it remained a best-seller and work for reference, especially after it had been translated into Arabic by 'Adil Zu'aytar (1897-1957). Needless to say, Zaidan was aware that Le Bon was not an Orientalist, but he still admired his polyvalence and even acknowledged him as "one of the greatest French scholars".[25] From the *Civilization des Arabes* he borrowed in particular the idea that the Arabs were by nature "*susceptibles de civilisation*", that is to say "inclined to" or "predisposed to civilization".[26] Besides Zaidan's readings, he also had connections with contemporary European scholars. He partly formalized such linkages through his membership in a variety of learned societies in Europe. As early as 1887 [27] he requested admission to the *Società asiatica italiana.* Founded in Florence in 1886, this Italian Asiatic Society had only been in existence for a year (or even a few months) when Zaidan submitted his application. Since it was a recent creation, his chances for admission may have been good, even if he was still young and unknown. Years later, in 1897, he became a member of the Royal Asiatic Society in London. Lastly he was elected a member of the Société asiatique of Paris, during the meeting held on June 13th 1912.[28] Among the other members elected that day was Dawud Bey 'Ammun,[29] who at the time was president of the Alliance Libanaise in Cairo; after World War I,

25 *Al-Hilāl* 21 (May 1913) pp. 511-512.

26 "*Musta'iddūn li'l-Ḥadāra*" and "*Min Akthar al-Umam Isti'dādan li'l-Ḥadāra*"; see "Al-'Arab wa'l-Tamaddun," (The Arabs and Civilization) in Zaydān, *Tārīkh al-Tamaddun,* vol.1 pp. 9-14, to be compared with "Les Arabes avant Mahomet," in Le Bon, *La civilisation des Arabes,* book 1, ch. 3 pp. 58-75.

27 Following the publication of *Al-Alfāẓ al-'Arabiyya wa'l-Falsafa al-Lughawiyya.*

28 *Journal asiatique,* dixième série 20 (1912) pp. 191.

29 Dāwūd Bey 'Ammūn (1857-1920).

he was to lead the first Lebanese Delegation to the Peace Conference. Zaidan was sponsored by Lucien Bouvat (1872-1942), the librarian of the Société asiatique and author of laudatory reviews of *History of Islamic Civilization* in the *Journal asiatique,*[30] and Clément Huart (1854-1926), both a diplomat and professor of Arabic and Persian at the Ecole des langues orientales in Paris. It seems, however, that Zaidan never attended any international orientalist conference.

Zaidan also corresponded with a number of renowned Orientalists. After the publication of *History of Islamic Civilization*, he was congratulated by Jan de Goeje (1836-1909), professor at Leiden, who also reviewed the first two volumes of the book in the *Journal asiatique;*[31] Hartwig Derenbourg (1844-1908), scion of a prestigious family of semiticists in Paris;[32] Victor von Rosen (1849-1908) from Saint Petersburg; Ignaz Goldziher (1850-1921), the great Hungarian Orientalist; Ignazio Guidi (1844-1935), professor of Semitics at the University of Rome; and David Margoliouth (1858-1940), professor of Arabic at Oxford University.[33] With Margoliouth, Zaidan maintained more personal links and asked him to translate his book, at least in part.[34] Zaidan visited him in Oxford when he returned to England in

---

30 See below.

31 *Journal asiatique*, dixième série 10/3 (1st semester 1904) pp. 356-9.

32 Messaoudi, Alain. "Derenbourg, Hartwig," in *Dictionnaire des orientalistes de langue française*, p. 288.

33 These names are listed by Zaidan himself at the end of his introduction to the third volume of Zaydān's *Tārīkh al-Tamaddun.* I have respected the order of names that he uses. Obviously he selected them on purpose, as a demonstration of the success of his book all over Europe.

34 See *Umayyads and 'Abbasids being the fourth part of Jurjī Zaydān's History of Islamic Civilization.* E. J. W. Gibb Memorial, vol. 4. (Leiden, E. J. Brill; London, Luzac & Co, 1907). In the preface, Margoliouth writes that, if he agreed to translate the book, it was because of its good reputation among orientalists, especially Professor de Goeje.

1912 and, thanks to his recommendation, was permitted to read rare Arabic books.[35]

Zaidan was also visited by some European scholars who came to Egypt to conduct research or to teach. Ignazio Guidi paid calls on him in 1909, during his employment at the brand new Egyptian University where he was in charge of the course in Arabic literature.[36] While preparing his thesis, the then young Ignaty Kratchkovsky (1883-1951) met him several times from 1908 to 1910. Their discussions were in English, French or Arabic. In his memoirs, Kratchkovsky notes that, when Zaidan heard him speak in Syrian dialect, he was so moved that he was on the point of bursting into tears.[37] This is the same Kratchkovsky who was later to write the entry "Zaidan" in the first edition of the *Encyclopædia of Islam* (1934). Zaidan was also an acquaintance of Martin Hartmann (1852-1918)[38] who describes him in his book *The Arabic Press of Egypt* as "an eminently industrious man",[39] but the aspect that Hartmann admired most in him was the journalist and entrepreneur more than the historian.

What did Zaidan represent for the Orientalists with whom he was in contact, and at the same time what did they mean for Zaidan? Above all, European scholars viewed him as the author of useful textbooks through which Arab readers were being initiated into their own scientific methodology. In *History of Islamic Civilization,* de Goeje

35 Zaydān, Jurjī. *Riḥlat Jurjī Zaydān ilā Ūrubbā sanat 1912* (Cairo, Idārat al-Hilāl bi-Miṣr, 1923) p. 148.

36 Letters from Jurjī Zaydān to his son Emile: 20 January and 20 March 1909 (not published, copies with the Zaidan Foundation).

37 Kratchkovsky, Ignaty. *Avec les manuscrits arabes (souvenirs sur les livres et les hommes),* original ed. 1942. Translated from Russian by Marius Canard (Algiers, Publications de l'Institut d'études orientales de la faculté des lettres d'Alger, 1954) p.18.

38 On Hartmann, see Kramer's article referred to in footnote 2.

39 Hartmann, Martin. *The Arabic Press of Egypt* (London. Luzac & Co, 1899) p. 35.

appreciated the comparisons made by Zaidan "between the state of the old Muslim Empire and the present state",[40] while Lucien Bouvat, reviewing the English translation of the book, even compared it to the French best-seller on Ancient Greece and Rome, *La cité antique* by Numa Denis Fustel de Coulanges (1830-1889).[41] It seems, however, that many European scholars did not really expect any new information or interpretation to emerge from Zaidan's work. They did not regard him as their peer. If they were interested in him, it was rather because he symbolized the Arab revival or because, like Martin Hartmann, they recognized him as a prominent figure in the development of a nascent Arabic press. It is thus not surprising to find reviews of his books in the new French periodical *La Revue du monde musulman*, which aimed to go beyond classical Orientalism and to give news of the present Muslim world from a more sociological and anthropological perspective. Zaidan was also a good "resource", someone who could provide assistance and give recommendations or access to various institutions—libraries for instance. This aspect appears in Kratchkovsky's testimony: not only did Zaidan inform him of the existence of Ahmad Taymur's rich library, but he also wrote him a letter of recommendation which opened the doors of the City of Alexandria library for him.[42]

As for Zaidan himself, it is obvious that the recognition that he received from European scholars and the mention of his books in scholarly Western reviews made him proud. He probably gave this recognition more importance than Orientalists intended because he was able thereby to gain scientific authority. Yet one should not overestimate his

---

40 *Journal asiatique,* dixième série, 10/3 (1st semester 1904) p. 357.

41 "Disons que les *Ummayyads and 'Abbasids* rappellent à quelques égards, pour l'ancien monde musulman, ce que la *Cité antique,* ce chef d'œuvre de Fustel de Coulanges, est pour l'ancien monde latin" in *Revue du monde musulman* 4 (Jan.1908) pp. 210-1. Cf. de Coulanges, Numa Denis Fustel. *La cité antique: étude sur le culte, le droit, les institutions de la Grèce et de Rome* (Paris, Durand, 1864 1st ed.).

42 Kratchkovsky. *Avec les manuscrits arabes,* pp. 25, 32.

connections with European Orientalists. They were merely part of a broader network that he constituted step by step and extended all over the world, both West and East. As an intellectual, he found it entirely natural to exchange information, books, and ideas. As a result of such exchanges he felt that he belonged to an educated elite, with a special commission to modernize society. Just as he had become a member of European learned societies, he also affiliated himself to diverse associations in Beirut and Cairo, including the Oriental Scientific Academy and Free Masonry. Asiatic Societies were simply a non-confessional, international and professional extension of his network, albeit beyond his initial missionary contacts and Syrian or Syrian-Egyptian connections.

Zaidan also maintained good relations with Arab or, more generally, Eastern scholars who shared his interests in the history of Islam and the role of heroes in history. He was a friend of the Damascene writer and politician, Rafiq al-'Azm (1865-1922), who also lived in Cairo (from 1894 onwards) and was the author of a book dealing with the period of the four first Caliphs: *The Most Celebrated Men of Islam in Wars and Politics*.[43] Zaidan was also acquainted with a prominent Indian modernist scholar, Shibli Nu'mani (1857-1914), who, under the influence of Sayyid Ahmad Khan (1817-1898) and Professor Thomas Arnold (1864-1930) at the Muhammadan Anglo-Oriental College in Aligarh, had become a specialist in the early centuries of Islam. A historian, biographer, literary critic and poet who wrote in Urdu, Shibli Nu'mani promoted the reform of religious education in India, all in an attempt to fill the gap between English-educated Muslims and representatives of the old learning. Serving as Professor of Arabic at the Muhammadan Anglo-Oriental College from 1883 to 1898, he later joined the Nadwatul Ulama' in Lucknow, a new institution in which he saw a proper alternative to Aligarh and the more conservative revivalist movement of Deoband.[44] His move from Aligarh to Lucknow

43 Al-'Aẓm, Rafīq. *Kitāb Ashhar Mashāhīr al-Islām fī'l-Ḥurūb wa'l-Siyāsa* in 4 vols. (Cairo, Maṭba'at al-Hindiyya, 1903-1905).

44 Haywood, J. A. "Shiblī Nu'mānī", *Encyclopædia of Islam,* 2nd edition (Brill Online, 2012); Troll, Christian. "Muhammad Shiblī Nu'mānī (1857-1914) and the Reform of Muslim Religious Education," in *Madrasa. La transmission du savoir*

corresponded more or less with his change of attitude towards Zaidan. Shibli had earlier visited Zaidan in Cairo during a journey through the Ottoman Levant in 1892. In 1894, he had sent Zaidan his travel account in which he praised the quality of the review *al-Hilal.*[45] In the following years, they continued to correspond with each other and exchange information. In Zaidan's opinion, Shibli Nu'mani was "the greatest scholar of India" (*akbar 'ulama' al-Hind*),[46] he considered him a friend and referred to his works in *History of Islamic Civilization.*[47] But for Shibli, Zaidan's history of civilization was a real challenge, as we shall see later.

Another name that deserves to be mentioned here is 'Alimcan al-Barudi (1857-1921), a Tatar scholar from Kazan, one of the leaders of Jadidism, the Turkish speakers' cultural and religious reform movement in the Russian Empire. Founder of a review entitled *Al-Din wal Adab* (1906-1908) and a prominent figure in the Muslim Union (a political party created during the Russian revolution of 1905), he was exiled in 1908.[48] Spending time in Cairo, he visited Zaidan and told him that he had read all his books. When Zaidan mentioned these visits to his son Emile,[49] he displayed the same pride as when he mentioned the visits of the Italian Orientalist Ignazio Guidi. The recognition of the "imam of Kazan

---

dans le monde musulman, edited by Nicole Grandin and Marc Gaborieau (Paris, éditions Arguments, 1997) pp. 145-57. About the Deobandi movement, see Metcalf, Barbara. *Islamic Revival in India: Deoband, 1860-1900* (Princeton, Princeton Univ. Press, 1982).

45 Mentioned in *al-Hilāl* 3 (Dec. 1894) pp. 279-80.

46 A letter from Jurjī Zaydān to his son Emile, 28 March 1912. See its English translation in Philipp. *Zaidān,* pp. 216-9.

47 Zaydān. *Tārīkh al-Tamaddun*, vol.1 p. 169; vol. 2 p. 7; vol. 3 pp. 4-5.

48 Bennigsen, Alexandre and Lemercier-Quelquejay, Chantal. *La presse et le mouvement national chez les musulmans de Russie avant 1920* (Paris, The Hague, Mouton & Co, 1964) pp. 59-60.

49 Letters from Jurjī Zaydān to Emile Zaidan, 5 December 1908 and 3 June 1909. op.cit.

Muslims", as he described Barudi, as well as that accorded by Rafiq al-'Azm and Shibli Nu'mani, were of major importance for Zaidan who knew how sensitive were the issues in which he himself was interested. He was eager not to appear as a mere imitator of European scholars.

Arabizing Orientalism?

As a matter of fact, Orientalism had already been discussed for years in Muslim modernist or reformist circles. As early as 1868, the Egyptian scholar and employee of the viceroys, Rifa'at al-Tahtawi, (1801-1873) had given his opinion on this issue in his book about the history of Egypt, *Anwar Tawfiq al-Jalil.* His main concern was the renewal of the Arabic language, a necessary medium for the understanding of sacred texts. He criticized the teachers at al-Azhar for their routine and intellectual laziness, as well as those others who thought that Arabic was a difficult language, impossible to master in an entire lifetime. Tahtawi's belief, on the contrary, was that the Arabic heritage was alive and should be enriched, a clear demonstration of which was provided by the works of European scholars. Consequently he thought that their methods should be used. In his struggle to renew the Arabic language, Orientalists were at once his allies and challengers. For him it was inconceivable that they alone were working to preserve and resurrect the Arabic heritage. This noble task needed to be accomplished primarily by the direct heirs of the Arabic language, that is to say the scholars of Egypt and other Islamic countries.[50]

In Zaidan's time, this debate was even more acute. It had become genuinely polemical ever since the famous controversy between the great French semiticist Ernest Renan (1823-1892) and the Persian philosopher

50 Al-Ṭahṭāwī, Rifa'at. *Anwār Tawfīq al-Jalīl fi Akhbār Miṣr wa-Tawṭīq banī Ismā'īl* (1st ed. 1868). See *Al-A'māl al-kāmila li-Rifa'at Rāfi'al-Ṭahṭāwī,*.edited by Muḥammad al-'Imāra in 5 vols. (Bayrūt, al-Mu'assasa al-'Arabīyya li'l-Dirāsāt wa'l-Nashr, 1973) vol. 3 pp. 623-4. My analysis relies on a commentary of these two pages by Professor Gilbert Delanoue during a conference held in Aix-en-Provence (France) in 1998 on the Egypt of the Khedives.

and "pan-Islamist" activist Jamal al-Din al-Afghani (1838-1897). On March 30 1883, Renan, who at the time was at the zenith of his career as philologist and historian of religions and a prominent figure in the French Third Republic, gave a lecture at the Sorbonne University in Paris on "Islam and Science". The text was published the next day in the French newspaper *Le Journal des Débats.*[51] Renan focused on the "Arab period" of Islam between the sixth and thirteenth centuries A.D. His first argument was that the intellectual movement that existed during those centuries in Islamic countries was not Arab at all, even if its medium was the Arabic language. Its primary sources were Greek, and its major scholars and thinkers were not of Arab origin. Renan added that this movement was no more Islamic than Arab. It had developed, he maintained, because Islam was weak. When Islam grew stronger, it was destroyed. Islam, according to Renan, failed to encourage science because of its dogmatism and the coincidence of the temporal and spiritual dimensions.

Al-Afghani, who at that time was living in Paris, reacted promptly to Renan's comments. His refutation, translated from Arabic to French, was published in the *Journal des Débats* on May 18 1883.[52] He responded that Islam was not a greater obstacle to science than Christianity and that the Arab people had conclusively proved its intellectual superiority when it disseminated the Greek sciences so extensively. According to al-Afghani, the distinction between Arabic speakers and people of Arab origin, or between language and race, was irrelevant, for there was no race, only language. These arguments did not entirely contradict Renan's. Al-Afghani was also a rationalist and agreed with the idea of the struggle between religion and philosophy. The main issue in this controversy was the capacity of Islamic societies, and especially Arab

51 "L'islamisme et la science," *Journal des débats politiques et littéraires* (March 30, 1883) pp. 2-3. This newspaper is available for free on Gallica, the digital library of the Bibliothèque nationale de France at www.gallica.bnf.fr

52 *Journal des débats politiques et littéraires* (May 18, 1883) p. 3. Jamāl al-Dīn al-Afghānī's name is transcribed there as Gemmal Eddine Afghan.

societies, to emerge from a period of intellectual decay. What was at stake was the Arabs' ability to create a civilization of their own. Two visions of history confronted each other here: for Renan, Islamic civilization was decadent; for al-Afghani, it was only behind the times because the essence of Islam had been perverted.

This debate did not merely pit Westerners against Easterners, but also divided Western Orientalists as well: Louis Sédillot, for example, who emphasized in his *Histoire générale des Arabes* the Arab contribution to science opposed Renan. What is more, the debate was not restricted to a purely academic milieu, but was popularized by writers such as Gustave Le Bon. His *La civilisation des Arabes* was published in 1884, just one year after the controversy between Ernest Renan and Jamal al-Din al-Afghani. Borrowing his terminology from racial anthropology, Le Bon asserted that the Arabs were a "superior race". He considered them to be the most advanced Eastern people and believed in their civilizing potential or at least their "predisposition" for civilization—a feature which he thought to be lacking among other Easterners such as the Turks. With such arguments, Le Bon openly condemned Renan's prejudices (while creating others!).[53] This helps explain in large part why he was so fulsomely praised in the learned circles of great Arab cities.

Zaidan was fully aware of this debate. We have already noted the impact of Le Bon's *Civilisation des Arabes* on his own vision of Islamic history. That led him to criticize Renan's belief that the Semitic peoples were not inclined to philosophy and that the Arabs had not renewed the Greek heritage.[54] This did not mean, of course, that he was condemning the scientific value of European Orientalism; his general view of Orientalism was rather

53 Le Bon. *La civilisation des Arabes,* pp. 32, 58.

54 See the biography of Ernest Renan in a*l-Hilāl* 7 (August 1899) pp. 634-7. Another allusion to Renan, who is not named however, is in Zaydān, *Tārīkh al-Tamaddun,* vol. 3 p. 3. Interestingly, Renan is not mentioned in the list of nineteenth century orientalists elaborated by Zaydān in *Tārīkh Ādāb,* vol. 4 pp. 144-63 (cf. the following footnote). Zaidan did not consider him an important participant in the Arab Nahda.

similar to Tahtawi's, even more enthusiastic. It is significant that he included modern and contemporary European Orientalists (*al-mustashriqun*) in the fourth volume of his *History of Arab Literature,* the very volume that deals with the nineteenth century, a period that he himself called the era of "the most recent Nahda".[55] He was thus suggesting that Orientalists (or at least, some Orientalists) were full actors in the Arab Nahda. He credited them for four things: 1) reliable editions of Arabic texts; 2) accurate studies on the Arabic language and the history of the Arabs; 3) efforts to collect and preserve manuscripts; and 4) the many translations that had made the Arabic heritage known all over Europe and the world.

But for Zaidan, the time had now come to challenge those pioneers and initiators that were the Orientalists. His feelings are reflected in his introduction to *History of Islamic Civilization.* Alluding to the question as to how the Arabs had been able to conquer both the Byzantine and Persian Empires despite their small numbers and weakness of means, he writes:

> This is a philosophical discussion that, to our knowledge, nobody has treated at great length in any language, with the exception of what we read in books by European researchers *(bahithin min al-Ifranj).* But most of those discussions are condensed and fail to quench one's thirst. European researchers should not be blamed for this because the subject is far removed from them and is only vaguely relevant to their situation, religion, customs and history. We, being the sons of this [Arabic] language, are the ones to be blamed because the Europeans (*al-Ifranj*) have preceded us in studying the history of our country, our community, our customs and our morals (*tarikh biladina wa ummatina wa adabina wa akhlaqina*).[56]

55 "*Al-Nahḍa al-akhīra.*" For "Al-Mustashriqūn wa'l-Lugha al-'Arabiyya," see Zaydān, *Tārīkh Ādāb*, vol.4 pp. 144-63.

56 Zaydān. *Tārīkh al-Tamaddun*, vol. 1, p. 6.

Zaidan's worry is clear enough: that the Arabs, here a community defined in linguistic terms, should be outdistanced in the writing of their own history. He does not deny that the Europeans are entitled to study Arab history and literature, but he suggests that they are unable to write a *national* history, that is to say a history participating in the building of an Arab nation. The reasons he gives are that their concerns do not coincide with those of the Arabs, and that some Europeans, such as Renan, fail to acknowledge the Arabs' scientific achievements and have disparaging views of Islam.

In fact, Zaidan's discourse on Orientalists was a reproduction of his global discourse on the Nahda.[57] He believed that the development of civilization was conditioned by the process of opening up to Europe. According to him, Europeans themselves had sown the seeds of modern civilization in the East, at the time of the French occupation of Egypt in 1798, for instance, or through missionary activities in Syria. Nevertheless, in his opinion, it was now the Easterners' task and obligation to make these seeds germinate. For him, Orientalists were actors in the Nahda process, as were foreigners like Cornelius Van Dyck or the famous Clot Bey (1793-1868) in Egypt, but they were not the only ones. Just as Zaidan included Cornelius Van Dyck and Clot Bey in the group of the eight "pillars of the most recent intellectual Nahda",[58] but always in association with a representative of the local (Syrian or Egyptian) learned elite—Butrus al-Bustani and Rifa'at al-Tahtawi respectively—he considered Orientalists to be collaborators or even models and teachers. But whatever they may be, Arab writers now had to undertake the task—the preservation of the Arab heritage—on their own. Orientalists had done a good deal for the Arab revival, Zaidan believed, but now their work had to be continued by Easterners, whose legitimacy in doing

57 For a detailed analysis of this discourse, see Dupont. *Ǧurǧī Zaydān 1861-1914,* ch.10 pp. 489-541.

58 "Arkān al-Nahḍa al-'ilmiyya al-akhīra," See Zaydān. *Tarājim Mashāhīr al-Sharq* in 2 vols. (Cairo, Maṭba'at al-Hilāl, 1903).

so was greater than that of the Europeans. Zaidan aspired to be one of these "continuators" or maybe even the first among them. He did not content himself with translations alone (which would have been mere imitations and would have weakened the national perspective that he wished to give to historiography) but tried to adapt Orientalist works for his Arab readers.

From the Orientalists Zaidan borrowed a methodology based on a search for the causes and consequences of past events, the notions of decline and fall, and a global perspective that would embrace every political, cultural, social or economic aspect of history. He also found in their works the central concepts for his own books: the histories of literature and civilization, with both of which he familiarized Arab readers. He even may be considered one of the first writers to search for an equivalent to "literature" and "history of literature" in Arabic. He proposed *ādāb al-lugha:*[59] *ādāb* was a plural, since the singular form, *adab*, that is used nowadays for "literature", at that time retained its broader sense of culture, belles-lettres, education and good manners. To translate "civilization" and "history of civilization", Zaidan had several Arabic equivalents at his disposal: *madaniyya, tamaddun, ʻumran* and *hadara* (the last being the most commonly used nowadays). For the title of his book about Islamic civilization, he chose "*tamaddun*". In Ibn Khaldun's *Muqaddima, al-tamaddun* implied "urbanization", to be understood as a result of the transition from the bedouin way of life (*al-ʻumran al-badawi*) to the sedentary (*al-ʻumran al-hadari*).[60] In late nineteenth

59 See "Tārīkh Ādāb al-Lugha al-ʻArabiyya," a serialized article published in *al-Hilāl* 2 as early as January - August 1894 and *al-Hilāl* 3, September 1894 - April 1895. This article constituted the basis of Zaidan's later book *Tārīkh Ādāb* published between 1911 and 1914.

60 I am referring here to analysis by ʻAbdesselem, Aḥmed. *Ibn Khaldūn et ses lecteurs.* Collège de France, Essais et Conférences (Paris, Presses universitaires de France, 1983) pp.68-70; and by Vincent Monteil in his translation of and introduction to Ibn Khaldūn's *Muqaddima*: *Discours sur l'histoire universelle : Ibn Khaldûn, al-Muqaddima* in 3 vols. (Paris, Sindbad, 1978) vol.1 pp. xxxiii.

century culture, one that was influenced at one and the same time by the age of Enlightenment and the law of evolution, this definition included the notion of progress: *al-tamaddun* became the transition from an inferior basic social state to a more complex and superior one. According to *Da'irat al-Ma'arif,* the great Arabic encyclopedia composed by Butrus al-Bustani, it was "the opposite state to that of savagery" (*hala didd halat al-khushuna*), the latest stage achieved by mankind after "the state of nature" (*al-hala al-tabi'iyya*) and "the period of barbarity" (*'asr al-tawwahush aw al-barbariyya*).[61] Its characteristics were urbanity, a complex political and economic organization, prosperity, and the development of arts and sciences. This stage had been reached throughout history in various locations: Ancient Egypt, Greece and Rome, the Muslim World, and Europe. Within this conception, Civilization with a capital C (*al-madaniyya* in Arabic) was the superior stage of development that human beings strove for; it successively incarnated itself in specific civilizations with a lower-case c *(al-tamaddun)*: the Egyptian, Greco-Roman, Islamic, and modern European civilizations. Thus, by choosing to use the word *tamaddun,* Zaidan was inserting Islamic civilization into the global course of history.

Zaidan's attempts to adapt European works had their limits. The border between adaptation and imitation was not always clear. It is likely that some passages of his books are direct quotations or compilations of external sources.[62] He was criticized for his dependence on Orientalists in both the very conception of the topics themselves and the general structure of his works. Father Louis Cheikho,[63] a renowned Jesuit from

61 "Tamaddun." *Dā'irat al-Ma'ārif* (Beirut, 1882) vol. 6, pp. 213-5.

62 We noticed that in Zaydān, *Tārīkh al-Tamaddun* some passages on the Caliphate (see vol. 1, p. 87) are copied from Ibn Khaldun's *Muqaddima*, book 1, ch. 3 "on the meaning of the Caliphate and Imamate" (*fī ma'nā al-khilāfa wa'l-imāma*). We believe this not to be a unique case. Only an in-depth comparison between Zaydān's works and the books he referred to would confirm our hypothesis.

63 See below.

Beirut who had himself composed a book about Arabic literature in the nineteenth century,[64] accused Zaidan of imitating Carl Brockelmann's *Geschichte der arabischen Literatur* in his *History of Arab Literature.*[65] According to Cheikho, the book was more of a translation into Arabic *(ta'rib)* than an original composition *(ta'lif).* Indeed, Zaidan, like Brockelmann, indicates where and when the works in Arabic he mentions have been printed and, if they have not, in which libraries there are manuscript copies of them. Most of all, his periodization of Arabic literature is apparently similar to that of Brockelmann. This was to be the major issue in his debate with Father Cheikho.

Brockelmann had divided his *Geschichte der arabischen Literatur* into eight books:

1. National Arab literature before Islam
2. National Arab literature at the time of Muhammad and his first three successors
3. National Arab literature in the Umayyad period
4. The Classical Age of Islamic Arabic literature from 750 CE to 1000 CE
5. The Post-Classical Age of Islamic Arabic literature from 1000 CE to 1258 CE
6. Islamic Arabic literature from the Moghul Empire to the conquest of Egypt by Ottoman Sultan Selim the First in 1517
7. Islamic Arabic literature from the Ottoman conquest of Egypt to Napoleon's campaign in Egypt in 1798; and
8. Islamic Arabic literature from Napoleon's campaign in Egypt to the present day.[66]

---

64 Cheikho, Louis. *La littérature arabe au XIX*[e] *siècle* (*Al-Ādāb al-'Arabiyya fī'l-Qarn al-tasi''ashar*) in 2 vols. (Beirut, Imprimerie catholique, 1908-1910).

65 *Al-Mashriq* 15 (August 1912) pp. 597-610.

66 We are relying here on the 2nd ed. of *Geschichte der arabischen Literatur* (Leipzig: C.F. Amelangs Verlag, 1909).

As for Zaidan, he organizes his history of Arabic literature in four chronological volumes and subdivides each of them into several periods. Volume One deals with Arabic literature during the pre-Islamic period, called *jahiliyya,*[67] the beginnings of Islam and the Umayyad period. He designates two stages for the *jahiliyya*: the ancient *jahiliyya* and the second *jahiliyya* corresponding to the two last centuries before the Hijra. Volume Two is about the 'Abbasid period from 750 CE to 1055 CE. Here Zaidan identifies three separate centuries: 1. From the founding of the 'Abbasid Empire to the beginning of Caliph al-Mutawakkil's reign (750-847 CE); 2. From the beginning of al-Mutawakkil's reign to the Buyid era (847-945 CE); and 3. From the Buyids to the conquest of Baghdad by the Seljuks (945-1055 CE). Volume Three deals with the final two centuries of the 'Abbasid period from 1055CE to 1258 CE, and then the Moghul and Ottoman periods until the French Expedition of Egypt in 1798. Volume Four is devoted to the most recent renewal (Nahda) of Arabic literature.

There are no real differences between Brockelmann's and Zaidan's periodization except that Zaidan's is more detailed. This constitutes the very argument that Zaidan used to defend himself against accusations that he was merely an imitator of Brockelmann. In his response to Cheikho, he emphasizes the distinction that he makes between two *jahiliyya* periods and his subdivision of the 'Abbasid age in four periods rather than the two to be found in Brockelmann's work.[68] This is not simply a matter of futile sophistry. By making such choices, Zaidan was able to emphasize both the periods of the Nahda and the "golden ages" (*'usur dhahabi*) in the history of Arabic literature. According to him, there were three: the second *jahiliyya* just before Islam; the first century of the 'Abbasid age between 750 CE and 847 CE; and the Buyid period between 945 CE

---

67 "jāhiliyya" literally means "the time of ignorance" i.e. the time before the revelation.

68 *Al-Hilāl* 20 (May 1912) p. 502.

and 1055 CE.[69] From Zaidan's perspective, there was a "more recent Nahda" that had started from 1798, and he devoted to it an entire volume of *History of Arab Literature*. In comparison, Brockelmann's work only devotes twenty pages to Arabic literature of the nineteenth century, without dubbing it either "a period of Renaissance" or "Revival".

Thus it seems that Zaidan's originality is to be found in his insistence on the concept of "Nahda". He was to make extensive use of this term, the original meaning of which, according to the *Lisan al-'Arab,* was "power and strength" (*al-taqa wa-al-quwwa*), something that was given a positive connotation in the nineteenth century. It came to be associated with upward movement, change, progress, and every aspect of the development of "civilization" in the East. Arab intellectuals eventually started using the term "Nahda" to designate a whole period, one that resulted from the confrontation with France in 1798; it was used in an analogous manner to the European Renaissance (also called "Nahda" in Arabic). Thus, the term "Arab Renaissance" or the "age of Nahda" is not the context in which Zaidan worked, but rather a discourse, an intellectual construction in which he vigorously participated. He contributed to the popularization of the concept and its historicization by associating it with particular periods of Arab political and cultural dynamism between the birth of Islam and his own day. To do so, he blended various ideas that he had found in Orientalist works and, more generally, in the historiographical conceptions of his time: the idea that Islamic civilization was a link between Greco-Roman civilization and modern European civilization; that the Arabs were a "superior race" predisposed to the notion of civilization; and that Napoleon Bonaparte's campaign in Egypt had brought back civilization to a declining East. Combining all these ideas, Zaidan could demonstrate that the Arabs had provided precedents to Europeans in many inventions and achievements, that they had played a major role in global history by transmitting the knowledge of ancient

69 For more details on the way Zaidan subdivided the history of Islam and Arabic literature and on the periods of Nahḍa he observed, see Dupont. *Ǧurǧī Zaydān*, pp. 518-37.

worlds to the West, and that they were now able to start a new process of civilization. This process of civilization was termed "Nahda".

Polemics

How were Zaidan's work and methodology received? At the time of their publication, his books were generally regarded as major literary events; they were reviewed in the press and found many readers. However, just because they were so appreciated, they also attracted sharp criticism. Nobody doubted their utility. What was at stake was their scientific validity and their writer's authority. Zaidan was faced with two kinds of critics: those who criticized him for misusing Orientalist sources, and others who reproached him for using them too extensively; those who thought he had only undertaken a superficial reading of such works, and others who thought that he was much too dependent on their interpretation of Islamic history. These criticisms were leveled by scholars who felt challenged by Zaidan because they regarded themselves as either better adaptors of Orientalism in the Arab world, or else as the only valid interpreters of Arab history, being specialists in the religious sciences.[70]

To the first category belonged two famous scholars and Roman Catholic clergymen, the Jesuit Louis Cheikho (1859-1927) and the Carmelite (al-Karmali) Anastase-Marie (1866-1947).[71] Father Cheikho was the founder and director of the Bibliothèque orientale at the Université Saint-Joseph of Beirut, Father Anastase-Marie ran a college in Baghdad. Both edited periodicals: respectively *al-Mashriq* which had been published since 1898, and *Lughat al-'Arab,* launched later, in 1911. As specialists in the Arabic language and literature, they both focused their criticisms on Zaidan's *History of Arab Literature* which they reviewed extensively.[72]

70 Ibid. ch.12, pp.627-74.

71 For more details, see ibid, pp. 642-50.

72 *Al-Mashriq* 14 (Aug. 1911) pp. 582-95; 15 (Aug. 1912) pp. 597-610; 16 (Oct. 1913) pp. 792-3. *Lughat al-'Arab* 1 (April 1912) pp. 392-7 and 447-53; 2 (June 1912) pp. 52-62; 2 (Nov. 1912) pp. 205-9; 3 (July 1913) pp. 73-82.

They criticized him mainly for idealizing the contribution of Arabs to the history of literature,[73] for confusing Arabs with Semites to such an extent that he saw an Arab in Hammurabi; for giving too much importance to libertine 'Abbasid poetry; and, above all, as mentioned above, for being a mere imitator of Carl Brockelmann. From a scientific point of view, these criticisms were generally justified, but their tone was very polemical. It is for that reason that we have suggested that, for Cheikho and Anastase-Marie, Zaidan had no legitimacy as an "Orientalist". Moreover because he was a Freemason, a deist and a scientist, Zaidan ideologically represented everything that they hated and feared.

Other criticisms came from Muslim scholars and reformers, according to whose opinions Orientalism was not a valuable model. Their main medium was the review *al-Manar*, founded in Cairo in 1898 by Muhammad Rashid Rida (1865-1935). Each time Zaidan published an important book, whether *History of Islamic Civilization, The History of the Arabs before Islam* or *History of Arab Literature,* he was criticized for making errors; his sources were also questioned. After the publication of the first volume of *History of Islamic Civilization*, for instance, Shibli Nu'mani noticed that Zaidan agreed with "many Orientalists in Europe" who traced diverse inventions and scientific findings to the Arabs: at first, Nu'mani suggested, one might feel a sense of pride, but, if one went in search of proof, one would soon understand that "they mistook the he-camel for the she-camel", in other words that they were completely wrong.[74] The polemical dimension involved in such an apparently justified criticism is visible in the journal *al-Manar* which reviewed each volume of *History of Islamic Civilization.*[75] It often happens that Zaidan

73 In his introduction to volume one, for instance, Zaidan suggests that Ibn Nadīm was somehow a pioneer in the history of literature when he composed *Al-Fihrist.*

74 A letter from Shiblī Nu'mani to Jurji Zaidan, quoted in the introduction to the second volume of Zaydān, *Tārīkh al-Tamaddun,* vol. 2 p. 8.

75 *Al-Manār* 5 (Oct.1902) pp. 551-2; 7 (May 1904) pp. 149-52; 7 (Sept.1904) pp. 514-18; 8 (Aug. 1905) p. 511; 9 (Dec.1906) pp. 873-4.

makes mistakes, the reviewer (maybe Rida himself) explains, but he has to be excused since such errors are commonly made by "those who study the religious science in the works of history without learning its rules from qualified people".[76] As a consequence, Zaidan is advised to take lessons from a Muslim scholar, something that would not be more difficult than visiting the Khedivial Library,[77] that is to say much more profitable. One could hardly disapprove more openly of Zaidan's training and methods. Later, still in *al-Manar,* Shaykh Ahmad al-Iskandari (1875-1938), a professor of Arabic literature at Dar al-'Ulum in Cairo, reviewed *History of Arab Literature*[78] and pretended to excuse Zaidan's errors of deduction (*instintaj*) by stating that his *ijtihad,* his method of interpretation, was of his own devising (*lahu ijtihad min 'inda nafsihi*); he meant that Zaidan was not qualified to interpret Arabic and Islamic sources because he had no knowledge of the religious sciences.

The most controversial topic involved Zaidan's representation of the relations between Arabs and non-Arabs in the first century of Islam. For Zaidan, the birth of Islam resulted from an Arab Nahda in the Hijaz.[79] The very beginnings of Islam itself, under the Rightly Guided Caliphs, was an Arab Nahda,[80] which brought unity to Arab tribes and created one unique Arab *'asabiyya.*[81] This was immediately criticized by Muhammad Rashid Rida. He agreed with Zaidan that there was an Arab Nahda in the Hijaz before Islam, but disagreed with the statement that

76 "Man yakhūdhu al-'Ilm al-dīnī 'an al-Kutub al-tārīkhiyya min ghayr talaqqī Aḥkāmihi 'an Ahlihi," *al-Manār* 7 (May 1904) p. 151.

77 *Al-Manār* 7 (Sept. 1904) p. 518.

78 *Al-Manār* 15 (Oct. 1912) p. 741-4; 15 (Nov. 1912) pp. 841-56; 16 (Jan. 1913) pp. 41-54.

79 Zaydān. *Tārīkh al-Tamaddun*, vol. 1 pp. 22-24; vol. 3 pp. 29-36.

80 Ibid. vol. 1 pp. 51, 171; vol. 3 p. 39; vol. 4 p. 30.

81 Ibid. vol. 1 pp. 43-62; vol. 4 pp. 30-49.

Islam was a purely Arab movement. He believed that the Companions of the Prophet defended the interests of Islam before those of the Arabs. For him the Arab awakening put an end to ignorance of God, the *jahiliyya*, and led to the triumph of true religion, whereas for Zaidan it was only a new step in their progress toward civilization.[82]

This debate however was nothing compared to the polemics that arose over Zaidan's portrayal of the Umayyads. This portrayal combined elements of the Shi'i as well as Sunni Islamic pietistic tradition, according to which the Umayyads were irreligious tyrants. It also involved a strictly political and secular interpretation of their Empire, one that was comparable to Julius Wellhausen's approach in *Das arabische Reich und sein Sturz* (1902). Wellhausen (1844-1918) was a German biblical scholar and Orientalist, who thought that religion played a minor role in the expansion of the temporal realm of Islam. For him, the Umayyad Empire resulted from the emergence of an Arab political power. The Umayyads were the founders of an Arab State, not an Islamic one.[83] Zaidan depicted them from the same perspective,[84] defining their power not as a religious caliphate but as a "temporal sultanate" (*saltana dunyawiyya*) [85] and "political monarchy" (*mulk siyasi*) [86] while at the same time underlining their cruelty and irreligion. He also insisted on their Arab chauvinism (*ta'assub al-'Arab*) and showed how they discriminated against both the *dhimmi* (non-Muslims) and *mawali* (non-Arab Muslims). Yet Zaidan also credited them with intelligent and efficient administration and, above all, the expansion of the Arab language in the conquered territories. In doing so, they had created the political and cultural conditions for the development of a great civilization, the golden

82 *Al-Manār* 5 (Oct. 1902) pp. 551-2; 7 (Sept. 1904) pp.515-6.

83 "Umayyads". EI[2] (Brill Online, 2012).

84 Zaydān.*Tārīkh al-Tamaddun,* vol.1 pp. 63-68; vol. 2 pp. 17-27; vol. 4 pp. 50-105.

85 Ibid. 1, p. 63.

86 Ibid. 1, p. 85.

age of which was reached under the ‘Abbasids, thanks to a better integration of Christians and Jews and non-Arab Muslim elements, especially Persians, into the State.

This was the contrastive and contested picture of the Umayyads' reign that was drawn by Zaidan in his *History of Islamic Civilization.* It was widely discussed in reviews of the book. For Jan de Goeje, Zaidan was influenced too much by the ‘Abbasids' perception of their predecessors and enemies, but he was not to be blamed since a number of European authors displayed the same anti-Umayyad prejudices.[87] Commenting on the English translation of the fourth volume of *History of Islamic Civilization,* Lucien Bouvat was less severe: for him Zaidan's pages about Arab chauvinism were among the most interesting in his book.[88]

If the attention of Orientalists was drawn to this issue, what can one say about Muslim scholars?! Many of them were shocked by such a picture of a true Arab dynasty as well as by Zaidan's insistence on constant struggles for power between Muslim peoples (Arabs, Persians, Turks, Mongols…). In their opinion, an Arab dynasty could only serve the interests of Islam. The issue was particularly sensitive in the first decade of the twentieth century, a period when the idea of an Arab nation was emerging. In such a context Muslim modernists, influenced by readings of works by Ibn Taymiyya and Ibn Khaldun, wished to rehabilitate the Umayyads as the first great Arab caliphal dynasty, whose political legitimacy, despite their irreligion, was unquestioned by Sunnis. From the perspective of Arab nationalism and the emerging *Salafiyya,* Umayyads were becoming a central and polemical issue in Arab historiography.[89]

87 *Journal asiatique,* dixième série, 3 (first semester 1904) p. 358.

88 *Revue du monde musulman* 4 (Jan. 1908) p. 211.

89 See Ende, Werner. *Arabische Nation und islamische Geschichte: die Umayyaden im Urteil arabische Autoren des 20 Jahrhunderts.* Beiruter Texte und Studien, vol. 20 (Wiesbaden, Franz Steiner, 1977). The dispute about Zaydān's *Tārīkh al-Tamaddun* was only the first of a long set; Ende analyzes it on pp. 32-55.

The first Muslim scholar to criticize Zaidan's depiction of the Umayyads was Rafiq al-'Azm in 1905, following the publication of the fourth volume of *Tarikh al-Tamddun al-Islami.*[90] He admitted the Umayyads' imperfections, but tried to excuse them: the community they were leading was a young one, and their State was still in the process of construction while remaining under the influence of bedouin traditions. Al-'Azm also said that Zaidan's picture of the 'Abbasid Empire was ambiguous because of the role that he attributed to the Persian element in it: from the reading of Zaidan's book one could deduce that the 'Abbasid Empire was great because it was *'ajami,* that is to say non-Arab. For al-'Azm Zaidan had interpreted tradition without basing it on reliable authorities; he had trusted historians rather than specialists on *hadith.* Zaidan of course protested against such interpretations of what he had written in *History of Islamic Civilization.* He replied to Rafiq al-'Azm's criticisms, noting that, while he may have blamed Umayyads for their political behavior, he had credited them with the spread of the Arabic language in state administration. He added that he had not the slightest intention of giving undue credit to non-Arabs.

The debate between the two stopped there. Al-'Azm's criticism may have been really sharp, but his tone was polite; he adhered to scientific principles. He and Zaidan were sharing their views as men of letters who had different interpretations of history but who respected each other. They used the medium of *al-Hilal,* Zaidan's own review that was generally open for discussion with its readers. The polemic on this issue broke out later (in 1912) and was orchestrated by Muhammad Rashid Rida with the contribution of Shibli Nu'mani. The latter published a serialized article in *al-Manar*, the entire contents of which were an attack on Zaidan's *History of Islamic Civilization.*[91] Even if

90 *Al-Hilāl* 14 (Nov. 1905) pp.104-11.

91 *Al-Manār* 15 (Jan. 1912) pp. 58-67; 15 (Feb.1912) pp. 121-8; 15 (April 1912) pp. 270-80; 15 (May 1912) pp. 342-52; 15 (June 1912) pp. 415-27. Rida soon edited separately Shiblī Nu'mani's diatribe: *Kitāb Intiqād Kitāb Tārīkh al-Tamaddun al-Islāmī*

Nu'mani's arguments were those of Rafiq al-'Azm, his text had nothing to do with scientific discussion. Zaidan was on trial. Nu'mani starts his diatribe with the assertion that the author of *History of Islamic Civilization* has no other goal than to denigrate the Arab nation (*al-umma al-'arabiyya*). He claims that Zaidan had deliberately altered the image of the Umayyads. In fact Nu'mani does precisely what al-'Azm had warned about, namely deducing from Zaidan's treatment of the Umayyads and the valorization of the Persian element in the early 'Abbasid Empire that he does not like the Arabs and ignores everything to do with their culture. Nu'mani assumes that there has to be a causal link between Zaidan's statement that the Umayyad Empire was purely Arab and the bad image that he gives of it. For him, Zaidan hates the Umayyads *because* they are Arabs and praises the 'Abbasids *because* they have abandoned power to the Persians. Noticing too that Zaidan has attributed the responsibility for the fire at the Alexandria Library to the second Caliph, 'Umar ibn al-Khattab, Nu'mani accuses him of presenting Islam as an obscurantist religion. Finally, he completely rejects Zaidan's methodology: Zaidan, he says, "does not take the measure of Islamic history as *we* do";[92] he does not care about the men who adhere to tradition (*rijal al-sanad*); he is "an alien to us" and "his perceptivity and knowledge are alien to ours" (*dakhil fina, gharib al-dhawq wa al-ma'rifa*).[93]

The question that needs to be asked is why Shibli Nu'mani and Muhammad Rashid Rida waited until 1912, ten years after the publication of the first volume of *History of Islamic Civilization,* in order to launch an attack on Zaidan's work. The first explanation lies in Zaidan's increasing influence and the simultaneous growth

---

li-Shams al-'Allāma al-Shaykh Shiblī Nu'mānī (Cairo, Maṭba'at al-Manār, 1912) pp. 1-76. Footnotes that follow refer to this edition.

92 "Innahu yazin al-Tārīkh al-Islāmī bimīzān ghayr Mīzāninā," *Kitāb Intiqād Kitāb Tārīkh,* p. 60.

93 *Kitāb Intiqād Kitāb Tārīkh,* p. 56, 70.

of criticisms against him. In 1910 he had been appointed professor of Islamic civilization at the new Egyptian University, but the Board of Trustees, fearing the reaction of "ignorant" Muslim opinion, had finally decided to dismiss him before he even started his lectures and to give the chair to an authentic and open-minded Egyptian *'alim*, Shaykh Muhammad al-Khudarī (1872-1927), a former student at Dar al-'Ulum and teacher at Madrasat al-Qudat (Islamic Justice School) in Cairo.[94] Even so, Zaidan aspired to be considered the historian of not only Islamic civilization but also of Arabic language and literature. He confirmed his intellectual authority with the publication of *History of Arab Literature,* a book which received an award from the Egyptian University in 1911,[95] but which was sharply criticized, as mentioned above, by a large array of scholars including Christian Catholic clerks and Muslim men of letters.

A second reason lay in the rapprochement between Rida and Nu'mani. During the spring of 1912, Rida was travelling in India while publishing Nu'mani's diatribe against Zaidan in *al-Manar*. Nu'mani himself had invited Rida to be the chairman of the annual conference of the Nadwatul Ulama'. This institution had more or less the same areas of interest as the new *Dar al-Da'wa wal Irshad* (Seminary for Predication and Religious Orientation) just founded in Cairo by Rida. Obviously both scholars wished to enhance their relationship and create what Rida later called (in Nu'mani's necrology) [96] a *hizb al-islah,* a "reform party", a group from which Zaidan was excluded because he was considered a *mutafarnij,* a mere imitator of the "Franks": in other words, according to Nu'mani and Rida, he had become a European. The publication of a

94 Dupont. *Ğurğī Zaydān 1861-1914.* On the Egyptian University, renamed Cairo University in 1925, see Reid, Donald M. *Cairo University and the Making of Modern Egypt* (Cambridge, Cambridge Univ.Press, 1990) pp. 629-42.

95 Reid. *Cairo University,* p. 37.

96 "Al-Shaykh Shiblī wa-Ḥizb al-Iṣlāḥ bayna al-Jāmidīn wa'l-Mutafarnijīn," *al-Manār* 18 (April 1915) pp. 233-8.

pamphlet against Zaidan's *History of Islamic Civilization* was thus the concretization of a religious and intellectual agreement between the two Muslim reformist scholars.

Finally, the launching of the Rida-Nu'mani campaign against Zaidan coincided with the publication of a Turkish translation of *History of Islamic Civilization* in *Ikdam*, an influential newspaper in Istanbul.[97] In a period of critical relations between the Ottoman government and Arab politicians and polemics about what Ottomanism or Ottoman citizenship should be, Rida feared that the Turks might exploit Zaidan's interpretations to charge the Arabs with chauvinism. The risk was that they might find historical arguments in Zaidan's book for accusing the Arabs of fracturing Islamic and Ottoman unity. This was a major reason why Rida decided to publish Nu'mani's pamphlet and wanted to have it rapidly translated into Turkish,[98] thus showing that Zaidan's vision was not shared by true Arabs and interpreters of Islamic history. The fact that the Umayyad dynasty was being defended by an Indian scholar reinforced the political dimension of Rida's posture: a non-Arab scholar was stating that it was inconceivable for a true Arab dynasty such as the Umayyads to put Arab interests above Islamic unity. Arabs were not chauvinistic, whether in the past or present. For Rida, the people who were chauvinistic and had fractured Islamic unity were the Turks. He could thus justify Arab nationalist demands: from his perspective, the emergence of Arabism was not the cause of the downfall of the Ottoman dynasty, but rather the consequence of the failure of Ottoman rulers to preserve Islamic unity. Arabism was a way of rebuilding an Islamic Ottoman unity that was fractured.

It should be noted that Zaidan was never openly attacked as a non-Muslim. Rida was too much of a politician and advocate for enlightened Islam to commit such an error. On the contrary, he inserted Father

97 At least two volumes were translated. They were first serialized in 1910 and 1911, then edited separately. *Revue du monde musulman* 14 (April 1911) p. 184.

98 See Rida's introduction to *Kitāb Intiqād Kitāb Tārīkh,* p. 7-8.

Cheikho's criticism of *History of Arab Literature* into his separate edition of Nu'mani's diatribe.[99] Thus he combined the criticisms of a non-Muslim scholar and Christian priest in order to reinforce his own campaign against Zaidan's work. Zaidan was the victim of a debate that arose first inside Muslim modernist circles. He was attacked, not as a Christian but as an *adīb,* a non-*'alim*, a secularized intellectual claiming authority in the field of Islamic history even though he had not the slightest knowledge of the methodology of Islamic tradition and the religious sciences. Muslim intellectuals were attacked for the same reasons as those invoked against Zaidan, especially within the framework of the new scientific institution that was the Egyptian University. Other scholars were similarly accused because of their multiple references to Orientalists and suspected of irreligion, including Mansour Fahmy for his book (in French) about the condition of women in Islam (1913) and, of course, Taha Husayn, for his book about pre-Islamic poetry (1926).[100]

Those scholars who attacked Zaidan had ambivalent attitudes towards European Orientalists themselves. Shaykh Ahmad al-Iskandari for instance, may have criticized *History of Arab Literature,* and yet he attended the Orientalist conference held in Athens in 1911.[101] We have noted earlier that Zaidan himself never participated in such conferences. While the Egyptian University's Board of Trustees may have hesitated to appoint Zaidan as professor of Islamic Civilization, they gave the

---

99 "Intiqād Kitāb Tārīkh Ādāb al-Lugha al-'Arabiyya bi-qalam al-Abb Louis Cheikho al-Yāsū'ī," in *Kitāb Intiqād Kitāb Tārīkh,* p. 127-46. This edition also included Shaykh Aḥmad al-Iskandarī's review of *Tārīkh Ādāb al-Lugha al-'Arabiyya* (p. 77-126) and an earlier criticism of *History of the Arabs before Islam* (p. 149-67) that the latter had written in 1908 and published in *al-Manār* 11 (Oct. 1908) pp, 681-7 and 11 (Nov. 1908) pp. 780-6.

100 Fahmy, Mansour. *La condition de la femme dans la tradition et l'évolution de l'islamisme* (Paris, Félix Alcan, 1913); Ḥusayn, Ṭaha. *Fi'l-Shi'r al-Jāhilī* (Cairo, Maṭba'at Dār al-Kutub al-Miṣriyya, 1926). On Mansour Fahmy's affair, see Reid, pp. 65-6.

101 Dāghir. *Maṣādir al-Dirāsa al-adabiyya*, p. 255.

chair of Arabic literature to the Italian Ignazio Guidi, without apparently arousing any particular polemic. At the same time, Muhammad Mas'ud (1872-1940), a translator and journalist who had started his career at the Cairo newspaper *al-Mu'ayyad*[102] and whom Zaidan privately described as "one of the Muslim writers of the old school" *(min kuttab al-muslimin al-qudama'),* intended to translate into Arabic Gustave Le Bon's *Civilisation des Arabes.* In doing so, he was supposed to fill a gap: the lack of any book in Arabic about such a subject. This decision deliberately overlooks Zaidan's own *History of Islamic Civilization,* the publication of which had started a decade earlier. Zaidan was conscious of the polemical dimension of Muhammad Mas'ud's project. Meeting him by chance, he asked why, if he thought *History of Islamic Civilization* was erroneous, he was satisfied merely to translate a French work rather than writing a book of his own. Mas'ud's answer, which infuriated Zaidan, was that readers would trust a foreign writer more than him.[103] These reactions illustrate the ways in which the works of European Orientalists were regarded in Arab learned circles. They were less criticized than those Arab writers who relied on their own works; or at least they were only *indirectly* criticized by reference to those scholars who relied on them. What was dangerous was not the way foreigners wrote Arab history, but rather the internal use of such historiography. Misinterpretations could be expected from European Orientalists, but they were not permitted when the writers were their Arab disciples.

Conclusions

Jurji Zaidan generally used his Arabic sources in the same way as European Orientalists. He was initiated into the latters' works by his American teachers in Beirut and continued to read them throughout his career. His choices were eclectic and often depended on what was

102 Ibid, p. 1080-81.

103 Zaidan related the whole story about Muhammad Mas'ud to his son Emile in a letter dated 28 March 1912. English translation in Philipp. *Zaidān*, pp. 216-19.

in vogue. He favored Orientalists who presented a good image of the Arabs and who celebrated their scientific achievements, without always distinguishing between academic scholars and popularizers. To tell the truth, this distinction was hard to make for a man of letters of his kind, a writer who defined himself as a *kātib 'amm*[104] and who was torn, as Taha Husayn noted, between two tendencies—one scientific *(naz'a 'ilmiyya)*, the other popular *(naz'a sha'biyya).*[105] In addition to his readings, he was also acquainted with some Orientalists of his time through travels, correspondence, membership in learned societies, and book reviews in scholarly periodicals. He felt simultaneously indebted to them for their pioneering role in the construction of an Arab historical and literary heritage, and challenged by their activities. He thought that the time had now come for Arab writers to appropriate the methodology and concepts of the Orientalists, such as "the history of civilization" and "the history of literature", and to compose books of their own in Arabic, for an Arab readership. Without being very original, he tried in his work to distance himself from his European models through extensive use of the concept of "Nahda", emphasizing the cyclical periods of it in Arab history until the most recent one that was said to have been initiated by Bonaparte's military expedition to Egypt in 1798 (that being the subject of the fourth volume of *History of Arab Literature*).

By so doing, Zaidan initiated a debate in reformist or modernist circles where the idea of "Nahda" was attractive but not consensual. There existed diverse interpretations of what an Arab Nahda was, and it was on those interpretations that the definition of the Arab nation and the place of Islam in it was to depend. For Zaidan, a Nahda was every movement

---

104 Zaydān. *Tārīkh Ādāb,* vol. 2 p.5. See Dupont. *Ǧurǧī Zaydān,* p. 359 and Dupont, Anne-Laure."What is a *Kātib 'āmm*? The Status of Men of Letters and the Conception of Language According to Jurjī Zaydān," *Middle Eastern Literatures* 13 (Aug.2010) pp. 171-81.

105 Husayn, Ṭaha. "Āthār al-Hilāl wa Munshi'i-hi," in *Al-Hilāl, Al-Kitāb al-Dhahabī 1892-1942* (Cairo, Dār al-Hilāl, 1942) p. 135.

or period whereby or when Arabs displayed their civilizing abilities and introduced their contributions to universal civilization. Those contributions included a great religion and culture—Islam—but Islam was neither its origin nor its end; it was only a single phase in the history of an Arab community based on language and culture that had existed long before it. For scholars such as Rashid Rida, and non-Arab Muslims like Shibli Nu'mani, an Arab Nahda could not be anything but Islamic. There was a state of Nahda when Arabs were united to fight religious ignorance and demonstrate the modernity of Islam. To those who had this vision of Nahda, Zaidan's works were dangerous, and they kept a close eye on errors and misinterpretations to be found in them. They questioned Zaidan's legitimacy in the composition of a history of Islam with no training in the science of *hadith,* and criticized his reliance on Orientalist sources. In the years following the Young Turk Revolution, when the historiography of Islam and the Arabs was to have an impact on the present state of affairs, they went on to politicize their criticisms. If they reproached Zaidan for his confidence in European Orientalists, it was not only for methodological reasons, based on his ignorance of the "religious sciences", but also because Orientalists were foreigners. Zaidan himself was attacked as an enemy of the Arabs, as somebody who was not an Arab anymore; he had become just like Europeans, a *mutafarnij.*

The violence of these polemics over the content of the Nahda and the proper methodology to be used in writing about Islam and the Arabs was proportional to Zaidan's success and the growing authority of intellectuals that resulted from the expanding press tradition and the emergence of a secular school system and new academic institutions. This also helps explain why, among Zaidan's sharpest censors, we find Roman Catholic clergymen and scholars, Father Cheikho at Beirut and Father Anastase-Marie at Baghdad. Even if they were themselves deeply influenced by European Orientalism, they did not admire

Zaidan whose education, academic training and religious beliefs had nothing to do with theirs. Just as Muslim scholars (*'ulama'*) could feel threatened by new secular intellectuals (*udaba'*), these Christian scholars were not willing to acknowledge that a self-made writer and journalist could challenge them in the creation of a local "arabized" Orientalism.

The debate on Zaidan's works was never completely closed. As late as 1983, a Syrian Islamist writer, Shawqi Abu Khalil, put Zaidan's historical novels on trial, making use of violent arguments very similar to those of Shibli Nu'mani's seventy years earlier.[106] Using his book on Zaidan, Abu Khalil inaugurated a series entitled "*Fil-mizan*" (In the Balance). After Zaidan, he selected the Arab American historian and professor of Semitic languages, Philip Hitti (1886-1978), for weighing in the balance, followed by Carl Brockelmann and Gustave Le Bon, whose works had all become very popular in the Arab world throughout the twentieth century. This time, it was not just Arab Orientalists who were directly attacked but also some of their European models. Abu Khalil concluded by generalizing his criticism to include the whole Orientalist vision of history and associating it with the proselytizing of Christian missionaries.[107] The underlying question remained and remains what it had been in Zaidan's own lifetime: to what extent may foreigners inspire a national history, especially when it is entangled in the history of Islam?

---

106 Abū Khalīl, Shawqī. *Jurjī Zaydān fī'l-Mizān* (Damascus, Dār al-Fikr, 1983).

107 Abū Khalīl, Shawqī. *Al-Isqāt fī Manāhij al-Mustashriqīn wa'l-Mubashshirīn* (The Overthrow of Orientalists' and Missionaries' Methods). (Beirut, Dār al-Fikr al-Mu'āṣir, 1995).

Between Enlightenment and Evolution: Arabic and the Arab Golden Ages of Jurji Zaidan

Marwa Elshakry

Jurji Zaidan is a seminal figure in modern Arabic thought and his works have done much to define the very meaning of the Nahda as a historical sensibility and as an era, though the exact boundaries of each are still up for debate. The term Nahda is a notoriously ambiguous one, and Zaidan was among those who critically expanded its definition and scope in Arabic while nevertheless giving it specific historical and temporal connotations. This essay will consider how he defined it in relation to both Arabic and the Arabs. Zaidan distinguished between disparate, yet connected, episodes of efflorescence. One was of a past Arab golden age that was predicated upon a series of *nahdat*—from the Year of the Elephant to the conquest and rise of a Muslim state from Baghdad to Andalusia. Yet with every golden age, comes a fall, and this one, too, was followed by a period of medieval decline or a "dark age". Yet, as this essay tries to argue, Zaidan's vision of an Arab golden age was also critically tied to his conception of a promised Arab Nahda. Indeed, Zaidan cast his age as one of re-naissance (a "Nahda"): not least through his biographies of modern Arabic "luminaries" from the time of the French occupation of Egypt to his own day. The chronology and characters he seized upon are significant and demonstrate how Zaidan appealed to an emergent, middle-class public readership that stretched from late Ottoman Beirut to British-occupied Egypt (if not beyond). Zaidan defined his own contemporary or anticipated future golden age largely as a "translation movement", whereby the East was to be inspired by scientific, technical, literary and political developments in Europe. Yet he did more than simply imply a reversed *translatio imperii et studii*; this transfer of knowledge and power from West to East was neither direct nor uncomplicated. And in the process of making the argument, he redefined the East, and particularly the Arab East, in novel ways. Racial kinship, language and science proved the key markers for Zaidan's narratives of Arab rise and fall, as, history, and the specific contours it took on in his work, gestured to a "golden" future.

This essay aims to explore Zaidan's popular writings on history, language and science in order to trace the genealogy of these ideas against the background of broader Arabic debates and events of the time. It is divided into three sections. First, I examine how the young Zaidan formulated his ideas on Arabic and the philosophy of language. I then trace his views on the idea of history and its particular significance for the Arabs. I see his analysis oscillating between, on the one hand, a subscription to what we might call enlightenment ideals of the march of reason (if not Spirit), and on the other, to nineteenth century notions of the evolution of humanity, particularly racial, or ethno-moral, ones. The former might be understood as part of a complex intermingling of a critically revised European Orientalist and Enlightenment historical temporality with a specifically neo-classical Arabo-Islamic one. The latter was formed by the new racial sciences and imaginaries of the nineteenth century, a view that also emerged against the background of numerous publications in Arabic (as in other languages) on the evolution of "civilizations". Finally, I examine how appeal to these multiple golden ages allowed Zaidan to mediate between the present (and future) and the past in novel ways, and in the process, helped to construct novel political imaginaries in Arabic.

The History (and Future) of Arabic and the Arabs

In 1885, Zaidan composed his first book on *Arabic Expressions and the Philosophy of Language.*[1] The influence of an evolutionary worldview on his theories of the origin of language was highly apparent in this work.[2]

1 Zaydān, Jurjī. *Al-Alfāẓ al-'Arabiyya wa'l-Falsafa al-Lughawiyya* (Beirut, Maṭba'at al-Qidīs Jāwrjiyūs,1886).

2 See Philipp, Thomas. *Jurji Zaidan and the Foundations of Arab Nationalism* (New York, Syracuse Univ. Press, 2014). Manuscript cited with permission of author.

He took the then common view that behind the multiplicity of contemporary languages rested an original one. His evidence for this confusion of tongues resulted from his interest in comparative philology. With the rise of "civilization" in Mesopotamia and then the subsequent development of the Semitic languages in particular, Zaidan also tied his view of language groups to a civilizational concern. For he saw Arabs and Arabic, as descending from Hammurabian Babylonia and their language. Hence, he thought the Arabs could also be said to have contributed the very idea of codes of law to the world of civilizational progress. Later, he argued, the Koran would standardize the language and give greater specificity and scope to the Arabs, even as it temporarily and, through standardization, necessarily slowed down the natural laws of evolution. Even as Zaidan highlighted the role of Islam in the formation of a common Arabic language, he replaced the view of its sacral origins, centered around an *umma* or community of believers, with an evolutionary, linguistic one, centered around the community of language or *ummat al-lugha*.[3]

One should not detach these ideas from the dilemmas of a young Syrian émigré intellectual in a precarious epoch of competing nationalisms in the cockpit of colonialism. For Zaidan, tracing the long gestation of Arabic beyond and including the Koran and his understanding of the evolutionary development of Arabic were tied to his desire to present a new Arab historical consciousness for novel, national ends. Yet as with many other colonial intellectuals in Egypt, this did not preclude his participation in the colonial state. In British-occupied Egypt, Zaidan had earlier offered his services to the British officials, and with his friend Jabr Dumit, who also wrote on the philosophy of language, he joined the British army as a translator during the Wolseley expedition to the Sudan.[4] As with his later emphasis on the positive force of syncretism

3 Philipp. *Jurji Zaidan and the Foundation of Arab Nationalism*, op.cit.

4 Dumit, like Zaidan, also published extensively on the need for language reform and simplification. Indeed, many of Dumit's essays on the evolution of language were first published in *al-Hilāl* and *al-Muqtaṭaf* between 1888 and 1928. These included such studies as "The Evolution of the Arabic Language"; "Arabic: What It Took

(and translation) for both language and history, he saw no contradiction between modern European (or colonial) modes of governance and statecraft and promised national ones; indeed, one might imagine how even the young Zaidan might here have seen the two as resting on a continuum that aimed at a proper universal order.

After his brief stint with the British army, Zaidan managed *al-Muqtataf* for two years, and later began publication of *al-Hilal*. The latter journal shared with the former a general evolutionist line that reflected the proprietors' common Syrian Protestant College training and sensibilities, though they themselves collectively and ultimately broke with their former patrons on the issue of evolutionary theory itself. Yet, Zaidan had a greater sensitivity to history, and from the start, *al-Hilal* differed from *al-Muqtataf* in that it featured numerous articles on the history and philosophy of language and writing—a subject that Zaidan paid special attention to and that he would continue to return to throughout his life. Of special interest was the preservation of ancient Mesopotamian and fertile crescent civilizations through the last great descendents of the "Semitic" philological line: Arabic.[5]

In his writings on language in *al-Hilal* and in later works on the subject, Zaidan also seized upon another key motif in his philosophy of language: the value of translation.[6] He emphasized the way Arabic, including and especially the Meccan dialect (as exemplified by the Koran) had gained its very shape and force through a series of linguistic borrowings.

---

and What It Gave"; "Origins of the Semitic Peoples"; and "America and American" (a study of deriving adjectives from assimilated words). Dumit was also interested in the genesis and historical development of Arabic as evidence of its ability to adapt to the times. These articles were published collectively as *Falsafat al-Lugha al-ʿArabiya wa-Ṭatawwuruha* (*The Philosophy of Arabic and Its Evolution*).(Cairo, Maṭb'at al-Muqtaṭaf, 1929).

5 See for instance his "Tārīkh al-Kitāba wa-Aṣl al-Ḥurūf," *al-Hilāl* 1 (August 1893) pp. 446-451.

6 See for instance his *Al-Lugha al-ʿArabiyya* (Cairo, Maṭbaʿat al-Hilāl, 1904).

Hence, while Zaidan saw Arabic as the key vehicle of Arab social and spiritual expression and as the basis of an Arab unity that was critically shaped by Islam, its progress and evolution over time was nevertheless inseparable from a series of translation movements.

This emphasis on acculturation was clearly linked to his general views on language and literary production. His interest in comparative philology in particular was what encouraged him to present a radically alternative vision of Arabo-Islamic history, one which sat at odds with both some of his own contemporary neo-classical reformers and with European Orientalists themselves.[7] Borrowing both from the works of classical Arabic authors like Ibn Khaldun who saw social solidarity, or *'asabiyya*, as the key to the rise and fall of peoples, as well as from European scholars (and here his influences included Enlightenment and evolutionary historians, alongside contemporary Orientalists), Zaidan fashioned a completely novel narrative and chronology for Arab history.

If the origin and evolution of language as a proxy for the progress and evolution of a people was a key theme for Zaidan, the idea of history and the importance of cultivating a proper historical consciousness for social solidarity and national unity was another. (As we shall see he also related the two.) Other early works included *The History of Egypt from the Islamic Conquest until this Age* in 1889 followed by *A General History since Creation until Today* in 1890. Both of these emphasize the importance of history—its proper method, scope and aims—and point to the ways in which Zaidan aimed deliberately to rekindle an Arab historical consciousness. They both follow a standard Victorian liberal trajectory and outline discrete epochs of history organized around the progressive development of peoples from primitive and barbarian to settled, civilized and (hopefully) modern stages of social evolution. Finally, they both hint at the influence of the East in critically refashioning the West's own past inheritance and its current sway, though this last point would be born out more fully in his later *History of Islamic Civilization*

7 See below for more.

and his *Arabs before Islam*, both of which utilized a similar historical methodology and offered a new periodization for Islamic history.[8]

Indeed, Zaidan proposed a series of novel periodizations for both Arab and universal history. In his general history, he divides mankind into nomadic, primitive, settled and civilized types (distinguishing between the latter two forms of settled civil communities as *al-hadara* versus *al-madaniyya*). In later writings, he pares this down to a triptych that charts the progression of humanity from barbarism and tribalism to the final stages of a *civitas* or a *civitates foederatae,* meaning a civil urban polity, now placed under one division, albeit undergoing a series of material, political and moral progressions. In other writings on world history, he would return to a tripartite division between antiquity, the middle and the modern ages. Nothing unusual there—except that in Zaidan's version, the universal middle ages was the story of Islamic civilization itself.[9]

In his histories of the Arabs and of Islam (published in the early 1900s) and in his later writings and his lectures on history (particularly those he composed for the newly founded Egyptian University in 1910), Zaidan turned from the subject of universal history to focus on Arab and particularly Islamic history.[10] And while he turned to a novel periodization for

8 In this respect, both *Tārīkh al-Tamaddun al-Islāmī* and *Al-'Arab qabla 'l-Islām* followed the works of Rifa'at Al-Ṭahṭawi, Buṭrus al-Būstānī, Khayr al-Dīn al-Tūnisi, and 'Alī Mubārak in this vein. See Khālidi, Ṭarif. "Reflections on Periodization in Arabic Historiography," *Medieval History Journal* 1 (1998) pp.107-124.

9 For more on this see Philipp, Thomas. "Approaches to History in the Work of Jurji Zaydan," *Asian and African Studies* 9 (1973) pp.63-86, especially pp. 68-74.

10 The university was renamed Cairo University in 1925. Zaidan was forced down from his appointment as lecturer on Islamic history before he could present any of his lectures (or even his thanks) because of controversy over appointing what some charged to be an unorthodox historian—though he was not openly attacked as a Christian—to the position. See ibid., pp.71-72, and for a translation of one of these "Al-Tārīkh al-Islāmī", first published in *al-Hilāl* 19 (Dec. 1910) pp. 154-161. See Dupont, Anne-Laure. "L'histoire de l'Islam au regard des autres histoires: un article de Ǧurǧī Zaydān (1861-1914)," *Arabica* 4 (1996) pp. 486-493. For more on this

that history, his basic commitment remained the same: it was through a Muslim efflorescence that the real power and strength of the Arab peoples contributed to the progress of history. The novelty of this golden age was that it was nestled between the fall of the greatest ancient empires of the world and the rise of Europe, with the latter's progression matching the Muslim world's own rate of decline.

From the start, Zaidan had been especially keen to popularize for Arabic readers the lives and contributions of key figures canonized over previous decades by European Orientalist scholarship because of their association with an Arab golden age of science and philosophy: biographies of Avicenna, Averroes, Avempace and Ibn Khaldun featured prominently in *al-Hilal* and in other of Zaidan's writings and these helped in the gradual consolidation of their reputations among Arabic readers.[11] Yet Zaidan's cast of characters was more eclectic than this suggests—and alongside these medieval thinkers one finds him writing on a range of other figures from Hammurabi and Cyrus to Muhammad 'Ali and his descendents. In short, the novelty of Zaidan's argument was to stretch out the historical temporality of the Arabs themselves and to disseminate an expanded sense of their role in history.

He highlighted the unification of the Arabs through the Islamic conquest, to be sure, but Zaidan also traced the origins of the latter's own sacred language, and of its very spiritual-legal codes, as far back as the Babylonians. Indeed, the ancient Phoenicians, Assyrians, Persians, Babylonians and others frequently appeared in Zaidan's articles on history in *al-Hilal*. Stretching the Arab ecumene in this way implied attaching Islam to a longer, and critically refashioned, sense of its own *jahiliyya*, or era of ignorance. In the process, Zaidan redefined

---

incident see also Dupont's essay in this volume. The book bringing all these lectures together was only recently published for the first time in *Miṣr al-'Uthmāniyya*, edited by Ḥarb, Muḥammad. (Cairo, Dār al-Āfāq al-'Arabiyya, 2002).

11 See Dupont, Anne-Laure. *Ǧurǧī Zaydān 1861-1914: Écrivain réformiste et témoin de la Renaissance arabe* (Damas, Institut Français du Proche-Orient, 2006) p. 494 for references to these.

the boundaries of what counted as an Arabo-Islamic antiquity. Thus Islam was connected to its own putative "dark ages" or *jahiliyya* on new terms.[12] Needless to say, set against the background of classical Arabic histories, this was an unusual and distinctive chronology. Yet we should bear in mind that he was among the first of many—Taha Husayn comes to mind in particular—who redefined the history of Islam by recasting the meaning and scope of the *jahiliyya* itself.

Zaidan's reconstruction of an Arabo-Islamic chronology and history was always cast against his reading of the categories of a universal historical time, and generally set against the rise of the "West". Indeed, East and West formed a critical suture for Zaidan and allowed him to rethink the history of the Arabs as a series of transitions along a dual timeline. We might briefly depict this as follows:

The West

Antiquity: Ancient Greece and Rome	European Middle Ages, beginning c. 476 C.E.	Renaissance to present

The Arab East

Antiquity: From Ancient Mesopotamia to the *Jahiliyya*, ends c. 330 B.C.E.	Muslim Middle Ages: With the rise and fall of an Islamic Civilization from c. 570 C.E. to 1258 C.E.	Nahda, 1798 C.E. to present

As we can see, Zaidan gave new meaning to the pre-Islamic era, the *jahiliyya*, by including the ancient kingdoms of the east as linguistic,

12 See his *Tārīkh al-Tamaddun al-Islāmī* (*History of Islamic Civilization*) published between 1902 and 1906, and his *Al-'Arab qabla 'l-Islām* (*The Arabs before Islam*) published in 1908, in particular.

political and even spiritual progenitors to the Arabo-Islamic ecumene. He also marked its demise with the death of Alexander. The rise, formation, and maturity of Islam thus constituted an ambiguous "middle ages" (*al-qurun al-islamiya al-wusta*): it began with the Year of the Elephant, followed a brief detour under the Ummayyads, achieved its final maturity under the 'Abbasids and marked its nadir with the fall of Baghdad. 1258 was thus both the final death knell of its golden age and the point at which Islam as a civilizing force ceased to be significant within a general universal historical timeline. The Muslim "middle ages" was therefore a strange hybrid: for the periodization binds it to both its golden and dark age progressions.

Zaidan thus created novel genealogies as well as periodizations. The heritage that interested him was clearly pre-Islamic, stemming from the Babylonians, falling briefly after Alexander and then culminating again with the Abyssinian conquests. This was then followed by a specifically Muslim golden age, one with its own internal periodization: from its rise, and then brief detour under the Umayyads, it achieved its final maturity under the 'Abbasids.[13] In short, this redefined the meaning of classicism and the classical tradition of Islam. Partly, this reflected the continued influence of European Hellenism and the powerful nineteenth-century liberal enthusiasm for the ancient Greeks. But the phenomenon had autochthonous roots too—for the real "neo-classical" revival occurred through the revival of Arabic literatures and histories themselves.[14] A new cor-

13 This latter chronology is most clearly laid out in his *Tārīkh al-Tamaddun al-Islāmī* but it is also extensively covered in numerous historical biographies and articles in *al-Hilāl* prior to that.

14 Texts previously untranslated, especially Greek epic and dramatic poetry, did also make their way into Arabic, such as Salīm al-Bustānī's 1904 rendition of the *Illiad*, Ṭaha Ḥusayn's translations of Sophocles' plays, Sa'ad Allah Bustānī's *Telemachus*, Adīb Ishāq's *Andromache* and Tawfīq al-Ḥakīm's *Pygmalion* and *Oedipus*. See Pormann, Peter. "The Arab 'Cultural Awakening (Nahda)' 1870-1950, and the Classical Tradition," *International Journal of the Classical Tradition* 13 (2006) pp. 3-20.

pus of classical Arabic works, many of which were being canonized or disseminated by contemporary Orientalist scholarship, were increasingly made available through the Arabic press. Of course, as is the case with the construction of a classical tradition for the West, this genealogy was no less re-invented and re-imagined for its present.

A prime exemplar of what Carl Schorske has called "thinking with history", Zaidan himself contributed much to this re-historicization. He covered numerous episodes in Arab history in *al-Hilal* as well as in literally scores of lengthier works—popular histories and particularly popular historical novels and novella serials. He wrote extensively on pre-Islamic and Islamic, particularly 'Abbasid and Andalusian, empires.[15] Meanwhile, the importance he placed on translations undertaken in Baghdad, and on the philosophical and literary aspects of the Arabo-Hispanic encounter in Andalusia, exemplified Zaidan's emphasis upon cultural transfers, borrowings and adaptation as the keys to civilizational progress and social evolution.

Translation was central to his vision of the past (and future) of Arabic and the Arabs. As we saw from his multiple chronologies earlier, Zaidan defined his expanded Arabo-Islamic middle ages—encompassing its own parabola of rise and decline—together with the epochs of universal history on the basis of their ability to bridge eras or worlds, both literally and figuratively. As the racial and linguistic heirs of the (eastern) Ancients, the real historical contribution of the Muslim empires of the eighth to thirteenth centuries lay in their ability to traverse civilizations and epochs through language, science and the arts, acting in effect as the translators and preservers of the best of the known "bounds of the human empire".[16]

---

15 Schorske, Carl. *Thinking with History: Explorations in the Passage to Modernism* (Princeton, Princeton Univ. Press, 1999).

16 Bacon, Francis. *New Atlantis* (Oxford, Clarendon Press, 1915) p. 35.

Driving this vision of the past were the realities of the present as well as Zaidan's hopes for the future. Saint-Simon had famously declared that "the Golden Age" lay ahead and not behind us; Zaidan certainly agreed. For the golden future of the Arabs, though it had its roots in the sixth, eighth and then eighteenth centuries, remained critically incomplete. In this sense, Zaidan followed Volney's depiction of a past Muslim golden age as a means to consider the possibilities of a future revival—this time bound by the realities of its place within the world of contemporary empires and measured against that decline which had retarded the Arab East until the era of a fortuitous European intervention.[17]

Zaidan's entire historiographical enterprise should be judged in light of the larger history of "golden ages". Early modern universal histories in Europe had begun from the problem of rewriting sacral history in the face of the onslaught of arguments from novel disciplines like comparative religion, philology, and archaeology, as well as from ideas of "natural religion" and of the "new science" of myths. By the late eighteenth and early nineteenth century, universal histories were beginning to be composed from a quite different vantage point from those of earlier scholars. It was not man's fall from grace that was now at stake, a loss that could only be recovered in the final reconstitution of the city of God through the destruction of the city of Man, but rather the rebuilding of the city of Man *as* the city of God—in other words, the story of human progress itself. This unraveling and refashioning of sacral universal histories was also accompanied by another, and I think allied, transformation. Consider Bacon's vision of a "New Atlantis", which envisioned a utopia governed by the craftsmen and natural philosophers of Salomon's House whose "foundation" was "the knowledge of causes, and secret motions of things; and the enlarging of the bounds of human empire", and whose ends were no less grand: "the effecting of all things possible".[18] We might view this techno-arcadian reverie, then, as rooted

17 For more on this subject, see Dupont, *Ǧurǧī Zaydān,* op.cit. p. 494.

18 Bacon, ibid.

both in a novel sense of the source of communal progress and harmony and in a very different picture of the origin of knowledge (which emphasized future discoveries and inventions over past divine inspiration or revelations).

Decoupling the notion of a golden age from a sacral or mythic past brought it into history. Once again, we can trace this against the background of novel disciplinary formations, particularly the rise of Orientalism in Europe as both a scholastic discipline, and later as the key narrative for the administration of knowledge in her colonies. By the late eighteenth and early nineteenth century, Orientalist accounts of golden age traditions throughout Asia had helped both to foster novel narratives of universal history itself and to account for the march of progress in the present. As a result, for many colonial intellectuals, uncovering, reclaiming and even redefining one's classical or golden age was crucial both for claiming one's place in the hierarchy of civilizations and for providing a blueprint for the future path to progress. If to be modern implied a return to one's true past, then it also entailed an embrace of the very vision of progress-in-the-present that European and colonial narratives had helped to spread. Among other things, this led many Arab (like Turkish, Indian or Chinese) scholars of the time, to construct a highly novel vision of the relation between their sacral and textual past to the present, and to redefine their civilizational contribution to the progress of knowledge itself.

Zaidan was a key exponent of this modernist construction of an Arab golden age. As we saw, his was a highly unique vision, borrowing from the terms of a sacral history but critically reworking these to encompass a broader civilizational heritage that could help define and measure the progress of universal history itself. And it was of course precisely this construction of a past Arabo-Islamic golden age that also provided the blueprint for his vision of the contemporary one. For Zaidan, the "latest Nahda", began both in Egypt, with the French occupation of 1798 and the destruction of Mamluk despotism (another favorite theme in Zaidan's popular historical writings). And in Syria, where European Catholic missionaries, followed by nineteenth century Protestant ones, had laid the foundations for a new literary, scientific, intellectual and spiritual awakening after years of torpor and the senescence of its own classical tradition of Arabo-Islamic sciences and *belles-lettres*. (Indeed it was no coincidence that the very terminology of "awakenings" presented by missionary acolytes like Zaidan clearly resonated with missionaries' own account of their activities in Syria and the Holy Lands.) Once again, translation as much as conquest and acculturation, pointed the way toward universal progress.

If the idea of a past renaissance is always critically tied to that of the future, what was Zaidan's vision of the latter? *Al-Hilal* posthumously published an intriguing set of "notes" found among Zaidan's papers, where he had begun to imagine a twenty-first century world. He begins with Egypt: with a population of thirty million, a sophisticated telecommunications and transportation system and a national university at Helwan serving as the intellectual center of the Arab world. Citizens would live a simple, yet modern pastoral life, with every man and woman tending to his garden to support his daily needs. Marriages would be contracted by the fit alone, ensuring public health. Everyone possessed knowledge of the basic medical arts and sciences and there was a universal language of communication (like "Esperanto"). *Al-Azhar*'s curriculum was finally modernized: subjects were taught in a range of arts and sciences, alongside training in theology and law. There would even be a statue in honor of Muhammad 'Abduh which Zaidan envisioned as a kind of national monument (replete with annual pilgrimages). Finally, religious faith itself was based on the twin principles of science and the public good.[19] As we can see, this futuristic vision was critically tied to a scientific and literary resurgence as much as to a political one. Indeed,

19 Zaydān, Jurjī. "Ba'd mi'at Sana" (After One Hundred Years) *al-Hilāl* 31 (Oct. 1923) pp. 18-21. For more on this, see Ware, Lewis Beirer. *Jurji Zaydan: The Role of*

as was typical of the Nahdawi intellectuals of his generation, Zaidan was little interested in the pragmatics of constitutional or parliamentary political reform, as his perfect state was governed more by technocracy than mass politics. (This was true of many other futuristic scenarios spelt out around the same time, including by Shibli Shumayyil, Zaidan's older Syrian Protestant College colleague and sometime nemesis. All of them had a Wellsian tinge and shared traits of much *fin-de-siècle* left-wing futurology.) Zaidan, like many of his generation, saw science as key to governing the future.

We might argue then that behind Zaidan's view of civilizational grandeur, and his explanation for the rise of the West itself, was his faith in the success of modern science. Science provided the narrative thread connecting his universal history. Modern civilization could but be firmly rooted in its principles and precepts and, like that of the Ancients and the golden or middle age Muslims, this too was a universal language whose providence and end was the result of the accumulation, translation and acculturation of human ingenuity and technical knowledge across the ages. This was one reason why Zaidan's *al-Hilal*, like *al-Muqtataf* before it, devoted so much of its energy to popularizing modern disciplines and findings, particularly in the natural and social sciences. Indeed, the very subsections of the journal reflect the deep interest Zaidan had in popularizing scientific and technical disciplines: in addition to the first general "Essay", typically a biography of a famous person or an article of historical or scientific interest, there were sections on "Family and the Home" (which revolved around the "domestic sciences"), "Wonders of Creation" (typically about oddities of nature), "News of Science and Industry" and "Social and Economic News". Zaidan clearly aimed to mediate between entertainment and education, and with sections on readers' suggestions and opinions, and on readers' critiques and reviews of new publications, they spoke of the

---

Popular History in the Formation of a New Arab World View (Princeton PhD Thesis, 1973) pp. 139-141.

creation of a flourishing popular Arabic literary market and appetite for popular science and history.

The Arabs, Islam and the Social Evolution of the Umma

Behind all this we can find a common motif and shared commitment: evolution, with all the ambiguity of the term and encompassing the then broad range of subjects and disciplines that fell within its rubric. Indeed, all of Zaidan's views on social reform and pedagogy were influenced by social evolutionary ones. Zaidan's vision of Arab history, which departed from classical histories of Islam in viewing "Islamic civilization" as merely the last re-sacralized (rather than desacralized) version of an ancient Arab culture, may have emanated from his philological interests.[20] Yet, over time, the influence of *fin-de-siècle* views of social evolution impressed itself upon his story of civilizational rise and fall as well.

For one thing, Zaidan, like many contemporary Arab intellectuals, often spoke of the Arab peoples as a "race" but in terms of an *umma* (*pl. umam*). Ahmad Fathi Zaghlul, in his translation of Gustave Le Bon's *Les Lois psychologiques de l'évolution des peuples* did much the same.[21] Substituting Le Bon's more squarely racial prognosis of the Arab (or Semitic) races for a socio-moral critique of the contemporary Arab *umma*, Zaghlul could subscribe to Le Bon's view of a ladder of civilizations without necessarily adhering to his view of a fixed hierarchy of races. Le Bon's influence upon Zaidan worked similarly.[22] To speak of races in this context as *umam*, as Zaidan did, with all the moral valences that that term implies in Arabic, shows how for Zaidan (as for Zaghlul), the emphasis was on socio-moral groupings rather than

---

20 Ware. *Jurji Zaydan*, p.170.

21 Lubun, Justaf. *Sirr Taṭawwur al-Umam,* translated by Aḥmad Fatḥī Zaghlūl (Cairo, Maṭba'at al-Ma'ārif, 1913).

22 This is the argument laid out by Samaḥ Selim in "Languages of Civilization: Nation, Translation and the Politics of Race in Colonial Egypt," *The Translator* 15 (2009) pp. 139-156.

physio-racial ones. Indeed, this was rather a Victorian notion of "race" itself: for Darwin too argues (in his *Descent of Man*) that it was the evolution of morality that provided the natural drive for human social selection. Tribes and nations of peoples rose and fell, and would continue to do so on the basis of the strength of their moral codes and hence their very social evolution and progress. Zaidan's subscription to contemporary views of race was coded similarly and it critically fashioned his own modernist reconstruction of the term for *umma* and the new criteria for the tribes, nations or races of peoples worldwide. Zaidan regularly featured articles in his journal on the latest ethnographic and anthropological findings and theories, just as he made liberal references to Ibn Khaldunian discussions of human geography in Arabic. Indeed, in a publication on the *New Physiognomy*, he used the classical term *'ilm al-firasa* while covering a squarely nineteenth century view of racial groups.[23] He also published a book under a similarly re-worked classical title, *Tabaqat al-Umam* that we might translate as "Peoples of the World" or "Races of the World", a popular title and theme for illustrated general histories at that time. Once again, Zaidan utilizes the term *umma,* while simultaneously relying on modern ethnographic notions of race or races. The translation is significant, for like many of his contemporaries, Zaidan understood race to be primarily a socio-moral category of human difference. Of course, it also had its attendant geographical and physical or bodily contours (as his many publications on race, and their accompanying illustrations, show). Indeed, the other main criteria for the nineteenth century construction of race—language—was also critical for Zaidan's own discussion of the classes of peoples or races, including the Arabs (as we saw). But the term *umma*, with its attendant religio-spiritual connotations in Arabic also allowed Zaidan to highlight moral, or in its nineteenth-century neologism "social", virtues when thinking about the worldwide geographic distribution of races of people. In his view

23 Zaydān, Jurjī. *'Ilm al-Firāsa al-jadīda* (Cairo, Dār al-Hilāl, 1958).

after all, Islam unified the Arabs on the basis of its moral commitment to patriotism and egalitarianism.

Zaidan's evolutionary concept of civilization was one he shared with earlier commentators like Le Bon and Guizot, as well as with Charles Darwin, particularly the *Descent of Man*. All three of these writers were hugely popular among Arab readers and writers of Zaidan's generation. As we might recall, Zaidan defined the Islamic civilization as having developed around "communities of interest" (*jami'at al-manfa'a*).[24] The influence of a classical liberal, utilitarian lens can be felt here as the attendant concern with the balance of self-interest and social utility demonstrates. Indeed, Zaidan was part of the generation of colonial Arab intellectuals who were influenced by classical utilitarianism and liberalism, as his very *penchant* for classical liberal virtues such as self-reliance, punctuality and hard work demonstrates. Even when re-inscribed with newly acquired socio-ethno or racial overtones, *umma* was still above all a moral community of shared or mutual interests. In this sense, Zaidan's depiction of the Arabs and their history mediated between Enlightenment views of civilization and nineteenth century evolutionary ones, understood in socio-moral and broadly conceived racial terms. It was not the march of reason alone that provided the guarantor of progress, as the Enlightenment universal histories would have it, but rather the moral development of humanity whose ebb and flow one could measure by the laws of social evolution. Focusing on the moral progress of a people also provided Zaidan a bridge between the past glory of the Arab civilization with the Arabs' future: for just as the past glory of one's own civilization was founded on the concern for the public good (*maslaha*), progress in the future was similarly guaranteed through a commitment to a project of reform (*islah*) that could be founded on the same attentiveness to the common good. Thus *maslaha* and *islah* would together provide the key to the revival and renaissance of the Arabs by a re-imagined and re-called Nahda.

---

24 See Thomas Philipp's essay in this volume and his *Jurji Zaidan and the Foundations of Arab Nationalism*. op.cit.

Awakenings and Genealogies for the Future

Zaidan was part of a new literary and political elite in Egypt; an era in which a new breed of "reformers" joined hands to pursue a program of pedagogic reform and to instill a new national consciousness and moral imagination. Zaidan's popular journalism and his fiction, which as we saw earlier aimed to educate as much as to entertain, was geared above all toward inculcating new social virtues and moral values for middle-class Arabic readers. Inspired by the print culture first of Beirut, and then of Cairo at the turn of the century, his publishing activities were highly popular examples of this construction of new bourgeois sensibilities in Arabic.[25]

But they operated within the specific parameters of a particular colonial or quasi-colonial predicament. Like many self-described Nahdawi reformers, Zaidan's evolutionary nationalism was both elitarian and pedagogic. His views of the evolution of the masses (*al-'amma*) in particular were connected to his views on the need for leadership from an elite (*al-khassa*). Education was, he judged, the best means of preparing a people for true independence and freedom. These values, he thought, had only been recently re-introduced to the East, thanks to the enlightened exemplar of Europe, after centuries of tyranny and political oppression.

Zaidan's faith in the leadership of an intellectual vanguard and technocratic elite colored his political prescriptions for the Ottoman empire (and its provinces). In thinking of the perfect state, Zaidan himself never made up his mind. For while he often spoke in positive terms of Ottoman constitutional reform movements, he was not precisely in favor of democracy. Indeed, he cautioned that earlier Ottoman revolutionary movements had failed due to the lack of readiness on the part of the masses. His faith in the guidance of an intellectual elite, whether as the manufacturers of citizen's social aspirations, virtues

25 For more on taste and class in the case of the former, see the work of Holt, Elizabeth and Abou-Hodeib, Ṭoufoul. "Taste and Class in Late Ottoman Beirut," *International Journal of Middle East Studies* 43 (2011) pp. 475-492.

and habits, or as a public check to monarchical authority, remained in place. Like so many *fin-de-siècle* evolutionists, Zaidan was clearly in favor of gradual, evolutionary reform rather than revolution. It was only through the classroom and the pen that Easterners, guided by elite discretion, could achieve true independence and freedom. Revealingly, among his "Famous People of the East", we find civil servants, students of missionaries and Muslim reformers, those in other words who had provided spiritual, intellectual or administrative leadership for a modernizing state.[26]

Zaidan's conception of the Nahda has proved surprisingly long-lived—indeed in many ways it has flourished in the historiography of Arab and Middle East history right to the present.[27] Yet, as recent scholarship suggests, this should not blind us to the alternatives that existed and were extensively voiced in the Arab press at the time. To go further: we might even view the pedagogic and political prescriptions of a Nahdawi writer such as Zaidan as responses, in part, to other radical, populist movements. New work on the popular press, theatre, music and other public expressions of mass sentiment and taste in late nineteenth and early twentieth century Egypt and the Levant has already pointed to the extent of these movements.[28] Hence, we might also see Zaidan's projected Nahda as a rise and fall story of its own—emerging, and then gradually waning, amid growing calls for new kinds of mass and populist politics.

Zaidan himself was not unaware of the importance of such social trends. Indeed he defined his own Nahda as a new "social awakening," one which

---

26 See his book *Tarājim Mashāhīr al-Sharq fī'l-Qarn al-tāsi''ashar* in 2 vols. (Cairo, Maṭba'at al-Hilāl, 1922). For more on this, see Dupont, *Ǧurǧī Zaydān,* op.cit.

27 For a critical account of this historiographical canon see the essay by Jens Hanssen in this volume.

28 See Khūri-Makdisī, Ilhām. *The Eastern Mediterranean and the Making of Global Radicalism* (Berkeley, Univ. of California Press, 2010) and Fahmy, Ziād. *Ordinary Egyptians: Creating the Modern Nation through Popular Culture* (Stanford, Stanford University Press, 2011) in particular.

offered a different foundation for political unity from that of past Eastern civilizations. It was for this reason that Zaidan spoke so often of the new varieties of nationalism, humanism and even socialism (defined more properly as an egalitarian social evolutionary reform movement) behind the coming awakening that was still to be completed in the East. And toward the end of his life, Zaidan showed himself to be in favor of the kind of evolutionary socialism that better-known early Arab socialists like Shibli Shumayyil, Farah Antun and Salama Musa were just beginning to advocate.[29] But this shift was not enough to win him a new following and his elitism and his faith in pedagogy under enlightened leadership cast him as the representative of a particular generation. Over time, as more radical socialist and nationalist ideologies gained ground, a new generation of Arabic audiences and authors rejected the elitism of his generation.

By this time Zaidan himself had come under fire for quite different reasons—his views on Islamic history. In particular Shibli Nuʻmani in his critical article included in the *Book of Critiques of the History of Islamic Civilization* published by Rashid Rida, accused Zaidan of basing his narrative too much on Western Orientalist scholarship.[30] Meanwhile, Lewis Cheikho, the Catholic writer who often took *al-Muqtataf* and *al-Hilal* as the object of his crusade against dangerously unorthodox views, had already said much the same. Cheikho accused Zaidan of relying on—if not outright plagiarizing from—Brockelmann's *Geschichte der arabischen Literatur* in particular. (Cheikho was also a staunch critic of the *Muqtataf* group's and Zaidan's *Hilal*'s views on evolution; hence he also took issue with Zaidan's views on the origin and evolution of language, and the Arabic language in particular, pointing out that Zaidan had completely ignored the sacral status of the Arabic of the Koran.) Cheikho and Rida published their

29 See my forthcoming *Reading Darwin in Arabic*, ch. 6.

30 The critique of Nūʻmānī was first published in al-Manār and then together with other critiques in *Kitāb Intiqād Kitāb Tārīkh al-Tamaddun al-Islāmī,* edited by Rashīd Riḍā (Cairo, Maṭbaʻat al-Manār, 1912).

criticisms in tandem, and indeed their critiques resonated easily—as did many others of the time who objected to Zaidan's historical arguments and periodizations for relying too heavily on the scholarship of Orientalists of the time.[31] This continued after his death as popular theologians and journalists turned his historical interpretations into an intellectual battleground. In 1936, for instance, Tantawi Jawhari published *The Innocence of 'Abbasa, Sister of al-Rashid.*[32] He claimed that he had been inspired by the spirit of Harun al-Rashid himself to compose it (and it seems they communicated through one of his spiritualist *séances*). According to Jawhari, Harun al-Rashid had been driven by the desire to defend his sister, al-'Abbasa, from the accusations of adultery, that had appeared some thirty years earlier in Zaidan's historical novel, *The Caliph's Sister.*[33]

Ironically, while nationalist and religious critics accused him of relying too heavily on Orientalist accounts of Arab history, European Orientalists themselves were certainly not always in agreement with his use of their work. It is true that Zaidan often referred to their scholarship. But much like the case with the translation of Le Bon's ideas on the Arab race, the very process of translating and transferring these ideas to Arabic audiences often transformed the very message of the original in ways that could alarm the original authors. One brief example: Zaidan often relied on the work of William Robertson Smith—particularly his 1885 book *Kinship and Marriage in Early Arabia* and his 1889 *Religion of the Semites*. Yet Zaidan rejected Smith's assertion that the culture of the early Arabs was totemic, and hence represented an inherently lower stage of civilization (something that D.S. Margoulith and Ignaz

31 See Ware, *Jurji Zaydan,* p.198, and especially Anne-Laure Dupont's essay in this volume.

32 Jawharī, Ṭanṭāwī. *Barā'at al-'Abbāsa Ukht al-Rashīd* (Cairo, Mustafa al-Babi al-Ḥalabi, 1936).

33 De Jong, F. "The Works of Tantawi Jawhari (1862–1940): Some Bibliographical and Biographical Notes," *Bibliotheca Orientalis* 34 (1977) p. 160.

Goldziher also supported against Zaidan's views).[34] Zaidan by contrast saw the worship of early female deities not so much as signs of a primitive idolatry but rather of the Arabs' egalitarianism and matrilineal kinship patterns.

If Zaidan and the Orientalists did not always see eye to eye it is because Zaidan clearly had other criteria and objectives in mind. That the Arabs had a past civilizational glory was key, as we saw, to Zaidan's vision of his own contemporary Arab efflorescence and, as he saw it, for the very future of the Arabs themselves. Reconstructing a novel genealogical philosophy of language and of history, of Arabic and of the Arabs, was also critical for his literary, technocratic and political prescriptions for the future. Orchestrating a neo-classical revival in literature and language, through translations and through novel histories and biographies of golden age luminaries, also allowed Zaidan to recast the Arab Golden Age as a blueprint for the present. For Zaidan, it was only through novel genealogies of their past that the Arabs could thus map the future.

34 For more on this, see Ware, *Jurji Zaydan*, pp.173-5.

Jurji Zaidan and the Ottoman Revolution: between Arab Nationalism and Ottomanism, 1908-1914

Thomas Philipp

In preparation for this essay I re-read Zaidan's novel *The Ottoman Revolution*. It was serialized first in his journal *al-Hilal* [1] under the title "The Ottoman Revolution: A historical, romantic novel, being the last part of the series of novels of the history of Islam". The novel is a perfect example of Zaidan's endeavor to present historical events, issues, ideas and ideologies in a popularized form by weaving historical knowledge and romantic entertainment into one texture. Fictitious persons and historical personalities encounter each other, interact and express their ideas, feelings and ambitions mainly through dialogue. All this is wrapped into a romantic story to which is added a fictional political testament by Midhat Pasha, the great reformer of the preceding generation that reflects more precisely the expectations and ideas of Zaidan concerning the actual revolution. On the whole, the reader takes away from the novel a balanced impression of the thinking of Sultan 'Abdulhamid, the political role of the *Mabayn*[2] and the ideas of the new educated, liberal professionals in the army, politics and society.

But for the historian a most important information comes as early as the title and Zaidan's introduction to the book. Zaidan had written historical novels for more than ten years with the idea of covering all of Islamic history in this easily digestible format. He wrote the novels in chronological order and in 1910 had reached with *'Abd al-Rahman al-Nasir* the

---

1 *Al-Hilāl* 19 (1910) p.11.

2 In Turkish, *Enderun*, signifying the secretarial offices in the sultan's palace.

tenth century in Andalusia. At that point he interrupted the chronological order, because he felt that the Ottoman Revolution was the most discussed and important topic of the day. He promised his readers to return after this disruption to the chronological order of things. He added that the novel *The Ottoman Revolution* would be the final one of the series implying that with this revolution the series on Islamic history had come to its end.

In Arabic terminology the revolution became known as "The Ottoman Revolution" (*al-Inqilab al-'Uthmani*). At the time Ruhi al-Khalidi reflected the general understanding of the term by defining "*inqilab*" as

> ... an important change in government and state and a transformation. It is not a rebellion (*thawra*), the meaning of which is insurrection and disobedience to the lawful government (*al-hukuma al-mashru'a*). The *thawra* greatly harms the interests and the welfare of the nation (*al-umma*) and obstructs its path to success. In contrast the *inqilab,* in spite of hurting and crushing the nation, progresses a step forward and climbs a step up the ladder of success.

Inqilab was a beneficial revolution, while "*thawra*" meant rebellion or revolt.[3] Only after world War I was the term "*inqilab*" dropped in Arabic and "*thawra*" came to connote "revolution".

Of greater significance is the term "Ottoman" in the name "Ottoman Revolution". In Western languages but not in Turkish this revolution is known as the "Young Turk Revolution". At the time of the event it was referred to in Turkish as "Hurriyet'in ilani" (declaration of freedom) or "II. Meshrutiyet'n ilani" (declaration of the second Constitution[al period]). While it was referred to as *inkilab* (revolution) even then the term "Jon Turk Inkilabi", an adaptation from the French *Jeunes Turks*,

3 Al-Khālidī al-Maqdisī, Rūḥī, "Al-Inqilāb al-'Uthmānī," *al-Hilāl* 17 (Oct. 1908) pp. 67-83; (Nov. 1908) pp.131-171.

was rarely used.[4] Clearly the emphasis in Turkish was on the political content of the revolution not on its actors. But the Arabic name for the same revolution signified the inclusiveness of all the Ottoman people. The use of different terminologies signaled the differences in understanding the meaning of this revolution and the intellectual and political tensions this would bring about.

In the following I shall try to analyze the expectations Zaidan had for this revolution and to answer the question as to why he clung so long to the idea of a multi-ethnic democratic empire, secured by the constitution, even though, on the eve of World War I the unsustainability of such an idea was already clear. How could he not acknowledge the explosive power that political nationalism carried within itself—neither in the case of the Balkan nations nor in the case of the Arabs to whose national identity he had contributed probably more than any other member of the Arab Nahda?

Zaidan's interest—not just in politics and political events—but specifically in political systems can perhaps be traced to the Russo-Japanese war of 1905, which drew the attention of the whole Middle East and other regions under the rule of European imperialism. It was the first time that a non-European nation defeated a European nation in modern warfare. The major conclusion that the non-European observer drew, was that Russia, the most reactionary state in Europe, was beaten by Japan, which was, formally at least, a constitutional monarchy. Constitutionalism had been tried and then suppressed a generation earlier in the Ottoman Empire. But the Japanese victory gave a new lease of life to constitutionalism, having an influence on both the Persian Constitutional Revolution, beginning in 1906, and the Ottoman Revolution in 1908. The Japanese example and constitutionalism were much discussed and Zaidan contributed to this discussion. The sensation was that the Japanese won this war, "even though", as Zaidan continued,

4 In historiography "Jon Turk Devrimi" or "1908 Devrimi" is used interchangeably with "II. Meshrutiyet'in ilani" and with "Hurriyet'in ilani". I thank Hasan Kayali for this information.

"[they] and other Mongolian people were considered to be on a civilisational level inferior to that of the Caucasian people".[5] He concluded this article with the observation, that the defeat had also a positive aspect for the Russians: the establishment of a constitutional government. A year later he had already developed a much more sophisticated view of constitutionalism. In an article titled "constitutional government" he developed three categories of government: "one man's rule"; *al-hukm al-istibdadi al-mutlaq,* rule of some elite of a clerical, military or nobility character; and self-rule by thc people, *tahakkum al-umma nafsuha binafsiha.* The latter could come either as a constitutional monarchy or a constitutional republic. But only in a republic would the people truly rule themselves through their representatives. Zaidan regarded the Ottoman Empire as an absolute monarchy while Japan had become a constitutional monarchy.[6]

On the eve of the Ottoman Revolution a veritable flood of articles about the system and form of governments appeared in *al-Hilal.*[7] Two articles discussed the US American independence and the rebellion in British India.[8] In the conclusion to both essays Zaidan made a comparison and asked the question: why were the Americans successful where the Indians failed, even though they had many times the number of people and armed men that the British had in India? After giving a detailed historical background of both situations, he found the answer in the education Americans enjoyed. This argument was elaborated in a further article in Feb 1908.[9] Zaidan claimed independence without

---

5 "Al-Ḥarb al-Rūsiyya al-Yābāniyya," *al-Hilāl* 14 (Oct. 1905) pp.3-8, p.4.

6 "Al-Ḥukūma al-Dustūriyya," *al-Hilāl* 15 (Oct. 1906) p.18-23.

7 *Al-Hilāl* 16 (Oct.1907 – July 1908).

8 "Istiqlāl Amrīka," *al-Hilāl* 16 (Oct. 1907) pp. 5-15. "Thawrat al-Hind," *al-Hilāl* 16 (Nov. 1907) pp. 67- 79.

9 "Al-'Ilm wa'l-Istiqlāl," *al-Hilāl* 16 (Feb. 1908) p.305.

knowledge—relying simply on physical force—was a thing of the past.[10] Now independence was closely tied to knowledge. He did not mean the acquisition of factual knowledge but a moral education, imbuing the student with values. He argued that in all cases the educated classes were those that raised the issue of independence and the people would just follow them. Of course, he added, the public, *al-jumhur,* had to understand the meaning of independence and freedom. For that, institutions of higher education were needed in society.

Similarly he discussed the role of parties.[11] In pre-modern times, he argued, there existed only two classes in society, the *'amma* and the *khassa*, the masses and the elite. The elite could split over issues of power and its control. The masses would follow one side or the other within the elite and spill their blood for that side, but power would always remain within the elite. Real political parties could only rise when parliaments were functioning. Parties had to have clear programs and defined aims, which all or part of society would join. But, somewhat distrusting his own argument, Zaidan added that even in the most advanced societies most people did not have the faintest clue as to what parties stood for. In addition we find in this volume a series of rather descriptive articles on the system and present situation of various states,[12] and a lengthy historical article on the French Revolution.[13]

The Ottoman Revolution occurred in July 1908. When in October 1908 the first issue of *al-Hilal* after the revolution appeared, it was packed with many and unusually lengthy articles all dealing with various aspects of

10 This was expressed as a criticism of Ibn Khaldūn's political theory.

11 "Tārīkh al-Aḥzāb al-siyāsiyya," *al-Hilāl* 16 (Dec. 1907) p. 141.

12 "Aḥwāl al-Duwal al-mu'āṣara:Yābān," *al-Hilāl* 16 (March 1908) p.358. "Aḥwāl al-Duwal al-mu'āṣara: al-Wilāyāt al-Muttaḥida," *al-Hilāl* 16 (April 1908) pp. 392.

13 "Al-Thawra al-Faransiyya," *al-Hilāl* 16 (April 1908) pp. 386-404; pp. 442-450.

this Revolution. In an introductory article[14] Zaidan gave a rapid survey of the development of constitutionalism in Europe. He then provided an insightful analysis of the reasons for the failure of the first attempt to introduce a constitutional system in the Ottoman Empire in 1876/77. He saw the overall cause for failure in the "lack of preparedness of the Ottoman people". They were too inexperienced to defend the constitution against its reactionary enemies; most had not understood the meaning of a constitution which had actually only been demanded by a few enlightened people in Istanbul; the electoral process was not understood; most candidates were government employees anyway; delegates came from different ethnic and religious groups which lead to completely different expectations from parliament, where particularistic interests dominated the interest in the common weal. This paralyzed the decision-making process. But, Zaidan insisted that the multicultural and multi-ethnic background need not be an obstacle as demonstrated by the Hapsburg Empire.

The survivors of the defeat of constitutionalism, whom he called loosely *al-Ahrar*, the Liberals, reassembled in Europe, went underground or found shelter in Freemason loges or charitable societies, the only kind of associations permitted under the 'Abdulhamidian regime. The worst aspects of this tyrannical regime, according to Zaidan, were that it lead to corruption on all levels and to disunity of the people. In the following thirty years the Liberals systematized their political thinking and became politically more demanding. They recruited new supporters, found a new ally in the army or parts thereof and they worked with great dedication. The Liberals, so Zaidan said, united all ethnic and religious groups in the common cause of establishing a constitutional, liberal Ottoman Empire. Perhaps even more important was that the Ottoman people had evolved through education and gained an understanding of the meaning of freedom and independence: "It was the victory of light over darkness, education over ignorance, of the pen over the sword." The latter referred to the fact that the revolution occurred without a shot

14 "Al-Inqilāb al-siyāsī al-'Uthmānī," *al-Hilāl* 17 (Oct. 1908) pp. 3-40.

being fired and blood being spilled, “which came as a greater surprise to the civilized world than the tyrannical suppression”.

There is no doubt that the enthusiasm and the hopefulness that comes through from this article reflected a widely spread mood that touched all groups of the Ottoman peoples immediately after the revolution. Freedom, secured by a constitution and representative government, would create unity among all Ottomans and a better Ottoman Empire. Zaidan mentioned here several themes which would return again and again in his further writings on the Ottoman Revolution: unity of all Ottomans across the boundaries of religion and ethnicity; constitution and representative government guaranteeing this unity; education; and the “preparedness” of the masses for constitutional government.

In early 1909 Zaidan wrote an article[15] about constitutional government in Great Britain and France, where he discussed the sovereignty of the people and made a subtle distinction between a parliament which is just tolerated by the monarch for reasons of tactical convenience and parliaments which truly represent the sovereignty of the people and carry the appropriate authority. By analyzing the issue against the background of historical development, he also made clear that the process would take a long time for people to participate in this power.

In the same issue he answered the question of a reader as to whether this revolution would be permanent or collapse like the previous attempt to introduce constitutional government. Zaidan pointed out that since the earlier time a new class of educated people had come into existence, “a class not inferior to the civilized people in advanced societies”.[16] A retreat from the feeling of personal freedom and unity, so he argued, was unimaginable and the return of tyranny impossible. Besides, the Ottoman liberals were actively involved in improving and reforming society.

---

15 “Tārīkh al-ḥukūma al-Dustūriyya: Injlitera,” *al-Hilāl* 17 (Jan. 1909) pp. 210-220. “Faransa,” *al-Hilāl* 17 (Feb.1909) pp. 280-292.

16 Answer to a reader, *al-Hilāl* 17 (Jan. 1909) p. 247.

In an article that appeared in April 1909 Zaidan was somewhat defensive.[17] It is a lengthy essay, which he began, as so often, with a detailed, historical introduction to the topic. Introducing then the debate of contemporary Arab-Turkish relations, he explained his concept of the "community of interest", *jami'at al-maslaha.* In a sweeping sociological reflection he explained: "We do not believe that true solidarity, *'asabiyya*, or real union, *al-jami'a al-haqiqiyya,* is based on anything but common interest, *al-maslaha al-mushtarika.*"[18] The Committee of Union and Progress (CUP) had been accused, he said, of manipulating parliamentary elections with the result that Turks obtained disproportionally a large number of seats, while Arabs hardly gained any. Some Arabs thereupon suspected the Unionists of practicing radical Turkish nationalism under the cover of loyalty to the Ottoman Community. If a Muslim Arab did not get the position he expected, he immediately would blame the Turks of Turkish *'asabiyya* [19] despising the Arabs. Similarly, Christian Arabs would claim the existence of a religious *'asabiyya* between Muslim Arabs and Turks.

Zaidan declared his own partisanship for the Arabs:

> Our concern is, of course, with the Arab cause, because we belong to them, speak their language and share their character. We are particularly concerned with this cause because of our personal interest, since we stand up for the Arabs and concern ourselves with their literature and history. We do our

17 "Al-'Arab wa'l-Turk qabla 'l-Dustūr wa-ba'duhu," *al-Hilāl* 17 (April 1909) pp. 408-417.

18 Zaidan developed this concept fully in an article two years later: "Jāmi'at al-Manfa'a," *al-Hilāl* 19 (Feb. 1911) pp. 280-5.

19 Best translated here as extreme loyalty to one's own group.

> utmost to advance their affairs and one of our greatest wishes is that the Arabs should have a powerful state, *dawla*. [20]

He conceded that the CUP had committed errors. But he felt the Arabs were responsible for having raised the suspicion of the Turks after the revolution when the main Arab reaction had been to found their own Arab political organizations. If the Unionists had indeed manipulated the elections, they had done so only to safeguard the constitution and the security of the state. Besides, the Turks simply had more experience in governing which the Arabs first needed to acquire. The Arabs should—and here Zaidan returned to his introduction:

> ...focus on the tie of common interest, which today means the Ottoman identity, through which we have obtained the Constitution, and through which alone we will be able to preserve and strengthen it. We must reach an agreement...which will benefit both [the Turks and the Arabs]. What is true for individuals is also true for groups. Agreement is essential for the survival of our state, *dawlatna*, and the wise man will overlook his friend's immoderate behavior so long as he does not fear it will harm the common good; he will argue with him amicably and discuss with him as an intelligent partner. When this state, *dawla*, stands firmly on its feet, with its affairs in order, all can demand their rights with the utmost insistence.[21]

He became even more emphatic defending the right of the CUP to rule the state:

> It may be objected that the CUP's autocratic use of power goes against the spirit of the Constitution. But we would

20 The term *dawla* means here the Ottoman state, not a state for the Arabs, as becomes clear from his further use of the term.

21 "Al-'Arab wa'l-Turk qabla 'l-Dustūr wa-ba'duhu," op.cit. p.416.

> reply: how splendid autocracy is, when it is the autocracy of the intelligent and the just! Sensible people agree that the East will never achieve its Nahda except under a just and wise autocratic ruler. In fact this is the best form of government for every people, and the ruler's power is only limited through a constitution because there are so few intelligent and just men. How different is the situation now, when we have been fortunate enough to have a committee bringing together the best of the wise and the just! If it is autocratic, it's autocracy goes hand in hand with consultation...[22]

In May 1909, perhaps somewhat shaken by the attempted countercoup in Istanbul,[23] Zaidan expanded on the issue.[24] He declared quite openly, that there existed resentment against the *ittihadis* or "unionists" as they were now called.[25] He wanted to take up their defense so that perhaps the Arabs would tone down their opposition. He posited that there were three conditions that had to be fulfilled for a revolution to succeed: 1) The state must have a need for it and the people must be ready. 2) If the revolution is for reform and improvement, the leaders have to have a policy for gaining the support of the people in fighting the tyrant and forming a new government according to the expectations of the age. 3) It will be necessary to cleanse the state apparatus of all the old elements by retirement, exile or execution, so that there will be no resistance, trouble or *fitna*, internal unrest or civil war.

---

22 Ibid. p.415.

23 "The 31 March [1909] incident was an uprising of conservative forces in Istanbul: religious students and functionaries, military cadres with traditional education...and loyalists to the old regime...It posed a profound challenge to the new regime..." Kayali, Hasan. *Arabs and Turks: Ottomanism, Arabism, and Islamism in the Ottoman Empire 1908-1909* (Los Angeles, Univ. of California Press, 1997) p.72.

24 "Jāmiʿat al-Ittiḥād wa'l-Taraqqin," *al-Hilāl* 17 (May 1909) pp. 491-496.

25 "Unionists" after the group or party which had been founded before the Revolution and now had taken complete power, the Committee of Union and Progress.

The Unionists had fought from the underground for a long time. Once they came to power, Zaidan continued, they forewent any act of revenge or provoking a bloodbath. It turned out, though, that this policy was a mistake, because many people opposing the revolution remained in power. The revolutionaries only could be blamed for being too noble and *evolué* in their virtue, "knowledge softens the soul and weakens the anger". But tyranny was needed in the early stages of a revolution to secure it!

After a lengthy visit to Istanbul in the summer of 1909 he demanded the mandatory teaching of Turkish in all Arab secondary schools and passing the Turkish language test a requirement for obtaining a diploma. Knowing the integrative force that language could have, he believed that knowledge of Turkish by all citizens of the post-revolutionary Ottoman Empire was a precondition for their active participation in the politics and the maintenance of a constitutional, democratic Ottoman Empire. This call for the use of Turkish on the political and administrative level contradicted his own preoccupation with and high esteem for the Arabic language and history as can be seen in his earlier quoted statement about his own work.[26]

The themes that preoccupied and troubled Zaidan and which he and other authors debated are perhaps best summarized in the political testament of Midhat Pasha in Zaidan's novel *The Ottoman Revolution* that was just then being serialized in his journal.[27] In this document Midhat Pasha supposedly addressed the next generation of Liberals, which actually carried out the revolution. Zaidan let him start with a dramatic

---

26 "Al-Ustāna al-'aliyya," *al-Hilāl* 18 (Dec. 1909) pp. 131-165, p.161. Zaidan was by no means the only Arab demanding this. See, for instance, Al-Bustānī', Sulaymān. *'Ibra wa-Dhikra aw al-Dawla al-'Uthmāniyya qabla al-Dustūr wa-ba'dahu.* First published in 1909 (Beirut, Dār al-Ṭalī'ah, 1978) p. 247 where he, too, demands the spread of the knowledge of Turkish and claimed that in 1909 it would take only twenty-five years for citizens to acquire a basic knowledge of Turkish.

27 *Al-Hilāl* 19 (Oct. 1910 - July 1911).

order: "Demand the constitution with the sword!" i.e. collaboration with the army was necessary because force would be needed. This is to be followed first and foremost by education: "Teach the nation and lift the masses! Ignorance is the cause of all deficiency and weakness." He gave here considerable importance to the need for the education of women. Second, he warned the revolutionaries of ethnic and religious splits in society and ordered them to unite under the flag of Ottomanism. The Ottoman constitution needed this support. Third, the revolutionaries should ally themselves through secret societies with the army, "since the soldiers are the nation and with their swords the constitution will be defended and freedom stabilized". Fourth, the liberals should not be naive but distrust their enemies, especially 'Abdulhamid and his secretive group of advisors. Fifth, Midhat Pasha observed that freedom was based on justice, kindness and peacefulness, "but freedom will not be obtained without bloodshed. ...Annihilate the evildoers ... kill all whom you find working against freedom and the constitution". Force is needed to obtain freedom—the conundrum in which Zaidan found himself at least since the countercoup. Finally, Zaidan added the demand that sovereignty (*haqq al-siyada*) should remain with a sultan from the Ottoman dynasty, on the condition that the successor to the throne would be chosen by the nation or the parliament.[28]

During the same time he analyzed in an essay[29] various systems of political rule and compared, in particular, constitutional monarchy with republican constitutionalism. After weighing the pros and cons he clearly tended now towards constitutional monarchy. Under the influence of the barely prevented countercoup, Zaidan felt that republican constitutionalism with its need for elections led to instability and conflict in parliament. Besides, he argued, republicanism professed that any

28 Zaydān, Jurjī. *Al-Inqilāb al-'Uthmānī* (Cairo, Dār-al-Hilāl, 1933) pp.171-173.

29 "Al-Jumhūriyya wa-sā'ir Ḍurūb al-Ḥukūma wa-ayyuhā afḍal," *al-Hilāl* 19 (Nov. 1910) pp. 77-84.

person could become a ruler, but this was an illusion because power always remained in the hands of elites.

Generally speaking, the number of essays or comments to the post-revolutionary Ottoman Empire dropped noticeably in *al-Hilal* between Oct. 1910 and July 1911.[30] In the following volume[31] he hardly mentioned the Ottoman situation and only indirectly refers to it in an essay on Ahmad Pasha al-'Urabi's attempted revolution in Egypt between 1879 and 1882, which he felt had been premature. In June 1913 [32] we find one relevant article, discussing once more the constitutional state.[33] But the tone has changed. He was no longer calling on the Ottoman leaders and the Ottoman populations to do the right thing, but only pointed out how difficult it had been in modern times to establish constitutional rule. He wrote in a detached and even pessimistic tone. Considerable progress was needed and a profound recognition of the individual's right to freedom before a constitutional system could be established. Lucky were those nations who had reached this state of affairs gradually in a slow process. Others had tried to do so in a single stroke, with the result that it took much longer for true constitutionalism to take hold. Some tore up their constitutions and in the end were ruled by other states, as was the case in Iran "*and—as we fear—might happen to the Ottoman Empire* [emphasis added]". Every change in political systems puts at risk the income, wealth and vested interests of large numbers of people. The dangers to constitutionalism remained the same: lack of preparedness by the people, lack of unity and, more than ever, the opposition of the old elites, whose vested interests were endangered.

A final reference to the Ottoman revolution came in a lengthy historical article on Europe and the Ottoman Empire in the last volume of *al-Hilal*

30 *Al-Hilāl* 19.

31 *Al-Hilāl* 20 (Oct. 1911 - July 1912).

32 *Al-Hilāl* 21.

33 "Ajyāl al-Duwal - Ajyāl al-Duwal al-Dustūriyya," *al-Hilāl* 21 (June 1913) pp. 522-528.

that Zaidan wrote and edited personally.[34] A revolution under the flag of Ottoman identity, originally supported enthusiastically by "the shaykh and the priest", i.e. by everybody, had run into obstacles. Zaidan mentioned the by now well established reasons but was especially harsh on the ethnic divisions, the ethnic rivalries for government jobs and the conflict between the Unionists and the Federalists, *al-I'tilafiyyin*,[35] in parliament. This partisanship had damaged the parliament "because our parties are not like those of other countries and our character is not like theirs".[36] The decline of parliament had left the government without representative support, at a time when the European powers exploited the Balkan Wars to expand their own power.

This almost stubborn holding fast to the idea of an empire integrated and stabilized by a constitution, raises the question as to how he could reconcile this political stand with his life's work which laid the foundations for a secular national history of the Arabs and contributed massively to the revival and transformation of Arabic into a modern print-language. Nationalist movements, clamouring for their own nation-states, emerged everywhere. In the Balkans former Ottoman provinces seceded from the empire guided by nationalist ideologies. Perhaps Zaidan did not recognize that his own work and that of other Nahdawis would develop its own dynamic and would almost inescapably result in a program of political action for Arab nationalism. He certainly believed that the Arab society was not yet prepared for national independence and more time was needed to achieve that stage.

Zaidan's compatriot of an earlier generation, Butrus al-Bustani, too, had made it his business to revive the Arabic language as a vehicle of modern communication and a carrier of Arab identity. Especially with the unrests and wars between Muslims and Christians in Lebanon, Damascus and also Aleppo and elsewhere in the 1840s and early fifties al-Bustani began

34 "Al-Dawla al-'Uthmāniyya wa'l-Duwal al-Ūrubiyya," *al-Hilāl* 22 (April 1914) pp. 323-338; pp. 416-425; pp. 505-512.

35 Meant are the members of the Decentralization Party.

36 "Al-Dawla al-'Uthmāniyya wa'l-Duwal al-Ūrubiyya," op.cit. p.509.

a campaign for a secular Arab identity bringing people together who had drifted apart, because of religion, to the point of threatening the dissolution of society. Syria as the Arab fatherland (*al-watan al-'arabi*) became a major theme in his writings and debates. With the famous *Hatt-i humayun*, announcing the Ottoman reforms, issued in 1856, he embraced the idea of an Ottoman political community fully. "Bustani lead the way, culturally to Arabism, politically to Ottomanism."[37] But he could not bridge the internal contradiction between the two. Perhaps for his generation this was not such an urgent issue. The political order of the Ottoman Empire had existed for some three hundred and fifty years and, though Greece had separated already from the Empire, the explosive centrifugal power nationalism would generate was not yet visible in the empire itself.

On the eve of World War I the Ottoman Empire had ruled the Arab lands for four centuries and there were many signs that not only Zaidan but his whole generation of Arab intellectuals could simply not conceive of a political future beyond the Ottoman system. To be sure, all saw the need for reforms in the empire. But the thought that the empire was perhaps beyond repair and reform did not occur to Zaidan's generation, even though nationalism had already acquired a much more aggressive form with the Balkan wars than was the case during al-Bustani's time.

Most members of the educated classes could see a danger looming from the European powers, desirous of splitting the Empire among themselves. Zaidan was aware of this danger. But the danger of imperialism could only be answered by internal reform and greater unity of the Ottoman Empire.

Zaidan's analysis of history focused most often on persons as the *agentes historiae*, their talents, their knowledge, their virtues or lack thereof. Thus *al-Hilal* issues were often introduced with an article on some remarkable historical personality. And he could never quite

---

37 For more details see Abu Manneh, Buṭrus. "The Christians between Ottomanism and Syrian Nationalism," *International Journal of Middle Eastern Studies* 11 (1980) pp.287-304.

decide whether the just ruler, albeit under check by the constitution, was not the best political system.[38] Similarly Zaidan gave great weight to the person of ‘Abdulhamid as the cause for the decay, the disunity and the oppression, which eventually lead to the Ottoman Revolution. The Unionists, on the other hand, had been in the aftermath of the revolution too virtuous to seek revenge on the ignorant supporters of ‘Abdulhamid, which provided the opposition with the opportunity to raise its ugly head barely nine months later. But his focus on the individuals as the cause for historical development also carried the great promise of the Enlightenment: the individual could become better, i.e. a more rational and responsible person, through education and knowledge. What was needed was time to educate and create the enlightened person. Hence Zaidan worried on repeated occasions as to whether the people were ready for reforms or revolution. “Lack of preparation” i.e. insufficient education of the individuals, was in his opinion the reason for the failure of the ‘Urabi Revolt in Egypt and the first Ottoman attempt to introduce the Constitution. With progress in education, society as a whole would become ready for political change and the complexities of parties, election, deputies and parliaments. This was Zaidan’s hope.

In the last years of his life Zaidan had articulated a theory of the “community of interest”, *jami‘at al-manfa‘a.* He argued that human beings always have to live in groups or communities with each other. But they will choose the group from which they expect the greatest benefits for themselves. The most stable social groups are those that give benefits, *manfa‘a,* and are useful to their members. People will be loyal to and associate with those groups that promise benefits to the individual. At the height of Islamic rule in the East it was useful for the people of the East to be loyal to Islam and join a countermovement to the European states. But today it is in the interest of the

38 See his article “Al-Jumhūriyya wa-sā’ir Ḍurūb al-Ḥukūma wa-‘ayyuhā afḍal,” *al-Hilāl* 19 (Nov.1910) pp. 77-84.

people of the East to safeguard the nation, *al-umma*, and they take to it on wings.[39]

He later elaborated a few issues in an essay on the relation between individuals and a group and the expected benefit from membership in that group.[40] Zaidan started again with the observation that association with others was a human instinct, because social groups are the essential instrument for the survival of the individual. After passing briefly over the primal associations such as the family or the clan, into which the individual is born and which are also mutual-help associations, he analyzed the societies or groups that individuals would form and join voluntarily, depending on their perceived benefit.[41] The identity-forming elements that would hold such societies together were of almost unlimited variety, from professional associations or racial similarity to language groups or religion—anything that could hold a group together. The perceived benefits could also differ and were not necessarily determined by the common identity. Most important, Zaidan asserted that individuals were simultaneously members in a variety of associations or societies, which might even have contradictory purposes or goals. They would shift the emphasis of membership in one or another group according to their needs at any given moment. They could also join additional societies or leave others, depending on changing circumstances and always according to their perceived benefits. Societies of one form could be replaced by societies of another form. The shapes and structures of such societies, their strength, endurance and benefits were limitless in their variety, but the driving force behind them remained the *jamiʿat al-manfaʿa* or "community of usefulness". Such a sociological model could actually fit very well multi-ethnic multi-sectarian empires such as the Ottoman one. Multiple loyalties could exist simultaneously to the state, the religion, the location

39 "Al-Taʿaṣṣub al-dīnī wa'l-Taʿaṣṣub al-siyāsī," *al-Hilāl* 19 (Oct. 1910) pp. 54-55. He means here the Ottoman *umma*.

40 "Jāmiʿat al-Manfaʿa," *al-Hilāl* 19 (Feb. 1911) pp. 280-5.

41 "*Li-mā yatawassamūhu min al-naf ʿ bi-wasīṭatihā.*"

or the linguistic ethnicity just as well as to social class. Multiple and overlapping loyalties did not need to lead to the break-up of the empire.

With the benefit of hindsight after almost one hundred years we can easily agree that from a rational and responsible point of view and an Enlightened point of view, a democratic, constitutionalist Ottoman Empire might have provided the greatest benefit to its multi-ethnic population and the intended reforms might have bettered the life of all citizens. It might or might not have been the best defense against European imperialism. But it presupposes that rational thinking would bring under these circumstances all human beings to the desired results and to mutual understanding—an assumption directly taken from the Enlightenment movement. It also presupposes that, having formulated a constitution and officially made it the law of the land, people would act rationally according to its provisions. What is completely lacking from this equation—and herein consists perhaps Zaidan's blind spot—are human emotions, subjective perspectives and the impact of ideologies or specific world views on human action.

It appears that this "blind spot" made it impossible for Zaidan, even though all his life he had labored hard to establish a secular Arab identity, to recognize the passions of political nationalism and the ease with which these could be mobilized for powerful, political action and different aims. This underestimation of the political power of nationalism applied not only to the nascent nationalism in the Balkans but also to Arab nationalism itself. Nationalism heralded a whole new set of perceived self-interests, not necessarily bound to democracy and constitutionalism or any other particular political system. By the time the constitution was reestablished in the Ottoman Empire, the time for multi-ethnic empires had already passed.

In conclusion we may say that a number of different factors made it impossible for Zaidan to envision a political order beyond the Ottoman Empire: his enlightened belief in human reason as well as the need for education, his confidence that the constitution alone would reintegrate the Ottoman Empire, his underestimation of the passion of nationalism and, finally, the justified fear that the disintegration of the empire would mean the colonization of the Middle East by the European powers.

At the end he might have sensed the futility of the project, called "Ottomanism". We only know that he ceased to comment much on it or to encourage people to pursue it. We cannot know how he would have reacted to the gigantic changes that were to follow: he died unexpectedly on the eve of World War I.

Zaidan the Novelist: The Image and Roles of Women in his Novels[*]

Zaïneb Ben Lagha

> *"This is how all men are, my lady,"* 'Utba said.*"They have dominion and are in command. They prefer themselves to women, allow themselves what they deny women, and enjoy what they forbid women. A man marries several women, and owns slave girls; yet he prevents a woman from marrying the man who loves her and whom she loves."*

With these words the servant and confidante 'Utba tries to comfort her mistress, al-'Abbasa, the sister of the caliph Harun al-Rashid, in the novel by Jurji Zaidan.[1] The caliph had effectively decided to formally arrange a marriage between his sister and his vizier and friend Ja'far al-Barmaki in order to enjoy their company at the same time. He, however, forbade them from consummating the marriage, since this would be a mismatch, and above all any child born from this union would threaten his power. Al-'Abbasa and Ja'far paid no attention to this prohibition and bore two sons from their romance, who were kept in hiding. Their mother was only allowed to see them once a year in secret in a slave-merchant's house.

---

* I would like to thank Thomas Philipp for his judicious remarks.

1 *Al-'Abbāsa Ukht al-Rashīd* [1906]; *The Caliph's Sister: Harun al-Rashid and the Fall of the Persians,* translated by Issa J. Boullata and published by the Zaidan Foundation, Inc. 2012, p.18. The quotes are all taken from the English translation of the novel as are all the quotes from *Saladin and the Assassins* translated by Paul Starkey and published by The Zaidan Foundation, Inc. 2012. Quotes from other works were translated by the author.

These remarks, which 'Utba uttered to the princess al-'Abbasa, are surprising in their anachronism. Imagine a servant talking to her mistress in this way in the ninth century! In fact the novel, from which these lines have been taken, was published several years after the violent polemic sparked by the 1899 publication of the book of Qasim Amin[2] on *The Liberation of Women*, followed two years later by *The New Woman.* But the debate over the question of the condition of women had already started in the 1890's. Zaidan, through this exchange between the princess and the servant provides us with a feminine point of view on this question, a reminder that there were two types of feminist viewpoints in his time, one held by women and the other by men, each viewpoint stemming from different priorities:

> In the main towns of Egypt or Syria, some women, who belonged most often to the Bourgeois or "middle" class, whether Christian or Jewish, had seen their status changing. [...] These changes fed into a feminist viewpoint held simultaneously by women and men. [...] the women, such as 'Aisha al-Taymuriyya (1840-1902), Zaynab Fawwaz (1860-1914) or the founders of the first magazines in the 1890's, were motivated by the concrete conditions of their existence. The male opinion on the status of women was part of a wider debate concerning the causes of their society's backwardness. This thinking was led by men and was above all targeted at men: it was they who determined what should change in the status of women.[3]

But it was certainly the work by Qasim Amin which would deal comprehensively with the question of the status of women. He criticized, in

---

2 Amīn, Qāsim. *Taḥrīr al-Mar'a* (Cairo, Maktabat al-Taraqqī, 1899) and *Al-Mar'a al-jadīda* (Cairo, s.n., 1900). At the time he was the most important Egyptian protagonist of the emancipation of women.

3 Dupont, Anne-Laure. *Ǧurǧī Zaydān 1861-1914: Écrivain réformiste et témoin de la Renaissance arabe* (Damas, Institut Français du Proche-Orient, 2006) p. 447.

particular, the reclusion of women and polygamy. For him, the veil, completely covering the woman, was not an Arab custom, but a foreign one adopted by the Arabs through contact with other nations. This practice was later legitimized by the scholars of Islamic Law. Since this was only a custom, it was possible to change it; this should be the task of the politicians. Amin also specified that there is no Koran-based text demanding the wearing of this type of clothing. Drawing inspiration from the law, he confirmed the contrary: that the processes of civil order, penal or financial, undertaken by women require them to be unveiled in order to avoid being exploited. Finally, Amin considered that the veil prevented the woman from having a professional activity when she needed one to look after her family.[4] In fact what created the polemic and the rejection of Qasim Amin's theses is the manner in which he treated all of these questions, especially in his last work *The New Woman*, comparing the oriental woman to the occidental woman:

> Look at the eastern countries; you will find woman enslaved to man and man to the ruler. Man is an oppressor in his home, oppressed as soon as he leaves it. Then look at the European countries; the governments are based on freedom and respect for personal rights, and the status of women has been raised to a high degree of respect and freedom of thought and action.[5]

Although the country was under British occupation, his attitude was felt as a veritable provocation by his opponents. He was thus accused of promoting a European viewpoint that blamed the status of women for the backwardness of Egyptian society and hence justified Great Britain's civilizing mission in the country. In his second work, *The New Woman,*

---

4 Abbès, Makram. *La femme au centre des débats intellectuels au Moyen-Orient dans la première moitié du XXe siècle*. Unpublished lecture in preparation for the national exam for teaching Arabic (cours de préparation à l'agrégation d'arabe), (Lyon, ENS-Lsh, 2006).

5 Amīn. *Al-Mar'a al-jadīda*, p. 1. Quoted by Ḥourani, Albert. *Arabic Thought in the Liberal Age 1798-1939* (Cambridge Univ. Press, Cambridge, 1962) p. 167.

the reference was no longer the word of the Koran but "the science and social thinking of the West". One of its main protagonists, Herbert Spencer, is often evoked by Amin.[6]

Zaidan took part in this debate starting in 1894[7] for almost twenty years in his magazine *al-Hilal,* via numerous articles, which include: "The Oriental Woman Yesterday and Today",[8] "The Nation is a Product of its Mothers",[9] "The Woman Between Indecency and the Veil",[10] and "The Arabic Woman Before and After the Veil".[11] The extract we quoted from *The Caliph's Sister* shows that Zaidan also tackled this question in his fictional work. This type of literature has the advantage of permitting the author to tackle the sensitive questions concerning the status of women without fear of provoking debate or risking being accused of attacking Islam. The fictional setting also allows the reader to be

6 Ḥourani, p. 167.

7 For Zaydān's approach to feminism see the following works: Philipp, Thomas."Women in the Historical Perspective of an early Arab Modernist (Ǧurǧī Zaidān)," *Die Welt des Islams* 18 (1977) p. 65-83; Dupont. *Ǧurǧī Zaydān*, p. 446-465 ; Ben Lagha, Zaïneb. *Le personnage historique dans l'œuvre romanesque de Ǧurǧī Zaydān (1861-1914): entre figure exemplaire et personnage de roman.* Unpublished doctoral thesis (Paris, Institut National des Langues et Civilisations Orientales, 2006) p. 305-332.

8 "Al-Mar'a al-sharqiyya Ams wa'l-Yawm," *al-Hilāl* 9 (March 1901) pp.350-357.

9 "Al-Umma Nasīj al-Ummahāt," *al-Hilāl* 16 (Jan. 1908) pp. 139-243. The page numbers in this issue are mixed up: after p. 200 the pagination continues with p.101 until p.140 and then shifts back to p. 241. The essay is four pages long, not 104 pages.

10 "Al-Mar'a bayna 'l-Tabadhdhul wa'l-Ḥijāb," *al-Hilāl* 19 (Nov.1911) pp.106-109.

11 "Al-Mar'a al-'Arabiyya qabla 'l-Ḥijāb wa-ba'duhu," *al-Hilāl* 22 (Dec.1913) pp.163-176. The article "Al-Mar'a al-sharqiyya: Ams wa'l-Yawm" which is presented by Zaidan as the history of the Christian woman in the Orient also tackles the Muslim woman in the period after the Nahda since he observed that before this period: "the [oriental] Christian woman's lifestyle was identical to that of a Muslim woman in almost all areas, and in particular over the subject of the veil and freedom, right up until the point where the Nahda separates them."

touched much more profoundly. The "experiences" of the female characters show very real situations that the readers feel intensely, something the historical analysis does not always manage to do. Tackling this question in his historical novels, which were highly successful from the moment they appeared, also gave Zaidan the opportunity to share his opinions with a much larger number of readers than those that read his articles. Thomas Philipp highlights the impact of Zaidan's novels regarding this question:

> The ideas of Zaidan about the role of women as they emanate from his popular historical novels had a greater impact upon the formation of public opinion than the far more radical and programmatic writings of a Qasim Amin, which drew certainly stormy but mainly rejecting reaction.[12]

The treatment which Zaidan accords the status of women in his novels is open to question and especially his views on their emancipation, given his minority position as both a Syrian *Shami* immigrant and a Christian, in a mostly Muslim country, Egypt.

The importance of the female character in Zaidan's novels

The place given to women in his novels is already apparent from the titles Zaidan gives them. Of his twenty-two novels, eight evoke female characters: *Armanusa the Egyptian* (1896), *The Gassanid Damsel* (1897-1898), *The Virgin of Quraysh* (1899), *The Young Lady from Karbala* (1901), *The Caliph's Sister* (1906), *The Bride of Farghana* (1908), *The Damsel of Kairouan* (1912) and *The Tree of Pearls*[13] (1914). This is almost as many

12 Philipp."Women in the Historical Perspective," p. 69.

13 In order of appearance: *Armānūsa al-Miṣriyya, Fatāt Ghassān,'Ādhrā' Quraysh, Ghādat Karbala, Al-'Abbāsa Ukht al-Rashīd, 'Arūs Farhgāna, Fatāt al-Qayrawān* and *Shajarat al-Durr* (a woman's name). See Bibliography for further details.

as the number of novels with titles of masculine characters (nine).[14] These titles refer either to fictitious characters, meant to represent a people, a dynasty or a town which played a particular role in history, or to historical figures. It is interesting to note that the titles referring to male characters are all real names. However, for the female characters, with the notable exception of *The Tree of Pearls*, their names are often indicated by generic terms and referred to by their tribal link—The *Virgin* of Quraysh, and The Ghassanid *Damsel*; by their patriarchal link—The Caliph's *Sister;* or by their country of origin—Armanusa the *Egyptian*, and The *Bride* of Farghana. It is in 1899, the date of publication of *The Freedom of Women*, that the historical female character entered into the historical novels of Zaidan and began to occupy an increasingly important place: 'Aisha bint Abi Bakr, a secondary character of *The Virgin of Quraysh*, al-'Abbasa, the heroine of *The Caliph's Sister* and Shajarat al-Durr who gives her name to his last novel. This presence brings across Zaidan's desire to show his readers that women have also played a role in history, even if these have been fewer than men. Among these female characters, may be quoted: 'Aisha the Prophet's favorite wife, considered to be an authority on the subject of prophetic traditions; Sukayna bint al-Husayn,[15] the grand-daughter of 'Ali, the son-in-law of the Prophet, renowned for the important role she played in the cultural life of her time, with her literary gatherings, where she brought together poets, musicians and singers; and of course Shajarat al-Durr, considered to be the first Muslim woman to have been in power as a Sultana.

The female characters, fictitious or historical, are central figures in the two interwoven storylines of each historical novel: the political storyline and the romantic storyline. The former, constitutes the "historical" part of the novel and, basing itself on historical events, is centered on the

14 In order of appearance: *Al-Mamlūk al-Shārid, Asīr al-Mutamahdī, Al-Ḥajjāj ibn Yūsuf, Shārl wa 'Abd al-Raḥmān, Abū Muslim al-Khurasānī, Al-Amīn wa'l-Ma'mūn, Aḥmad Ibn Ṭulūn, 'Abd al-Raḥmān al-Nāṣir* and *Ṣalāḥ al-Dīn al-Ayyūbī.* See Bibliography for further details.

15 In the novel *The 17th of Ramadan.*

conquest of power, or the defense of power when under threat. The latter corresponds most of the time to a thwarted love story, often the story of a broken family following a trauma, trying to put the pieces back together. The female character often plays a major role in the first and is always the heroine in the second. In *Saladin and the Assassins*, Sittalmulk is the heroine of the thwarted love story with 'Imad al-Din, Saladin's Kurdish officer, who saved her life. She is also at the heart of the political storyline of the novel, where she is the conduit for wresting power from the hands of her brother, al-'Adid,[16] a weakened Fatimid caliph. Two protagonists in the caliph's entourage desire to marry her to take over the caliphate: Abul-Hasan, a fictitious character of obscure origin, who claims to be the caliph's cousin; and his vizier, Saladin. This omnipresence of the female character in the two storylines allows Zaidan to fully tackle the question of the status of women.

Women's emancipation: a necessity

For Zaidan, women's emancipation is vital and urgent in the context of the issues prevalent at the time. All the more so because he believed that the position held by women regressed through the centuries, especially in certain areas when we compare the pre-Islamic period with the Islamic era:[17]

16 It should be noted here that Zaidan does not reflect historical facts accurately: the Faṭimid princess Sittalmulk is not the sister of the caliph al-'Āḍiḍ (1160-71), but of the caliph al-Ḥākim (996-1021) and was not alive at the time of Saladin.

17 Thomas Philipp rightly remarks that the vision that Zaidan has of the status of women in the pre-Islamic period has greatly evolved: "Highly interesting in this context is his treatment of women in pre-Islamic times. When in 1899, Qasim Amīn published his *Taḥrīr al-Mar'a*, it stirred up a great many discussions. Zaidan [...] described with great disgust the lowliness of her position and the cruel habit of female infanticide [...] Zaidan's opinion about the status of women in pre-Islamic society [...] radically changed some seven years later. Now Zaidan went to great length to explain that during the pre-Islamic time and early Islamic period, the Arab woman had a position almost equal to man. She was independent, often well educated, and appeared in public without restrictions. The habit of killing female babies he minimized in extent and importance. This change of view can only be explained with Zaidan's generally

> The Arab woman during pre-Islamic times and the early Islamic periods had a generous spirit, a strong character and determination. Among Arab women, several stood out for their intelligence, wisdom and political sense. They exerted a great influence on society and political change.[18]

A refusal of confinement

The confinement of women is without contest the principal cause of this regression from which all the others stem. Zaidan denounces this and, following Qasim Amin, states that this is not prescribed by the Koran:

> [Confinement] is in no situation a requirement in Islam, as many believe, since if we refer to the Koran, what we find there on this subject only serves to bring confinement into question.[19]

The women benefited, according to him, from a certain freedom of movement during pre-Islamic times up to the Umayyad period. In *The Virgin of Quraysh*, 'Aisha bint Abi Bakr and especially Asma', a fictitious character, frequently moved from one place to another. In the novel, we meet 'Aisha for the first time in Mecca, to where the "Mother of the Believers" had fled seeking refuge from the troubled political climate reigning in Medina. Later she leaves the town for Basra, where Asma' found her during the Battle of the Camel. Each time, these movements are taken at her own initiative. Showing a historical character of this importance moving with total freedom, without having to refer to any masculine authority, must have had a striking impact on the reader. As for Asma', the heroine of the romantic plotline, she undertakes a pilgrimage throughout the

---

changed approach to the time of the *jahiliyya*." Philipp. "Women in the Historical Perspective," p. 81-82.

18 "Al-Mar'a al-'Arabiyya qabla 'l-Ḥijāb wa-ba'duhu," p. 166.

19 Ibid. p. 254.

novel, bringing her first to Medina, which she leaves upon the death of the caliph 'Uthman, then goes to Mecca where she meets 'Aisha, and then on to Basra where she witnesses the Battle of the Camel. The reader later finds her in Kufa whose inhabitants swear allegiance to 'Ali. She then sets off in search of her roots in Damascus before proceeding to Jerusalem and Antioch. She also turns up in Siffin where she witnessed the conflict between Mu'awiya and 'Ali. Her journey ends in Egypt in Fustat. These travels occur in both the romantic and the political storylines as Asma' serves as an eye-witness for the reader to the historical events.

For Zaidan the confinement of women begins with the introduction of *jawari* or "slaves" into society that men take as "concubines", of which they may have an unlimited number, contrary to the number of wives. Through the power these slaves hold over the men, they exude a highly negative image of femininity, which results in the creation of a sense of mistrust between the sexes. Zaidan considers that the practice of taking concubines degraded the social status of women. Thomas Philipp summarizes Zaidan's position on this subject very well: "Since women became a purchasable merchandise, men began to doubt the integrity and virtue of their own free wives and began to lock them away."[20]

For Zaidan, the confinement of women became a common practice in the Orient during the Umayyad period and peaked at the time of the 'Abbasids, as illustrated perfectly in the novels *The Caliph's Sister* and *Saladin and the Assassins*. The women are described as living in total seclusion and subject to armed-guard surveillance, both to prevent their movements and to report their every action back to the relevant authority. In *The Caliph's Sister* it was the Barmakid viziers who held the keys to the palace of the women; Zubayda, the wife of the caliph Harun al-Rashid, saw her freedom of movement hindered. Referring to the fictionalised version of al-Itlidi,[21] Zaidan writes:

20 Philipp. "Women in the Historical Perspective," p. 73.

21 Muḥammad Ma'rūf Diyāb al-Itlidī, Egyptian author about whom very little is known. He died ca. 1689 and wrote *Nawādir al-Ḥulafā'* better known as *I'lām al-Nās bi-ma waqa'a li'l-Barāmika min Banī 'Abbās*.

> Harun al-Rashid allows [...] Yahya the Barmakid to move freely within her appartments and palace [so it seems] and charged him with keeping watch over her, as well as the harem, to the extent that he took the keys away with him after locking the doors.[22]

In the novel *Saladin and the Assassins*, the palace of Sittalmulk is watched over by a man in Saladin's trust, who allowed himself, as a result of a denunciation, to rifle through the princess' apartments against her will. The young woman did not hesitate to complain of this to her loved one, considering herself a prisoner: "I am a prisoner in this palace... I wish I could leave it with you this very instant!"[23]

For Zaidan the confinement of women transforms the woman into the "living-dead" and corrupts her morals.[24] Zubayda represents this image of the reclusive, affected woman that Zaidan denounces, a woman driven to vice through idleness. She appears in al-'Abbasa's portrait of her as an unfit wife, who encourages her husband's infidelity:

> But I remind you of the numerous slave-girls and concubines in your palace, whom you enjoy and have pleasure with and find nothing wrong in that, believing the laws allow you this. You don't see any problem with enjoying them even though the law forbids you from having them ... *Your own wife Zubayda gave you ten of the most beautiful slave girls as a gift. She did so without believing that this was demeaning for you or her, nor a crime either.*[25]

---

22 *The Caliph's Sister*, p. 48.

23 *Saladin and the Assassins,* p. 130.

24 "Al-Mar'a al-'Arabiyya qabla 'l-Ḥijāb wa-ba'duhu," op.cit.

25 *The Caliph's Sister*, p. 190; emphasis added.

The Woman and Marriage

As Thomas Philipp rightly notes, marriage remains the only accomplishment for the heroines of Zaidan's novels, at least for those who are not already married.[26] In his novels, Zaidan evoked the question of marriage exclusively from the woman's point of view, whereas in articles in *al-Hilal*, it was mostly the man's point of view which is prevalent. Zaidan thus denounces in his journal the traditional criteria upon which a man bases his choice of a future wife: the fortune of her family and her social position, her beauty and lack of knowledge. The young man only sees his bride to be on the day of their engagement; and she only hears about her future husband once everything has already been decided. Zaidan warns of two major risks for spouses and their families due to these arranged marriages—which are often forced marriages: adultery, or the young woman running away with another man when she doesn't like the husband chosen for her.[27]

In the fictional work by Zaidan, the question of marriage is always associated with the double issue of the *nasab* or "noble birth" and the *kuf'* or "equality of birth". The husband-to-be must at least be the woman's equal, as any mismatching must be avoided. In *Saladin and the Assasins* the Fatimid caliph tells his sister, whom he wishes to marry to his confidant, Abul-Ḥasan, in a very straightforward way: "Divine providence has set you among the class of caliphs and has given you a distinguished, noble heritage. So it is not right for you to marry someone who is unsuitable."[28]

This type of mismatched marriage is presented in the novels as a forced marriage. For Zaidan it reflected the expression of familial tyranny, which is comparable to political tyranny. It is represented by a very negative father figure, and in his absence, of the young woman's legal guardian, her brother. This is the case in the novel *Saladin and the*

26 Philipp. "Women in the Historical Perspective," p. 77.

27 "Al-Mar'a al-sharqiyya: Ams wa'l-Yawm," p. 353.

28 *Saladin and the Assassins*, p. 92.

Assassins where the caliph al-'Adid reminds his sister of the reasons why she must obey him and accept the man he wants her to marry: "You should know that it is the Commander of the Faithful, who is speaking to you and making this demand, and he is your guardian."[29]

This negative representation of familial authority, as Thomas Philipp remarks, may be related to Zaidan's own life experiences, being constantly in conflict with his father, whom he reproached for having cut short his education in order to have him work in his restaurant, thereby preventing him from preparing a better future for himself.[30] In Zaidan's novels, the women are always opposed to these forced marriages. In *The Fugitive Mamluk*, Salma runs away from home in order to avoid the marriage her father wishes to impose on her, and thus tarnishes the honor of her entire family. Her cousin, the wife of the emir Bashir al-Shahabi, believing her to be dead, would say of her "this poor girl, the victim of her father's fanaticism".[31] The emir himself would forgive her this action when he finds her. In *Saladin and the Assassins*, Sittalmulk would rather not marry at all, even if this means an infringement of the law, than to marry a man that she doesn't love: "Marriage is not necessary for me" she says and later, "She resolved to do as she pleased, even if it was contrary to law and custom."[32]

In Zaidan's novels, the heroine always marries the man she loves, who is often from a lower social class: Salma, the descendant of a Qurayshi family and the cousin of the emir Bashir al-Shahabi, married a mamluk emir; al-'Abbasa, the descendant of a Hashemite family, a "client" Ja'far al-Barmaki; Sittalmulk a descendant of Fatima, the Prophet's daughter, a Kurdish lieutenant from a servant background.

---

29 Ibid. p.91.

30 Philipp."Women in the Historical Perspective," p. 67-71.

31 *Al-Mamlūk al-Shārid* (Cairo, Dar al-Hilal, n.d.) p. 28.

32 *Saladin and the Assassins*, p. 92.

The recurrence of this theme of a young girl of noble descent marrying a socially inferior man is without doubt the echo of the violent polemic, which in 1902 was sparked by the planned marriage in Egypt between 'Ali Yusuf, the founder of the famous newspaper *al-Mu'ayyad* (1889), and Safiyya bint al-Shaykh al-Sadat, a young girl belonging to a family of *Ashraf* ("descendants of the Prophet"). The young woman had agreed to marry the journalist, but her parents were firmly against this, complaining of the young man's common roots. In the face of the young woman's obstinacy, her parents brought this affair before the press in order to prevent the union. This affair created a great public outcry, dividing society into two camps: those opposed to the marriage, which included the Khedive, and the institution of al-Azhar; and those supporting the marriage in the name of equality, including Muhammad 'Abduh, Qasim Amin and Ahmad Lutfi al-Sayyid.[33]

Although Zaidan carefully avoided evoking the prickly issue of polygamy in his magazine, he does speak of this in his fictional work, albeit with certain limitations. Incidentally, this issue takes second place in importance to that of forced marriage. In *The Damsel of Kairouan*, polygamy is presented as a danger to men. Condemning polygamy head-on was without a doubt considered as too daring by Zaidan. The Fatimid caliph al-Mu'izz advocated monogamy to his men:

> I am particularly afraid of my men taking several wives. I consider that each should only have one, in order not to complicate their lives in dealing with unwelcome consequences. This would tire out their bodies and weaken their forces.[34]

In *The Caliph's Sister*, the question is tackled in a round-about way via the issue of the slaves which populate the caliph's harems. In order

33 Moghith, Anwar. " Le roman et la fabrique de l'histoire," in *L'écriture de l'histoire*, conference at Cairo University, December 2003. Unpublished manuscript.

34 *Fatāt al-Qayrawān* (Beyrouth, s.n., n.d.) pp. 12-13.

to demonstrate the position they occupied at the time, Zaidan devotes seven whole chapters of his novel to them, a total of thirty pages:

> ...while most of [al-Rashid's] other wives were freed slave girls, like the wives of most of the 'Abbasid caliphs who preceded him. That is why there was no Caliph among them whose mother and father were both Hashemites—the exception being al-Amin...[35]

The accent here is systematically placed on the number of slaves which populate the harems and the prices they command. Drawing reference to al-Tabari[36] and Ibn Khallikan,[37] Zaidan informs the reader that Harun al-Rashid had bought a slave for one hundred thousand dinars and his vizier Ja'far forty thousand, which represented colossal sums.[38] The objective is to show that polygamy exists only to satisfy man's own pleasure and that it detracts from his responsibilities: Harun al-Rashid delegates all of his responsibilities to his vizier Ja'far who eventually becomes very powerful. Al-'Abbasa is outraged by her brother's behaviour:

> Why then does he marry slave girls and sire children from them whom he appoints as heirs apparent? ... Why does he not limit himself to his cousin Zubayda for a wife, whom he appears to love and respect?[39]

---

35 *The Caliph's Sister,* p.6.

36 Abū Ja'far Muḥammad b. Jarīr b. Yazid al-Ṭabarī (839-923), *Tārīkh al-Rusūl wa'l-Mulūk.*

37 Aḥmad b. Muḥammad b. Ibrābīm b. Abī Bakr b. Khallikān (1211-1282), *Wafayāt al-A'yān wa-Anbā' Abnā 'l-Zamān.*

38 *The Caliph's Sister,* p. 39.

39 *The Caliph's Sister,* p.19

Women's emancipation is not an end in itself

Although Zaidan firmly condemns the confinement of women because it contributes to the corruption of customs, he does, however, remain a supporter of the veil:

> Most important is to free the woman from her prison so that she may go out into the world, and there to gain knowledge, learn about the state of society, learn the customs of everyday life and [finally] understand her rights and obligations. However we support those who defend the wearing of the veil, since "unveiling women and freeing them at the same instant could corrupt their morals and lead them to wrongdoing". And this would contravene the customs of society.[40]

The veil as a mark of modesty

Referring to the fact that women had worn the veil since ancient times, appearing before Christianity and remaining popular subsequently, Zaidan considers the veil as a sign of modesty:

> It is not the veil that is detrimental. If it were used with moderation it would be indispensable to women [since] it would give them more modesty and bearing. This is above all valid in the Orient since the veil closely reflects its Oriental origins and traditions.[41]

The title of one of his articles published in *al-Hilal* in November 1911 is highly revealing in this respect: "The Woman Between Indecency and the Veil". In the novels, the veil is never an issue for the women. Moreover at the time, the veil "did not yet represent a major stake in the emancipation of

40 "Al-Mar'a al-'Arabiyya qabla 'l-Ḥijāb wa-ba'duhu," p. 175.

41 Ibid. p. 254.

women, in contrast to the interwar period".[42] In his portrayal of the character 'Aisha bint Abi Bakr, the veil appears as a means of demonstrating feminine beauty: "She wore a silk cape which covered all of her clothes, as well as a veil covering her head, emphasizing her nobility and majesty."[43]

In the novel *Saladin and the Assassins*, the unveiling of Sittalmulk before 'Imad al-Din during their secret meeting in the princess' apartments is by choice and a sign of her intentions: it is a privilege that she accords to her loved one, a proof of her love and trust. She takes off her veil in front of him "before the right moment", as he is the one that she wants to marry and will marry.

In contrast, affectation and vanity are often brought up by Zaidan. They are presented as vices. The character of Zubayda is a perfect incarnation of this. It is the surest method for her to manipulate her husband and son, over whom she holds a real influence:

> [The caliph] could not stop himself, despite his fury, from breaking into a smile at her sight. Then he took his place on the ceremonial bed, seized her hand and made her sit beside him. He looked in amusement at all of the jewelry she was wearing and upon which the light that shone on them magnifying their beauty and luster.[44]

She always greets them in her palace adorned in the most splendid of her dresses and maquillage, behaving just like these "ignorant and vicious" women that Zaidan denounces in an article in *al-Hilal*, and who pass their time making themselves beautiful: redrawing their eyebrows, *tazjij*; applying *kuhl* on their eyes, *takhil*; tattooing themselves, *tahtit*; coloring their hair with henna, *takhdib.*[45] Zaidan concludes this

---

42 Dupont. *Ǧurǧī Zaydān*, p. 455.

43 *'Adhrā' Quraysh* (Cairo, Dār al-Hilāl, 1965) p. 146.

44 *The Caliph's Sister*, p.172.

45 "Al-Mar'a al-sharqiyya Ams wa'l-Yawm," p. 352-353.

passage, which he consecrates to this type of woman, stating that they are only able to bring up their daughters in their own image, that is in vice.[46] Zubayda appealed to the weaknesses of her son and husband, offering them slaves. Zaidan additionally observes that slaves destined for her son dressed themselves as men, implicitly making reference to his homosexuality. It is through all these methods that Zubayda came to play her part in the destruction of the vizier whose downfall she precipitated in the novel, holding her son under her control and choosing to encourage his distractions instead of inciting him to prepare to take power as the caliph's successor, in the hope of playing herself a political role the day he succeeds his father.

As is often the case in his novels when he evokes societal issues, Zaidan draws a parallel with the contemporary era. This is the case in the passage he devotes to the headband of al-'Abbasa which she wore in order to hide a disfigurement on her forehead and which subsequently became "the fashion". Zaidan even uses this anachronistic term:

> Headbands were still new at the time, but common women did not wear them. They were limited to the womenfolk of caliphs and princes—very much like modern fashions [*al-muda*] in every age, worn first by a notable high-class woman and then imitated by her friends before it becomes prevalent among common people.[47]

This passage echoes the harsh opinions he held over the issue in one of his articles in which he evokes the unwelcome moral and economic consequences of certain extremely vain women: the habit of stepping out of the family home and spending money, depleting the family budget, associated with an excessive appetite for entertainment:

---

46 Ibid. p. 353.

47 *The Caliph's Sister*, p.112. The term '*al-mūda*' is the Arabicized Italian word for fashion.

> But we notice today that certain women have exceeded their limits, which calls us to regret the era of confinement and ignorance. We have made ourselves pine for this time when young girls stayed at home and were confined to their domestic chores [...]. This period when they knew nothing of [fashionable] clothes and where their only concern was to dress simply. This period when poor girls didn't try to dress like the rich ones, when they didn't put their appearance before their health in wearing iron corsets, risking compressed organs [...]. This time where they knew nothing of any of these channels of distraction.[48]

Which Role for Women?

Women's emancipation according to Zaidan is not an end in itself but a means of serving the nation's superior interest. Zaidan's hope is for women to play a role in the evolution of modern society. The title of one of his essays "The Nation is the Product of its Mothers" published in January 1908 describes very well the nature of this role: a woman takes her place in society in the role of the wife and of the mother. The dream of his heroine al-'Abbasa, from the very beginning of the novel, is to be able to devote her life to looking after her children from whom she is separated: "How lovely these two boys are and how lovely their names are, al-Hasan and al-Husain! Will God allow me to live with them, even in a simple hut or a tent in the desert?"[49]

Weary of the dangerous life she led, especially after her secret was discovered, al-'Abbasa and Ja'far make the decision together to leave Baghdad and its luxurious life to go to Khorasan, in order to live peacefully there with their children. For Zaidan, the fundamental role of women in society is to respectably take care of their home, supporting

48 "Al-Fatāt al-sharqiyya fī ākhīr al-Qarn al-tasi''ashar," *al-Hilāl* 6 (Nov. 1897) pp.169-174; p.170.

49 *The Caliph's Sister*, p.23.

their husband and educating the children. And it is in this context that women's education may serve a purpose. The issue is only fully tackled in *The Young Turk Revolution*, since women's education is not yet an issue in the novels that take place during earlier periods. The accent is above all placed on the intelligence, wisdom and morality of the heroines, who act as if they had received a proper education. In *The Young Turk Revolution*, the heroine is presented as a well-educated young girl, interested in the political debates of her time. However, her goal is not to work and even less to take part in politics. She puts her intelligence and wisdom in the service of her fiancé Ramiz—a journalist—proof-reading and correcting his articles, in which he often gets carried away. She also supports him in his political activities opposing the Ottoman sultan. Effectively, as rightly highlighted by Anne-Laure Dupont, Zaidan "was very reserved over the work of women and frankly hostile to their political participation", since "his deepest conviction [is] that woman was created to bring up children, which for him seems incompatible with a professional life. She should be taught how to accomplish 'natural chores' within the family home. In carrying out the work of a man, she is stepping outside her *raison d'être*"[50]—looking after her children. For Zaidan the world of politics is reserved for men. In his historical novels, the women are never the heroines of the political storylines. Even Shajarat al-Durr for whom the novel was named, is not the heroine of the political plotline, which is the ascension of Baybars. For it is unnatural for women to try to play a political role; such women are presented as unfit wives or mothers. Shajarat al-Durr, newly widowed, is as ruthless as can be in the pursuit of power: she has the son of her late husband, Turan Shah, killed, with the help of Aybak whom she loves and marries, but who betrays her. She then has him killed and will end up being herself assassinated. Zubayda, as we have seen, encourages her son and husband towards vice and at the end of the novel pushes the latter to assassinate al-'Abbasa's children. In contrast to Zubayda, Shajarat al-Durr evolves

50 Dupont. *Ǧurǧī Zaydān*, pp. 438-439.

during the novel: once destitute, she becomes more humane and recognises that women are not made to bear such heavy poltical burdens. In fact, for Zaidan women and politics do not go together and in this respect he is no different than other reformist historians. As Jocelyne Dakhlia states, they have all been much less sympathetic to women who played a role in history than their predecessors, the historians of the classical period:

> If the nineteenth century, with its grand Reform thematic, opens little by little a place for political reflection on the role of women and on the subject of the female figure in society, it is then equally remarkable that the suggestions of this contemporary reformist are those of women's education and "moral" citizenship [...] Even better, many nationalist reformists from the turn of the nineteenth and twentieth centuries without a doubt radicalized, under the pretext of moral resistance to the Occident and the regeneration of Muslim societies, the exclusion of women from the political scene.[51]

In his fictional work, Zaidan seems to want to inscribe the status of women in history, setting out in his twenty-two novels the different stages of their evolution, stating in note-form historiographical references. In fact, his approach to the status of women remains strongly affected by the conventions prevailing at his time and by his own reformist ideas which are inscribed in the continuity of contemporary reformists. The concerns of his female characters often correspond more to those of his own time than to those from the societies in which the characters lived. This is no doubt by choice—to make it easier for the reader to identify with the characters and

51 Dakhlia, Jocelyne. *L'empire des passions. L'arbitraire politique en Islam* (Paris, Aubier, 2005) pp. 139-140.

thereby promote the publication of his works. This omnipresence of the present-day and the reformist issues in Zaidan's historical novels allows us to appreciate the feeling of urgency which was typical for the author and his contemporaries to reform society. This also makes his fictional work a witness to an era, that of the Nahda of which he constitutes one of the greatest figures.

Part III

Jurji Zaidan—The Historical Novelist

Jurji Zaidan and the Development of the Arabic Novel

Roger Allen

> During my working life as a writer, the historical novel has been frowned on, and disapproved of, both by academic critics and by reviewers....I think it can be argued that the "historical" novel has proved more durable, in my lifetime, than many urgent fictive confrontations of immediate contemporary reality...I want to ask, why has history become imaginable and important again?[1]

> [T]he increasing prominence of historical themes in current fiction suggests that the novel's perennial valence for history has acquired new strength in recent years...A sense of urgency—sometimes even an air of desperation—pervades the historical novel since mid-century [twentieth], for its author probes the past to account for a present that grows increasingly chaotic.[2]

Introduction

Any survey of the development of Arabic fiction in recent decades (I am writing these words in 2011) will surely be convinced that the literary tradition in the Arabic-speaking world joins with the broader tradition

---

1 Byatt, A.S. *On Histories and Stories: Selected Essays* (Cambridge MA, Harvard Univ. Press, 2001) p. 9.

2 Cowart, David. *History and the Contemporary Novel* (Carbondale, Southern Illinois Univ. Press,1989) p.1.

of world literature, as reflected in the above two quotations, by noting the increased importance of historical fiction. In the particular case of Arabic novels, one might suggest that the aftermath of the June 1967 débacle, *al-naksa*, with its renewed quest for the quality of *asala,* cultural authenticity, and its fabled but often ignored *turath* (heritage) provided a ready impetus for such initiatives in fiction and its modes of innovation. Whence comes, of course, the need to trace the trend back into the past and automatically, one might suggest, to the foundational figure of Jurji Zaidan (1861-1914).

As part of any assessment of Zaidan's role in the development of a tradition of modern fiction in Arabic, there are certain parameters that need to be addressed, most especially within the trans-cultural context within which his career inevitably has to be situated and investigated. Of those parameters I would like to identify two in particular for closer consideration here. The first is the genre of the novel, its nomenclature and attempts at its definition, not to mention consideration of its precedents in earlier Arabic narrative. Since all but one of Zaidan's contributions to fiction take the identifiable form of "historical novels", we will also consider some of the critical issues associated with that particular sub-genre.[3] The second parameter involves the notion of "development" cited in my title; more specifically, the placement of Zaidan's works into a historical framework and a process of cultural change that is generally subsumed within the Arabic-speaking context under the term "Nahda", implying a revival of some kind. Before turning to a consideration of the novels themselves, I will therefore briefly consider the process of change into which Zaidan's career and fictional output needs to be placed, and not least because he himself was a major contributor to the examination of the period in question and its terms of reference through his own historical and literary-historical works. His journal, *al-Hilal* was to play a

3 We need to acknowledge at this point, albeit in passing, that Georg Lukacs refuses to allow for the existence of a particular sub-genre termed "the historical novel", insisting instead that the novel genre is itself by nature historical. See Lukacs, Georg. *The Historical Novel* (London, Merlin Press, 1962). First published in Russian in 1937

major role in the revival of interest in the heritage of Arab culture and in the development of the language and textual modes by which such interest could be fostered and developed.

The novel and the historical novel

Several European literary traditions, in using the term "*roman*" in order to identify the longer fictional genre, choose thereby to link its emergence to the earlier narrative example of the romance, utilizing Cervantes' wonderful subversion of the genre in his renowned *Don Quixote* as a model and purported starting-point—and, in an aside, one can observe that there seems to be an acknowledgment of the earlier Arabic tradition of narrative in Cervantes's use of an Arab historian, "Cidi Hamete Benengeli", as the narrator of at least the second half of that famous narrative.[4] The decision within the anglophone world to adopt the term "novel", with its connections to the older genre of the "novella", ties and continues to tie the genre to the processes of change and to emphasize that the fictional narrative thus described is a restless entity, never content to remain the same. Indeed, while Hegel may term the novel "the burger's epic", and Lionel Trilling may dub it "an especially useful agent of the moral imagination", it is perhaps best identified as the fictional genre whose major topic is the process of change, its forms thus inevitably reflecting its subject matter.[5] In such a context it is M.J. Abrams who, in a somewhat despairing tone, suggests that "the term novel is now applied to a great variety of writings having in common only the attribute of being extended works of prose fiction…" [6]

---

4 See page 459 of the superb translation by Edith Grossman of Cervantes, Miguel de. *Don Quixote* (New York, Harper Collins Publishers, 2003).

5 See Trilling, Lionel. *The Liberal Imagination* (New York, Scribners, 1950) p.vii. I have discussed the history of the Arabic terms used to define fictional genres in Roger Allen, "Narrative Genres and Nomenclature: a comparative study," *Journal of Arabic Literature* 23 (Nov. 1992) pp. 208-214.

6 Abrams, M.J. *A Glossary of Literary Terms* (New York, Holt, 1971) p.110.

Within such a context the sub-genre of the historical novel has been a significant and indeed "historic" participant in the developmental process. One might begin a consideration of the connection between history and fiction, and its apparent relevance to the present day as cited by A.S. Byatt's comment with which I started, by noting that literary theoreticians such as Hayden White have long since asserted that the principal linkage involved is that of *narrative* and *narration*: history, biography and autobiography all share with fiction their basic adherence to the principles of inclusion and exclusion. While annalistic historians, whether Western or Middle Eastern, may have insisted on the primacy of other, more chronologically-based principles of presentation, Hayden White emphasizes the aspects of narration that these seemingly different genres have in common. Byatt herself points out the direct linkage to fiction, noting that:

> Hayden White observes that novelists like Balzac and Flaubert could believe they were writing "history" because the forms of their fictions coincided with the forms of nineteenth-century histories, written by bourgeois historians, who believed that their historical narratives were a form of science.[7]

As we will see in what follows, Jurji Zaidan himself studiously included lists of references to his historical sources as part of the front-matter of many of his novels, including several of those "nineteenth-century histories" and their historians.[8]

---

7 Byatt, A.S. *On Histories and Stories: Selected Essays* (Cambridge MA, Harvard Univ. Press, 2001) p. 38, quoting from White, Hayden. *The Content of the Form* (Baltimore, Johns Hopkins Press,1983) p. 33.

8 For example, Zaidan's novel *The Conquest of Andalusia* cites as its sources works in Arabic by such renowned historians as Ibn Khallikān, Ibn al-Kathīr, and al-Maqqarī, but also Charles Romey, Reinhart Dozy, and Edward Gibbon, not to mention the *Encyclopedia Britannica.* Similarly, the novel *Saladin and the Assassins* lists works by Ibn al-Athīr, al-Maqrīzī, al-Suyūtī, Ibn Khallikān, al-Maqdisī (*Kitāb al-Rawḍatayn*) and Ibn Abī Usaybiʿa, along with J. L. Burkhardt's *Travels in Syria and the Holy Land* (1823).

The prominent Scottish literary critic, David Daiches, equally renowned on both sides of the Atlantic Ocean, is in no doubt that the genre of the historical novel, at least in its modern manifestations, begins with Sir Walter Scott. His opinion is worth quoting at some length because the comments that he makes are of obvious relevance to the career of Jurji Zaidan within the Arabic context:

> Scott not only invented the historical novel, but made it available for a great variety of new kinds of writing. Balzac in France, Manzoni in Italy, Gogol and Tolstoy in Russia, were among the many writers of fiction influenced by the man Stendhal called 'notre père, Walter Scott...' What Scott did was to show history and society in motion: old ways of life being challenged by new; traditions being assailed by counterstatements; loyalties, habits, prejudices clashing with the needs of new social and economic developments.[9]

Adding the names of these prominent European exponents of the novel genre, whether historical or otherwise, to that of Flaubert already cited by Hayden White, makes it clear that Scott was to play an enormously important and indeed international role in the development of the novel genre in general; and in the particular sub-genre of the historical novel he was to cast a very long shadow. The renowned Russian literary critic, Mikhail Bakhtin, is also among those who assess Scott's central importance in his often cited analysis of the juncture of time and place in narrative that he terms the "chronotope". Analyzing different categories of narrative according to the way in which these two elements are utilized, he begins with what he terms "adventure time", a category in which the role of chance is a unifying force. Citing Scott's historical novels as an example, he

---

9 See David Daiches' "Foreword," in Scott, Sir Walter. *Ivanhoe* edited by Graham Tulloch (Edinburgh, Edinburgh Univ.Press, 1998) p. v.

points to elements that will surely be familiar to those who have also read Zaidan's works: "undercover activities of secret benefactors and villains, the specific role of chance, various sorts of predictions and premonitions".[10]

As we consider A.S. Byatt's question posed above as to the current significance of the historical novel (and, one might add, the reasons for the continuing popularity of Zaidan's novels), the analysis of the American critic, David Cowart, becomes useful, in that he devises a list of four separate categories for historical fiction:

(1) The Way It Was: fictions whose authors aspire purely or largely to historical verisimilitude;
(2) The Way It Will Be: fictions whose authors reverse history to contemplate the future;
(3) The Turning Point: fictions whose authors seek to pinpoint the precise historical moment when the modern age or some prominent feature of it came into existence;
(4) The Distant Mirror: fictions whose authors project the present into the past.[11]

While many more contemporary novels in Arabic seem to fall into the fourth category (and here one thinks in particular of Jamal al-Ghitani's *Al-Zayni Barakat*[12] or Salim Himmish's *Majnun al-Hukm,*[13] both of which use not only specific historical periods but also their actual historical records in order to comment on the abuse and manipulation of

10 Bakhtin, Mikhail. *The Dialogic Imagination* edited by Michael Holquist (Austin, Univ.of Texas Press, 1981) pp. 94 and 96.

11 Cowart, p. 8-9.

12 Al-Ghīṭānī, Jamāl. *Al-Zaynī Barakāt* (Damascus, Wizārat al-Thaqāfa, 1971) translated by Farouk Abdel Wahab (London, Penguin Books, 1988).

13 Himmīsh, Ben Sālim. *Majnūn al-Ḥukm* (Rabat, Maṭba'at al-Ma'ārif al-Jadīda, 1988). English version: *The Theocrat* translated by Roger Allen (Cairo, American Univ. Cairo Press, 2005).

power),[14] Zaidan's novels appear to fit fairly exactly into the first of the four categories, where "the novelist attempts to recreate the past as vividly as possible, dramatizing a world whose values may diverge radically from those of the present age", and not least because of their already noted explicit reference in the front-matter to the historical sources that have been used in their composition.[15] And, in that those sources are culled from both pre-modern Arabic and nineteenth-century historical traditions, that combination may serve as a convenient segue into a brief discussion of the other major parameter that I have identified above, that of the Nahda during the nineteenth century, a movement to which Zaidan himself was a major contributor.

The Nahda and the Arabic novel

As all commentators on the Nahda have pointed out, it involved the Arabic-speaking world in renewed and intensified contact with Europe.[16] However, the nature and duration of that contact varied widely from one region to another. For example, while Lebanon, the region of Zaidan's birth and upbringing, may have had contacts with Western Europe for several centuries, largely based on the Maronite community's linkages with Rome, there can be little doubt that the situation with regard to Egypt, the country to which he emigrated in 1882, differed considerably, in that its encounter with the European other took the far more abrupt form of Napoleon's invasion in 1798. These regional variables, which

14 I have explored issues connected with more contemporary Arabic historical novels in Roger Allen "Lords of Misrule: history and fiction in two Moroccan novels," *Middle Eastern Literatures* 9 (August 2006) pp.199-209; and "Historiography as Novel: Ben Sālim Himmīsh's *al-'Allāma*," in *Transforming Loss into Beauty:Essays on Arabic literature and culture in honor of Magda al-Nowaihi* edited by Marle Hammond and Dana Sa'idi (Cairo, American Univ. Cairo Press, 2008) pp. 269-280.

15 See note 8 above for details. Among novels in this first category written in English to which Cowart refers are those of Mary Renault.

16 Ibrahim Abu Lughod, for example, composed a study on the topic with the title *The Arab Rediscovery of Europe* (Princeton, Princeton Univ. Press, 1963).

become even more accentuated when we take into account the widely variant pre-modern histories of, for example, the Gulf region and the Maghreb, quite apart from the roles and policies of different European colonialisms, suggest strongly that any attempt to produce a single model of the Nahda process is doomed to inaccuracy, if not outright failure. With Zaidan, we are, of course, talking primarily about the case of Egypt, the long-acknowledged centrality of which, both geographically and culturally, has led the majority of commentators on cultural trends in the nineteenth century (and I include myself in this category, at least for the first half of my career) to use it as a matrix that can be applied across the region.[17] Just to provide a single illustration of the background to this situation, we can take the process in which Zaidan himself was involved: the emigration of those Syro-Lebanese Christians who had benefited from a good education to Egypt following the civil strife of the 1850s and beyond. An Egypt-based version of cultural trends leading to the emergence of the novel genre, with the publication of Muhammad Husayn Haykal's *Zaynab* in 1913 as the first "artistic" novel in Arabic—itself a highly suspect and historically nonsensical ascription as it stands[18]— emphasizes the welcoming atmosphere of Egypt in the era of the Khedive Isma'il and the role of those new immigrants in fostering the lively press tradition that expanded rapidly from the 1880s onward and served as a major conduit for the publication of works of fiction (as will be discussed below) and, equally important, the development of a readership for it. Let me emphasize that there is clearly a good deal of truth to that interpretation, but, in the context of the linkage between

17 More recently I have been calling for a broader and more variegated approach to the writing of a literary history of modern Arabic fiction: see, for example, "Literary History and the Arabic Novel," *World Literature Today* 75/2 (Spring 2001) pp. 205-13; and "Rewriting Literary History: the Case of the Arabic Novel," *Journal of Arabic Literature* 38 (2007) pp. 261-92.

18 I have discussed the problematic status of Haykal's *Zaynab* in *Modern Arabic Literature, The Cambridge History of Arab Literature* edited by M.M. Badawi (Cambridge, Cambridge Univ. Press, 1992) pp. 190-92; and *The Arabic Novel,* 2nd edition (Syracuse, Syracuse Univ. Press, 1995) pp. 32-37.

Lebanon and Egypt that is represented by the career of Zaidan, it downplays, if not ignores, the obvious fact that the earliest examples of fictional narrative in Arabic—whether you choose to call them "novels" or not does not concern me here—appeared in Lebanon.[19] In a recent dissertation, Elizabeth Holt has not challenged the basic interpretation of cultural trends that I have just essayed, but through her detailed research on the press tradition in Lebanon has clearly demanded a redress to the relative roles involved, demonstrating that not only was there a thriving press in Lebanon at this time, but also the serialized novels of Salim al-Bustani often commented directly on contemporary social and cultural trends.[20] In brief then, the novels of Jurji Zaidan join with other fictional narratives penned during the nineteenth century in demanding that the early history of the development of the novel genre in Arabic be rewritten with a view to redressing the balance in terms of sub-regions and local histories. In that process, ongoing research on the role of the press, the functions of translation, and an emerging awareness of the role of women, can contribute in valuable ways to such a reassessment.[21]

---

19 I would note here the seemingly obvious notion that literary genres (like their biological analogues) do not "begin"; there can be no "firsts" and no "inventors". Instead, under the impetus of changing cultural times and priorities, they emerge from previously existing forms. The Arabic narrative genre of the "*maqāma*" can serve as a classic example of this trend. Examples of these early Lebanese narratives would include: Marrāsh, Fransīs. *Ghābat al-Ḥaqq* first published in 1865 (Cairo, Maṭba'at al-'Imrān, 1922) and al-Bustānī, Salīm. *Huyām fī Jinān al-Shām* (New York, Idārat al-Mir'āt, 1874).

20 Holt, Elizabeth. "Narrative and the Reading Public in 1870s Beirut," *Journal of Arabic Literature* 40/1 (2009) pp. 37-70.

21 Any listing of recently published works that address these issues would be a lengthy one. I will simply refer interested readers to the works of Marilyn Booth, Elizabeth Holt, Samaḥ Selīm, Stephen Sheehi, and Shaden Tageldin. A special issue of the journal *Middle Eastern Literatures* 13 (Aug. 2010) is devoted to the period in question, including an article by Anne-Laure Dupont on Zaidan's views on language, "What is a *Kātib 'āmm*?" pp.171-81. Much earlier Matti Moosa had addressed himself to the same period in *The Origins of Modern Arabic Fiction* (Washington, Three Continents Press, 1983).

In spite of the variation in the indigenous cultural heritage of the Arab world's various sub-regions, they all had one particular feature in common that, while not a constant, displayed certain elements of unity, namely the heritage of the past and, above all, the language in which it was couched. It is a feature that, needless to say, is a major contributor to any assessment of the nature of the process of change that was to occur during the nineteenth century. However, it is also here, I would suggest, that the assessment of the relative roles of the imported and indigenous that contribute to the Nahda, fails us, and for an easily identifiable reason. The pre-modern era (however one chooses to define it, but I will here suggest the sixteenth to eighteenth centuries) presents us, even within the generally dismal scenario created by the designation "period of decadence" as a means of describing the cultural environment between the thirteenth and eighteenth centuries, with a very large hole in our appreciation of developments and continuities in the Arabic literary tradition and its genres.[22] What is significant about this situation is that, as what might be termed the "discipline" of Arabic literary historical studies developed as an intrinsic part of the Nahda movement, Arabic-speaking scholars who were sent to Europe to study returned to their homelands fully aware of the radically different esthetic norms that they had encountered during their time away and proceeded to project them retrospectively on to their own pre-modern cultural heritage. One of the earliest of these scholars was, of course, the renowned Rifaʿat al-Tahtawi (1801-71), who was

22 I should observe at this stage that the process of re-evaluating these attitudes has been in process for some time now, but a great deal remains to be undertaken. The many contributions of Thomas Bauer, for example, are leading to a complete re-evaluation of the literature of the so-called "Mamluk period" (roughly coterminous with the thirteenth to sixteenth centuries), while *The Post-Classical Period* volume of the Cambridge History of Arab Literature (edited by Roger Allen and D.S. Richards, 2006) and, in particular, *Essays in Arabic Literary Biography,* vol. 2, edited by Joseph E. Lowry and Devin Stewart (Wiesbaden, Harrassowitz, 2009) constitute initial steps in the re-evaluation of the entire period between the thirteenth and eighteenth centuries.

to play a major role in Egyptian cultural life in general and through his activities in the field of translation in particular, but he and later such figures as Ahmad Amin (1886-1954) and Taha Husayn (1889-1973) were among the leaders in the process of denigrating the immediate past (including some less than complimentary attitudes towards Ottoman Turkish culture) and advocating a return to a much earlier period that would thus be designated Arabic's "classical" period, analogous to its European equivalents. Some scholars have even begun to term this trend one of "self-Orientalization".[23] And, lest this essay seem to err on the side of hagiography, let it be admitted that Jurji Zaidan participated in this process, not least in his pioneering work on Arabic literary history.[24]

Jurji Zaidan

Since one of my goals in this essay is to attempt a "re-situation" of Jurji Zaidan and his novels in the development of the modern Arabic novel, I have allowed myself to indulge in this somewhat lengthy exploration of some of the issues that seem to me to impinge upon that process, both in terms of fictional genres and the principles of literary history. At this point, I trust that it is fairly clear that, through his foundation and editorship of his influential journal, *al-Hilal*, his composition of a series of historical novels, and his deep concern with the establishment of a sense of "national" identity for the Arabs through a deeper knowledge of their history, Zaidan clearly belongs in the modernizing camp that sought inspiration in European culture while continuously seeking to revive the heritage of the Arab and Islamic past through resort to a Western genre and a careful adaptation of the literary language that had been the pride of all Arabs for many centuries. It is in the context of this "re-situation"

23 See for example, Mehmet Akif Kirecci, *Decline discourse and self-orientalization in the writings of al-Ṭahṭāwī, Ṭahā Ḥusayn and Ziya Gökalp* (PhD. Dissertation, University of Pennsylvania, 2007).

24 *Tārīkh Ādāb al-Lugha al-'Arabiyya* (Cairo, Maṭba'at al-Hilāl, 1911).

that I have insisted that, if we are to dismiss claims as to the historical primacy of Haykal's *Zaynab* (1913) in this context, then the field becomes open to a wide variety of other narrative texts, all of them preceding Haykal's work, not least being Ahmad Faris al-Shidyaq's (1804-87) *Al-Saq' 'ala 'l-Saq fima huwa al-Faryaq* (1855), a pioneering work in terms of its autobiographical content, and Muhammad al-Muwaylihi's (1858-1930) *Hadith 'Isa ibn Hisham* (1898; book form, 1907), which presents a lively and accurate portrait of *fin-de-siècle* Cairo, both of them including conscious revivals of the narrative tradition of the *maqama* that had flourished during the pre-modern era. In other words, the nineeenth century in the Egypt where Zaidan resided and worked reveals a fascinating blend of different cultural trends. While his own role may have reflected one strand in those different trends, the assessment of his total oeuvre needs to be fully cognizant of all the factors that were at play.

It is into this particular era of rapid change that Jurji Zaidan's remarkable career needs to be integrated. Anne-Laure Dupont effectively expresses the tensions involved:

> Fluctuating between the turn to the past and an equally necessary modernisation, of literary content and style, he was involved in this constant tension that characterized the spirit of the Nahda.[25]

In a similar vein Thomas Philipp points out that:

> The task of the Arab intellectual was to respond to a two-fold challenge: to adapt himself and his society to life in the modern, European-dominated world on the one hand, and to assert the independent identity and viability of his society on the other...[Zaidan] tried to educate and instruct his Arab

25 Dupont. "What is a *Kātib āmm*?", *Middle Eastern Literatures,* p. 175.

> contemporaries about the modern world, as well as their own past and national identity.[26]

What is truly remarkable about the extent to which Zaidan managed to blend these concerns and to achieve his pedagogical goals is that he was largely an autodidact, albeit one who clearly had a voracious appetite for reading works on a wide variety of topics. His early and abortive career in medicine, terminated, it appears, over a dispute at the Syrian Protestant College (which would later become the American University of Beirut) about the theories of Charles Darwin, may have provided him with many insights into the subfields of the natural sciences and the scientific method in general, but his major works on Islamic history, the Arabic language, the heritage of Arabic literature, and the historical novels all reveal a vast erudition that is coupled to the instincts, activities, and principles of an avid historian and story-teller. The means by which he was able to succeed in so many different spheres involved him in displaying his talents in a number of roles: firstly, as a journalist, with *al-Hilal* as a monthly outlet for both articles and novels in serialized form; secondly, as a littérateur contributing through both fiction and literary history to a new awareness of the great Arabic literary heritage and to the development of new genres of writing; and thirdly, as an advocate of language reform, *islah*, in that, as the style of his novels and their continuing popularity clearly show, he was determined to demonstrate that the written level of Arabic language, *al-fusha*, did not have to be restricted by its sheer elaboration to the élite classes, but rather could and should be accessible to a more general readership that was being fostered by the burgeoning press tradition in Egypt in the 1880s and 90s and the newly convenient availability of data and opinion that it offered.[27]

---

26 "Introduction" to *The Autobiography of Jurji Zaidan* translated and edited by Philipp, Thomas. (Washington DC, Three Continents Press, 1990) p. 1.

27 For more detail on Zaidan's works on the Arabic language and his views on the topic, see Dupont. "What is a *Kātib 'āmm*?" especially pp. 177-78. An idea of the extent to which the press tradition in Egypt expanded during these decades can be

The historical novels

Turning now to a consideration of Zaidan's historical novels themselves, we should begin by noting that in the Introductions to both his five-volume *History of Islamic Civilization*[28] and also in his novel, *al-Hajjaj ibn Yusuf* (1902), he includes specific statements about his methods and motivations for writing works that combine the functions of history and novel writing.

> We have started preparing readers' minds—with all their variety in terms of class, knowledge, and attainment—to read about history by publishing a series of historical novels in *al-Hilal*. That was because studying pure history is too hard for normal readers, especially in our country where such learning is still in its infancy. We have therefore had to adopt particular strategies so as to publish academic materials in a form that people will want to read. Novels are clearly the best way of achieving such goals.[29]

He emphasizes the fact that his purpose is to write history in novel form. His general goals are educational; the novel form is being selected because it allows for the presentation of historical data in a more palatable form than that offered by more traditional modes of historical writing. While, as we have already noted, the thread of narrative is a

---

gleaned from de Tarrāzī, Philippe. *Tārīkh al-Ṣaḥāfa al-'Arabiyya* (Beirut, Dār Ṣādir, 1960) [original publication, 1913].

28 *Tārīkh al-Tamaddun al-Islāmī* (Cairo, Maṭba'at al-Hilāl, 1902-6).

29 See the Introduction to *Tārīkh al-Tamaddun al-Islāmī* (Beirut, Dar Maktabat al-Hayāt, n.d. [1958?]) p. 7. I have consulted two editions of the novel *Al-Hajjāj ibn Yūsuf* but neither of them includes the introduction of Dār al-Hilāl (Cairo: n.d.) and Dār Maktabat al-Ḥayāt (Beirut, n.d.). I have thus relied for this account on: Barmū, 'Abd al-Raḥmān. *Al-Riwāya al-tārīkhiyya fī'l-Adab al-Sūrī al-mu'āṣir* (Damascus, Dār al-Shajara, 1996) p. 48; and Ḥamarneh, Walīd. "Jurji Zaidan," in *Essays in Arabic Literary Biography* edited by Roger Allen (Wiesbaden, Harrassowitz Verlag, 2009) vol 3 p. 385.

common feature associated with both categories of writing, Zaidan's emphasis, as illustrated by these statements of purpose and method, differs to a certain extent from that of his great European forebear, Scott. In the "Dedicatory Epistle" to his novel, *Ivanhoe*, amusingly addressed by its fictional narrator to a certain Reverend Dryasdust, Scott writes:

> It is true, that I neither can, nor do pretend, to the observation of complete accuracy, even in matters of outward costume, much less in the more important points of language and manners...It is necessary, for exciting interest of any kind, that the subject assumed should be, as it were, translated into the manners as well as the language of the age we live in....

In the context of this essay's concerns with the Arabic literary tradition and its forebears, it is interesting to note that this statement of purpose by Scott is immediately followed by fulsome praise of Antoine Galland, the translator of the fourteenth century version of *Alf Layla wa-Layla* (*A Thousand and One Nights*) into French (1704-17). In Scott's opinion, Galland has accomplished a similar task, in that he has "abridged the long-winded narratives, curtailed the monotonous reflections, and rejected the endless repetitions of the Arabian original". The author of *Ivanhoe* then proceeds to detail his priorities with regard to language and its use to portray character:

> I have so far explained our ancient matters in modern language, and so far detailed the characters and sentiments of my persons, that the modern reader will not find himself, I should hope, much trammeled by the repulsive dryness of mere antiquity.[30]

Such disparaging comments about the oral tradition of Arabic popular narrative were, of course, an anticipated reaction to the as yet unappreciated and unstudied narrative frameworks of popular folktale traditions,

---

30 Scott, Sir Walter. "Dedicatory Epistle," in Tulloch, Graham. *Ivanhoe* (Edinburgh, Edinburgh University Press, 1998) p. 9.

but Scott's particular ascription of "dryness" to writing about "mere antiquity" finds a clear echo in a criticism leveled by one of Zaidan's more contemporary readers, 'Abd al-Rahman Barmu, who comments specifically on the "*jafaf*" (dryness) of certain segments of the novelist's writing, namely those in which the narrative is temporally halted so that the omniscient narrator can impart some specific information or opinion.[31] However, rather than question Zaidan's method, it seems more useful to point to his expressed educational purpose, not to mention the considerably different time-period into which his novels were being introduced and the expectations of the expanding readership to which they were addressed.

In surveying the list of historical novels that Zaidan wrote, it is interesting to observe clear patterns that emerge. At the surface level, it appears that he would concentrate on a particular era for more than one novel. At the outset in the early 1890s, for example, he published three works that are set in what was then fairly recent history. His first novel, *The Fugitive Mamluk*,[32] tells the tale of the famous massacre of the Mamluk grandees of Egypt in 1811 as engineered by Muhammad 'Ali, the Albanian commander of the Ottoman forces who took control of Egypt after the departure of Napoleon's forces. Zaidan's only entirely fictional novel, *Lovers' Struggle*,[33] is a love-story set in Cairo and Alexandria in the latter half of the nineteenth century, and the second historical novel, *Mamluk Tyranny*,[34] places the family of Sayyid 'Abd al-Rahman, a rich merchant, into the turbulent era of civil war between 'Ali Bey al-Kabir and Muhammad Abu Dhahab (1769-73), the historical

31 Barmū, *Al-Riwāya al-tārīkhiyya*, p. 49. In the context of this criticism of Zaidan's use of historical materials, we should point out that Scott also occasionally allows himself reference to actual historical sources (including footnotes), as, for example, in his use of the Saxon Chronicles in Tulloch. *Ivanhoe,* p.192.

32 *Al-Mamlūk al-Shārid* (Cairo, Maṭba'at al-Hilāl, 1891).

33 *Jihād al-Muḥibbīn* (Cairo Maṭba'at al-Hilāl, 1892).

34 *Istibdād al-Mamālīk* (Cairo, Maṭba'at al-Hilāl, 1892).

period immediately antecedent to Napoleon's invasion of 1798. Several other sets of novels fall into this same clustering pattern, covering early Islamic history, for example, developments in Spain and Islam's contacts with Europeans, and the history of the 'Abbasid caliphs beginning with *Abu Muslim from Khorasan.*[35] That such planning and sequencing on Zaidan's part was deliberate (and, needless to say, a reflection of his own patterns of research and writing at the same time) can be gauged from the very first sentence in the novel, *Al-Hajjaj ibn Yusuf*: [36]

> In my previous novel, *The Young Lady of Karbala*[37] we reached the point of the deaths of al-Husayn ibn 'Ali and his family at Karbala near the city of al-Kufa and ensuing events up to the death of Yazid, Mu'awiya's son, in the year 64 AH [683 CE].

And a further example from *Saladin and the Assassins*: [38]

> The novel *The Damsel of Kairouan*[39] finished with Egypt coming under the control of the Fatimid dynasty in 357 AH [967 CE] at the hands of General Jawhar and the end of the Ikhshidid dynasty.[40]

As we look at the techniques used by Zaidan in composing his novels, it becomes immediately obvious that the process of publishing each work in serialized form and its subsequent conversion into book format clearly lead to the development of a matrix that changes very little in

35 *Abū Muslim al-Khurasānī* (Cairo, Maṭba'at al-Hilāl, 1905).

36 *Al-Ḥajjāj ibn Yūsuf* (Cairo, Maṭba'at al-Hilāl, 1902).

37 *Ghādat Karbalā'* (Cairo, Maṭba'at al-Hilāl, 1901).

38 *Ṣalaḥ al-Dīn al-Ayyūbī* (Cairo, Maṭba'at al-Hilāl, 1913).

39 *Fatāt al-Qayrawān* (Cairo, Maṭba'at al-Hilāl, 1912).

40 See *Al-Ḥajjāj ibn Yūsuf*, p. 5; and *Fatāt al-Qayrawān*, p. 5.

spite of the passage of actual time in the life of the author and of fictional time in the works themselves. His educational goals are fully evident from the front-matter. The title and title-page are designed in such a way as to attract attention: the title itself is direct and unambiguous, referring either to a well-known figure in Islamic history or to an event which is already well known to prospective readers—all of which is amplified by an illustration in the *Maktabat al-Hilal* editions involving colorful images of the principal character or characters in the work itself.[41] On the title page and below the title itself, readers are provided with a paragraph-length précis of the novel's historical context; on the obverse side there is a listing of the "*dramatis personae*", along with a short description of their primary position or function within the narrative itself. The novels that deal with events in more recent periods—from the late eighteenth to the twentieth century—do not include a listing of sources that have been used (on the assumption perhaps that readers may themselves be familiar with the events involved), but, as we have already noted, the novels that portray events further back in Islamic history include not only reference to the historical sources used but also footnotes throughout the course of the novel in which the specific sources of particular data are to be found.

The opening strategy of Zaidan's always omniscient narrator involves the need for the placement of events in both space and time. In *The Young Turk Revolution*, for example, the place is Salonika and the time is 1907; with *Al-Hajjaj ibn Yusuf* the year is 683 CE and the scenario is in both Iraq and Syria. Because of the lengthy physical and temporal distances involved, the novel *The Conquest of Andalusia* provides a particularly vivid example of its author's educational goals and methods.[42]

41 The cover of the Maktabat *al-Hilāl* edition of the most modern of all the novels, *Al-Inqilāb al-'Uthmānī* (*The Young Turk Revolution*, 1911) includes an obvious facsimile of a well-known portrait of the dour visage of Sultan 'Abd al-Hamīd II, who was indeed deposed in 1909.

42 Since I have recently translated this novel for publication by the Zaidan Foundation, Inc. and thus have that kind of familiarity with the text that only translation can

The Conquest of Spain (Andalusia)

In spite of this work's title, the focus of the narrative is very much on the era immediately preceding the Muslim invasion of Spain that began in 710 CE. In fact, Tariq ibn Ziyad, the commander of the invading forces who lends his name as a subtitle to the novel, is only introduced towards the end of the narrative. The primary focus for much of the novel is on the intrigues at the Visigothic court in the city of Toledo.[43] The Roman Catholic bishops of Spain have bested their ecclesiastical rivals who have long adhered to Arian beliefs and are now the dominant religious group in Spain. Having succeeded in deposing King Wittiza, they have placed Roderic on the Spanish throne. Toledo, its surroundings, and its magnificent cathedral are all introduced to the reader through a narrative that describes the king's procession from the royal palace to the great church. Roderic has succumbed to a heinous passion for the lovely Florinda, the daughter of Count Julian, the governor of Sabta, the North African province, but she is already engaged to Prince Alfonso, the son of the now deposed King Wittiza. Alfonso, the former heir-apparent is now cruelly kept at court as a retainer to the usurper of his father's throne. In this way, the novel *The Conquest of Andalusia* differs from many of Zaidan's other historical works, in that the "local interest" provided by a family saga and its accompanying love-story is not his own fictional insertion into the narrative but rather an intrinsic and central part of the historical record itself. Adding to the complications and intrigues that already form part of the actual historical narrative is the fact that, in spite of wide doctrinal differences, King Wittiza's own brother, Oppas, retains his position as the Metropolitan Bishop of Spain. He has arranged the betrothal of Florinda to his nephew, Alfonso, and continues to uphold

---

provide, I will make primary use of it in order to illustrate those aspects of the author's narrative method that seem symptomatic of his compositional techniques.

43 A convenient echo of Bakhtin's comment concerning Scott's historical novels (see footnote 10 above).

the honor of the Visigothic dynasty that has been so cunningly disrupted by the Catholic bishops.

In this case then, we might suggest that the historical sources themselves seem to have most of the elements needed for a wonderful novelistic account, and Zaidan's narrative makes full use of the possibilities afforded by the characters and events themselves. The novel's events begin on Christmas Day in Toledo; as the narrative opens, all the principal characters save Count Julian are residing in the capital city. The titles of the initial chapters, "Spain, the Goths, and Toledo", "Florinda", and "Alfonso", provide a clear indication of the way in which Zaidan begins his novels by laying the groundwork in terms of time, place, and principal actors.[44] As noted above, the major focus of this particular novel is to be the multiple ways in which two of those principals, Florinda and Alfonso, are to be the victims of the machinations of others, and most notably King Roderic. While the two lovers manage a clandestine meeting in the palace gardens (duly described in detail) on this particular Christmas Day, they are soon to be separated. Florinda has already been transferred to the royal palace where the King can more easily launch his evil plan to seduce her, and Alfonso is deliberately removed from the scene by being dispatched by the King at the head of a small armed force to quell an uprising in the southern city of Astigi. Still in Toledo, Bishop Oppas manages to rescue Florinda from Roderic's clutches and in a notable scene confronts the king for his outrageous behavior. At the same time the bishop organizes Florinda's escape from the royal palace on a proverbial "dark, stormy night". The furious monarch now proceeds to put Oppas on trial in Toledo Cathedral before the assembly of Catholic bishops (beginning with chapter 34), but, when the whiff of

44 At several other points in the sequence of chapters, the forward movement of the narrative is suspended while information relevant to the events is presented. In chapter 7, for example, there is a lengthy explanation of the doctrinal disputes between the Arian and Catholic clergy, while chapter 51 opens with a lengthy précis on the history of the Umayyad Caliphate in the East following the death of 'Abd al-Malik (704 CE).

scandal points in Roderic's direction, he rapidly dismisses the assembly but keeps Oppas in prison.

As the narrative of this novel progresses then, we find the different characters in a variety of locations; this is to become a central factor in the organization and sequencing of chapters. Dictated in large part by the principles of serialized publication, no doubt, one strand of the elaborate plot involving one character—Florinda in seclusion at a monastery, Alfonso billeted in Astigi, Oppas in prison, Count Julian in Sabta—is pursued over the course of several chapters. When a point is reached at which it is possible to leave that character "hanging", the narrative is switched to another location and character. Chapter 22, for example, "Back at the Palace", begins thus:

> Let's leave Alfonso now, as he prepares to travel, and go back to Roderic's palace. We left Florinda in her room pondering her situation after finishing her prayers, during the course of which she had placed all her burdens on God.[45]

Chapter 58 (entitled "Escape") provides another example of this switching of venues:

> A while ago we left Florinda, her aunt, and the two men, Ajilla and Chantilla, making their way around the Toledo outskirts.[46]

The arrest and trial of Oppas on trumped up charges (chapter 30-38) provide the novel with some of its most dramatic episodes, and it too is concluded with the initial sentence in chapter 39 (entitled "Alfonso and Ya'qub"):

---

45 *The Conquest of Andalusia*, p. 85.

46 Ibid. p. 225.

> Let us now leave Oppas to his problems, and return to Alfonso to see what happened to him after he followed the king's orders and went away.[47]

Through this technique, which, following those of movie westerns, we might perhaps dub "meanwhile back at the ranch", Zaidan is clearly catering to his readership by adopting one of the more traditional strategies of public story-telling, namely the need to maintain interest by providing specific elements of continuity to the narrative even though, as in this case, it has to combine depictions of events at different locations and in different time-frames. Here also he seems to be taking a leaf from Scott who noted:

> Like old Ariosto, we do not pique ourselves upon continuing uniformly to keep company with any one personage of our drama.[48]

As I noted earlier, the character whose name is part of the title of *The Conquest of Andalusia: Tariq ibn Ziyad*, plays no active part in the narrative until chapter 52, although reports of his imminent arrival occur in earlier chapters. However, as his forces cross the straits towards the rock that is to carry his name (Gibraltar), accompanied by Count Julian who has now learned from his daughter, Florinda, about Roderic's evil ways, all the widely separated strands of the narrative come together at Guadelete in southern Spain where the crucial battle between the Muslim forces and Roderic's army is fought in 711 CE. With Roderic's death and the defeat of his army, the Muslim conquest of the Iberian Peninsula can continue.

The above summary of the principal events in this novel and the participation in them of the main characters has shown clearly enough, I would suggest, what are Zaidan's goals and priorities in this and his other

47 Ibid. p.147.

48 Scott. *Ivanhoe*, p. 152.

historical works of fiction. As is suggested by his own statements of pedagogical goals that we have cited above, the primary focus is indeed on a presentation of historical events that is firmly anchored in both time and place. The characters in the narrative are drawn in the main from the upper echelons of society—rulers, statesmen, and their subordinates; they all play their part in the narrative in accordance with the functions of their position within the societal hierarchy. Roderic is the tyrannical and lecherous king, aided and abetted by his Machiavellian counselor, Father Martin; Florinda is his victim, young, beautiful, and devout; Alfonso is the young prince, handsome and bold, also assisted by a loyal servant, Ya'qub, who later in the narrative emerges as a major leader of the Jewish community; and Oppas, the ecclesiastical figurehead, remains steadfast to his beliefs, fearless in confronting the monarch, and also fiercely loyal to the cause of Christian Spain, to the extent of siding with Roderic in his battle against the invading Muslim army. As the narrative of the novel progresses, time and place will change, but the character traits that are identified in the early chapters remain much the same throughout. With that in mind, we need to point out that examples of historical fiction culled from the earliest phases in the subgenre's development do indeed rely for the most part on detailed narration of events, institutions, and "undercover activities" (to cite Bakhtin's phrase once again). Zaidan's pioneering contributions to the Arabic genre clearly conform to that pattern.

Conclusions

In 1999 the Egyptian literary critic, Gaber Asfour, published a collection of articles under the title *The Novel's Era*, which was intended as both an echo of, and a challenge to, the title of an earlier work by the poet-critic, Adunis, *Poetry's Era.*[49] During the last half-century it is certainly the case that fiction has become the most widespread and popular mode of literary creativity in the Arabic-speaking world. As a direct consequence

49 *Zamān al-Riwāya* and *Zamān al-Shi'r* (Beirut, Dār al-'Awra, 1972).

of the processes whereby the Arabic novel in particular has diversified and assumed an enormous variety of guises over that period—and, one might suggest, particularly in the era following the disastrous June War of 1967 when so many previously held political and cultural assumptions have been challenged—it has become almost automatically necessary to reconsider the history of the genre's earlier development along with the analysis of the works themselves, if only to incorporate new sets of precedents that were not previously appreciated as such. It is in such a context, I would suggest, that the need to re-examine the earliest phases in the development of modern Arabic fiction, and thus the central role that Jurji Zaidan played in it, becomes important. If Oscar Wilde can suggest that history needs to be rewritten on a continuing basis, then we may claim the same imperative for literary history as well. In the earlier sections of this essay we have already considered the ways in which current versions of such a literary history are unsatisfactory. We have then gone on to examine in some detail the specific techniques that Zaidan employs in composing his novels. Those topics addressed, we should now attempt a reconstruction of the scenario into which they need to be inserted and consider the nature of his role in that process.

I would begin that process of reconsideration by asserting once again that the quest for a single strand in the emergence and development of any literary genre is a virtual impossibility; as a corollary of that assertion, any claim of "firstness" for a particular work is bound to be of limited validity and value. Instead, I would suggest, in the particular context of the Arabic novel's early development we need to examine a whole series of different cultural trends not only in the nineteenth century itself but in the period anterior to it. Earlier in this essay I suggested that the Nahda movement involved both imported and indigenous elements and that any assessment of generic development demanded an examination of the relative balance between the two. The example of Jurji Zaidan, his career and the novels that he wrote, provide us with an excellent model through which to test these principles. As noted above, his use of sources, conscientiously listed in his novels, reveals clearly his reliance on a combination of the principal pre-modern Arabic source-texts on Arab-Islamic history and of Western historical sources that provide an external commentary on the particular periods and regions involved. That desire on his part to fuse his diverse source-materials into a popular educational project through the medium of fiction is clearly a reflection of the cultural atmosphere in Egypt within which the bulk of his career needs to be placed. It was to play a crucial role in the development of not only a sense of Arab identity but also of the fictional genres whereby that identity could be explored and elaborated; in the creation of what Benedict Anderson has so appropriately termed one of a series of "imagined communities".[50]

That very atmosphere involved a stimulating mélange of different cultural forces, Western and Arab-Islamic, Egyptian and Syrian, traditional and modern, political and social. Two of those forces, however, managed not only to include elements from each of those separate pairings but also to combine them, and both were clearly to be of overriding importance in the realm of fiction, namely the emergence of a press tradition and an increase in translation activity; to which we should add the increasing availability of the former as a ready means of publicizing examples of the latter.

We can begin with the emergence of the press, and in both senses of that word, namely the introduction and availability of printing and the almost concomitant appearance of a newspaper tradition. It is Walter Ong in his now classic study, *Orality and Literacy*, who points out the perhaps initially surprising but eventually compelling argument that "the print world gave birth to the novel", to which we can add that, whether we talk about the careers of Dickens or Zaidan, it was the newspaper publication medium that contributed in inestimable ways to the creation and maintenance of, indeed the huge increase in, that crucial element in the development of

50 Anderson, Benedict. *Imagined Communities: Reflections on the Origin and Spread of Nationalism* (London, Verso, 1983).

any novel tradition, a reading public for works of fiction.[51] To be sure, we have information about the early development of a press tradition in Egypt, although *al-Waqa'i'al-Misriyya*, the government gazette edited by the renowned figure of Rifa'at al-Tahtawi (1801-71), clearly functioned within the official and highly controlled environment of Muhammad 'Ali's regime and reflected its policies and priorities.[52] As has long been recognized and as recent research (cited earlier in this essay) has emphasized, it was within the lively atmosphere of Syro-Lebanon that the kind of press tradition that would foster the development of fictional genres originated and thrived. Jurji Zaidan himself would surely have been aware of the potential presented by this new communication medium, fostered by such families as the Bustanis and Shidyaqs. When he joined many of his fellow countrymen in emigrating to Egypt, he was thus poised to play a major role in the establishment and popularization of not only fiction but also the Arab heritage in general.

The role played by al-Tahtawi in the sphere of translation has also long been acknowledged, and indeed his function as translator (of Fénélon's *Les aventures de Télémaque*, for example) and trainer of other translators such as Muhammad 'Uthman Jalal (1829-98) was to lay the groundwork for many subsequent developments in Egyptian culture.[53] The latter half of the nineteenth century was to witness a significant growth in translation activities, and once again recent research has begun the process of investigating in more detail the precise nature of these exercises in cultural transfer and the methodologies involved (making use of the increasingly theoretical approaches to the study of the entire translation process).

---

51 Ong, Walter J. *Orality and Literacy: The Technologizing of the Word* (London and New York, Routledge, 1982) pp.149-50.

52 For a detailed discussion of Al-Ṭahtāwī's career, see *Essays in Arabic Literary Biography 1850-1950*, vol.3 pp. 339-50.

53 On the role of Jalāl, see Bardenstein, Carol. *Translation and Transformation in Modern Arabic Literature: the indigenous assertions of Muḥammad 'Uthmān Jalāl* (Wiesbaden, Harrassowitz, 2005).

Among the many things that these investigations have revealed is that, in our current context, the term "translation" actually needs to describe a wide variety of transfer strategies, from the most extravagantly adaptive (as in, for example, Mustafa Lutfi al-Manfaluti's (1876-1924) immensely popular version of Bernardin de Saint Pierre's *Paul et Virginie* (*al-Fadila*)—and we can note here that al-Manfaluti knew no French or any foreign language) to several more precise versions of Alexandre Dumas *père's Le comte de Monte Cristo*—a novel that was a clear favorite with readerships throughout the Middle East.[54]

It is within this vibrant and rapidly developing cultural environment that Jurji Zaidan's project for the establishment of his journal, *al-Hilal*, begun in 1892, and his subsequent use of its serialized opportunities for education and entertainment need to be placed.

What emerges with crystalline clarity from our investigations here and those of many other scholars is that the narratives published by Arab writers beginning at some median point in the nineteenth century are indeed novels, if, that is, we adopt a broader perspective on the question of generic definition that is now mandated by developments in world narrative genres during the course of the twentieth century and into the twenty first. These narratives display a variety of inspirations, some clearly imported, others—such as those of *al-Shidyaq* and *al-Muwaylihi*—seeking a blend of the principles espoused by the indigenous and imported traditions. All of them need to be incorporated into an expanded version of the early history of modern Arabic fiction, not merely for the sake of a more plausible historical account but also

54 See Moosa. *The Origins of Modern Arabic Fiction.* For details concerning the translation into Turkish in 1871, for example, see Evin, Ahmet. *Origins and Development of the Turkish Novel* (Minneapolis, Bibliotheca Islamica, 1983) pp. 41-49. I should also draw attention here to Maya Kesrawany's *Stranded in Arabic: Tales of the Novel in Translation* (Ph.D. thesis, Emory University, 2011) in which she analyzes many of these translated texts in great detail and also provides invaluable information about their publication venues and the large increase in journal outlets in which serialized fiction, both original and in translation, was published.

because more recent trends in Arabic novel-writing demand a consideration of precedents that are otherwise absent. In this revised scenario the novels of Jurji Zaidan can be seen as playing a significant and central role, because they illustrate not only the effective use of historical fiction as a means of fostering a sense of national identity and heritage, but also the ways in which the Arabic press was to become the major means for encouraging and maintaining a readership for fiction—that being a situation that has prevailed until recent times, as the career of one of Zaidan's successors, the 1988 Nobel Laureate Naguib Mahfuz, makes clear.

Jurji Zaidan and Modern Historical Representation[1]

Michael Cooperson

Over the past decade, Arab production companies have released a surprisingly large number of historical dramas: by my count, some thirty.[2] Meanwhile in Iran, a smaller but nevertheless significant number of historical series have appeared, mostly dealing with the lives of the imams and other religious figures.[3] To a large extent, these productions, whether in Arabic or in Persian, depict the past in ways that seem very much in the spirit of Zaidan's historical novels. This essay takes a particular historical moment—the 'Abbasid empire in the first few decades of the ninth century—and looks at how it is represented in three works: Zaidan's 1907 novel *Al-Amin wa'l-Ma'mun*, which I translated for the Zaidan Foundation as *The Caliph's Heirs*,[4] and two television productions, one in Arabic and

1 I would like to thank the Zaidan Foundation, the Library of Congress, and my fellow participants at the Symposium where a draft of this paper was presented.

2 As a sample, Arabic dramas set in the pre- and early Islamic period produced between 2000 and 2006 include *Salāḥ al-Dīn* (2000); *Dhī 'l-Qār* (2001); *Imru 'l-Qays, Abū Firās al-Ḥamadānī, al-Mutanabbī, Ṣaqr Quraysh, Zamān al-Waṣl*, and *Hūlākū* (all 2002); *al-Ḥajjāj* and *Rabī' Qurṭubah* (both 2003); *Fāris Banī Marwān* and *Sayf b. Dhī Yazin* (both 2004); *al-Ẓāhir Baybars* and *al-Murābiṭūn wa'l-Andalus* (both 2005); *al-Sayf al-Maslūl: Khālid b. al-Walīd*; *Abnā' al-Rashīd* (both 2006). These and many others are indexed at http://www.aflam.ws/index_2.htm (last visited June 21, 2012).

3 These include *Velāyat-e eshgh* (2001), and *Maryam-e moqaddas* (2002), *Imām 'Alī* (2003), and *Yūsuf payāmbar* (2008), as well as the time-travel series *Panjomīn khorshīd* and *Qahve-ye talkh* (both 2010).

4 Zaydān, Jūrjī. *Al-Amīn wa'l-Ma'mūn* (Cairo, Maṭba'at al-Hilāl, 1907). In English: *The Caliph's Heirs, Brothers at War and the Fall of Baghdad*, translated by Michael Cooperson, published by the Zaidan Foundation, Inc. 2011.

the other in Persian. The overlap in subject matter provides an opportunity to discuss the ways in which mass-media historical representation remains indebted to the premises established by Zaidan. It also gives us a chance to look at how contemporary historical dramas offer distinctive and divergent readings of the past.

The early years of the ‘Abbasid dynasty are commonly described as the golden age of Islamic civilization. The idealization of this era can be dated as far back as the tenth century, but it seems to have become standard only in the nineteenth.[5] It was then that the idea of “civilization” (*al-tamaddun, al-tamassur*), adopted from European historiography and expressed in Arabic by such figures as Rafi‘ Rifa‘at al-Tahtawi, became part of the vocabulary of self-understanding.[6] With this idea came the conviction that the Arabs, or the Muslims, were emerging from a period of decline, one that supposedly began with the advent of the Ottomans, or the Mongols, or even the Buyids. This way of looking at things raises a number of problems. For our purposes, the most important is how to represent the golden age that supposedly preceded the decline. If the early ‘Abbasid period was the golden age, what is its relationship to the period of the revelation: that is, the period from 610 or so, when the earliest chapters of the Koran were revealed, to the death of the Prophet

5 The universal historian al-Mas‘ūdī (d. 956) depicts an *akhbārī* (collector of historical reports) from Khurāsān as telling the caliph al-Qāhir (r. 932-934) that the people remembered the reign of al-Rashīd as “the wedding days” because they were “lush, prosperous, and fecund,” and witnessed “so many things too wonderful to describe”. Al-Mas‘ūdī. *Murūj al-Dhahab wa-Ma ‘ādin al-Jawar* in 7 vols. edited by Charles Pellat (Beirut, al-Jāmi‘a al-Lubnāniyya, 1966-79) vol. 5, p. 122, paragraph, 3449.

6 The locus classicus is al-Ṭāhṭāwī, *Al-Dīwān al-Nafīs aw Takhlīṣ al-ibrīz fī talkhīṣ Bārīs*, of which the best edition seems to be that by ‘Alī Aḥmad Kin’ān (Abu Dhabi, Dār al-Suwaydī li'l-Nashr; and Beirut, al-Mu’assasa al-‘Arabiyya li'l-Dirāsāt wa'l-Nashr, 2002). For the discussion of civilization and the valorization of the ‘Abbasid period, see 25ff. An English translation with very helpful annotation is *An Imam in Paris* translated by Daniel L. Newman (London, Sāqī, 2002); the relevant section begins on p. 101. The importance of al-Ṭahṭāwī’s discussion of civilization was brought to my attention by James Gelvin.

Muhammad in 632? It would hardly do to claim that the ʻAbbasids were more accomplished, or more authentically Arab and Muslim, than the Prophet.

A long-dominant strain of Arabic-language Sunni historiography responds by asserting that the Prophet's generation exemplifies the purest Islam, but that the subsequent conquests, which brought Muslims into contact with Jews, Christians, Zoroastrians, and others, led to the corruption of religion and the growth of heresy.[7] Moreover, conflicts between free Arab Muslim male protagonists in this—and indeed all periods—are the unfortunate result of plotting and scheming by slaves and women.[8] The traditional Sunni narrative thus posits a corruption of the pristine Arab-Muslim character through exposure to the frivolity and self-indulgence associated with a nebulous category of non-male, non-Muslim, and non-Arab others. In religious—and therefore moral—terms, then, the ʻAbbasid period was an age of decline—even if the ritual hand-wringing over the debaucheries of the caliphal court allows the Sunni tradition to insinuate a flattering equivalence between the high ʻAbbasid period and other famously debauched empires such

7 In the following passage, for example, the influential Egyptian literary critic and educator Ṭahā Ḥusayn sees bawdiness, irreligion, and non-Arab ethnicity as conjoined: "During the Umayyad period, the literary expression of heresy was feeble, attenuated, and covert, and attracted few; but when one of the Umayyad caliphs made an overt display of debauchery, it grew in strength. Then, when the Persians triumphed, heresy triumphed with them." Ḥusayn, Ṭahā. *Ḥadīth al-Arbaʻā'* in 3 vols. (Cairo, Dār al-Maʻrif, 1957-1962) vol. 2 p. 161; cited in Abū Zayd, ʻAlī Ibrāhīm. *Zuhd al-Mujjān* (Cairo, Dār al-Thaqāfa; Alexandria, Maktabat al-Maʻārif al-Ḥadīth, 1986) p. 25.

8 "As political conditions deteriorated; as women came to interfere in the administration of the country, to dominate the caliphate, and to dictate the conduct of the caliphs; as non-Arabs assumed many positions of leadership in ʻAbbasid society, whether in administration, government, or the army; and, furthermore, as morally, intellectually, and ideologically destructive elements insinuated themselves into ʻAbbasid society, many people felt compelled to turn away from the pleasures of life, renounce earthly enjoyments, and embrace asceticism" (Abū Zayd. *Zuhd*, p. 38).

as the Roman and even the American.[9] Against this background, the major figures of the period can be seen as engaged in a great struggle over the future of the faith. Harun al-Rashid (r. 786-809), for example, can be praised for his piety and orthodoxy; Ibn Hanbal (d. 855) lauded for his revival of the Prophetic tradition; and al-Ma'mun (r. 813-833) condemned for his alleged affection for all things Persian, including Shiism.[10] With these strategies, Sunni historiography disciplines the past by back-projecting orthodoxy as well as dubious notions of race, gender, and national character.[11] Obviously this way of looking at things is not the only one, though it is surprisingly hardy, turning up in Arabic works published by professional academics well into the twentieth century.[12]

Although Zaidan was not a Sunni Muslim, his historical writings helped form this particular understanding of "the golden age." The notion that the 'Abbasid period was one in which ethnicity—here meaning Persian self-assertiveness—becomes a force in history is implicit in the following passage from his *History of Islamic Civilization*:

> Whatever one may say about the Umayyad dynasty, it was distinguished from the 'Abbasid by being truly Arab (*'arabiyya haqiqiyya*): its governors, judges, and other officials were Arabs, with the exception of certain scribes, physicians, and the like. Under the 'Abbasids, however, it was the Persian

9 For an example of the latter position, see Khulūṣī, Ṣāfā. *Abū Nuwās fī Amrīkā* (Baghdad, Dār al-Ma'rifa, 1955).

10 Or al-Rashīd can be condemned for his libertinism, Ibn Ḥanbal criticized for his narrow-mindedness, and al-Ma'mūn praised for his promotion of free inquiry. The reversibility of these terms of judgment—and indeed the prevalence of such terms in the first place—emphasizes the incoherence of the traditional Sunnī view. For examples see the discussion of *The Caliph's Heirs* below.

11 Shi'ite historiography has its own very different but equally tendentious take on the period; see further below.

12 The passage quoted in footnote 7 was published in 1986.

> element that gained ascendancy, as it was the Persians who had brought the ‘Abbasids to power. The ‘Abbasids, who were the first rulers to appoint viziers, thus chose Persians to fill the post; and indeed derived the office itself from them.[13]

It is easy enough to draw a line between this way of speaking and later, more blatantly racialist depictions of “Arabs” and “Persians”. Yet Zaidan’s presentation here is more nuanced—or perhaps simply more incoherent—than one might expect. The idea that the Umayyads “were distinguished” (*tamtazu*) by being “truly Arab” implies that being Arab is a good thing. A few lines later, though, Zaidan praises the “Persian” Abu Muslim for leading the ‘Abbasids to power, and describes the era of al-Rashid and al-Ma’mun—an era supposedly dominated by Persians—as the apex of ‘Abbasid glory.[14]

In *The Caliph’s Heirs*, this ambiguity is even more pronounced. The novel depicts the struggle between the caliphs al-Amin (r. 809-813) and al-Ma’mun (r. 813-833) as one between Arabs and Persians. The latter are determined to avenge themselves on the ‘Abbasids for executing two of their heroes: the missionary Abu Muslim and the vizier Ja‘far al-Barmaki.[15] Admittedly, Abu Muslim and Ja‘far had designs on the throne: thus it was that the ‘Abbasid caliphs were forced to do away with them. But it is also true that the Persians have a genuine grievance. In Chapter 35, the physician Behzad exhorts his fellow conspirators as follows:

> How could you let yourselves be defeated by Arabs who once came to you to beg for food to eat and clothes to wear? The best of them fought for you as vassals, but then turned their swords against you. You rushed to their aid, but they betrayed

13 Zaydān, Jurjī. *Tārīkh al-Tamaddun al-Islāmī* in 5 vols. (Cairo, Maṭba‘at al-Hilāl, 1902-6) vol.1 p.70.

14 Ibid. vol.1 pp.70-71.

15 See *The Caliph’s Heirs*, Ch. 35.

> and slew your lords, and placed their feet on your necks. And yet: are the keys to power not in your hands? Are the viziers, the generals, the scholars, and the statesmen not all Persians like yourselves? How can you bow your heads to weaklings who overcame you only by trickery and stealth?

In the context of the novel, this speech is especially effective since Behzad is depicted as brave, honest, and sincere, while his enemy al-Amin is portrayed as a malicious drunkard easily manipulated by his mother and his viziers. Whatever Zaidan the historian may have written about "Persians", Zaidan the novelist not only fails to sustain the racialist narrative but positively undermines it.

One result of this emphasis on ethnicity—or perhaps indeed the justification for it—is that it removes religion from consideration as a cause of historical change. In his *History*, even when he alludes to religious conflict, Zaidan frames it as a struggle for power rather than the result of particular convictions about the moral order of the universe. The early Muslims chose Abu Bakr as caliph, he says, "because they did not want the Banu Hashim to have the office of prophet and the office of caliph both".[16] In *The Caliph's Heirs*, similarly, Zaidan hardly alludes to the religious element of the struggle between al-Amin and al-Ma'mun, or to the mighty struggles over interpretation and authority that characterize this period. "If you are Khurramis", he has Behzad tell his fellow conspirators, "then you are fighting for an ancient imam and a great leader: Abu Muslim of the black banners, founder of the 'Abbasid dynasty. He calls on you from his grave to overthrow the 'Abbasids and bring back Persian rule with the help of the Party of 'Ali." [17] The fact that the historical Khurramis had a distinctive religious identity does not concern the novelist; in the story, they are Muslims who happen to be Persian nationalists.

---

16 Zaydān. *Tārīkh al-Tamaddun*, vol 1 p. 69.

17 *The Caliph's Heirs*, pp.134-35.

Having decided what the motive force of historical conflict was, Zaidan invented characters to embody this force. In *The Caliph's Heirs*, for example, Behzad and Fatima represent the resurgent Persian particularism that he imagines to have been at work in the early ninth century. In this respect, Zaidan was following the example set by Walter Scott, who believed that history was most effectively narrated by telling the stories of invented characters who live lives peripheral to the great events of the past.[18] This invention serves another purpose as well: it creates a mechanism for narrative resolution. The novel's major plotline, in which the "Khurramis" manipulate al-Amin and al-Ma'mun into fighting each other and thus restore Persian ascendancy, is impossible to reconcile with the facts of history, as al-Ma'mun, upon defeating his brother, did away with two figures whom Zaidan understood to symbolize the Persian cause: the vizier al-Fadl ibn Sahl and the heir apparent 'Ali ibn Musa al-Rida. In this respect, the novel ends badly. Fortunately, there is a second plotline: the romance between Behzad and Maymuna, who, after many tribulations, are reunited and live happily ever after. Zaidan's invention of new characters thus allows him to achieve a certain kind of plot resolution—one centering on emotional fulfillment—that mitigates the dissatisfaction entailed by the recalcitrance of historical reality.

Having sketched out a few salient features of *The Caliph's Heirs*, let us turn to the Arabic television series that covers the same period. Titled *The Sons of al-Rashid: al-Amin and al-Ma'mun*, it was written by a team of writers, one Jordanian (Ghazi al-Diba) and one Syrian (Ghassan Zakariyya), and directed by a Tunisian (Shawqi al-Majiri). The principal actors are Syrian and Jordanian. The series aired during Ramadan 2006.[19] It consists of thirty episodes, and some of the most

18 Lukács, Georg. *The Historical Novel*, translated by Hannah and Stanley Mitchell (Lincoln, Univ. of Nebraska Press, 1983) pp. 19-88. I thank Stuart Semmel for this reference.

19 Produced by *Al-Markaz al-'Arabī li'l-Khadamāt al-sām'iyya wa'l-bashariyya*, 2006. I thank Awaḍ Awaḍ for drawing my attention to the series. Many of the episodes have been posted on YouTube.

celebrated incidents of the early ‘Abbasid period, including the division of the caliphate between the two sons of al-Rashid, the execution of the vizier Ja‘far al-Barmaki, the civil war between Iraq and Khurasan, and al-Ma’mun’s persecution of literalist Hadith-scholars. As with all productions of this type, one has to watch only a few minutes to realize that the premises of representation established by Zaidan are alive and well. The series is full of palace intrigues and romantic subplots, and little attention to likelier causes of historical change. There are also several invented characters, though few of them are as interesting as Zaidan’s. In *The Caliph’s Heirs*, Zaidan gives us a Christian tavern-keeper, a Sabean sorceror, and a Persian physician. In the television series, by contrast, all of the invented characters are Muslims—though not all of them are Arabs. In this respect, at least, the series falls short of the example set by Zaidan.

Even so, the series follows in the tradition of Zaidan, and goes beyond it, in several respects. As we have seen, Zaidan the historian appears to have thought—if only in a tentative and inconsistent fashion—that being “truly Arab” was a good thing, while his Sunni successors made a virtual cult of the misogynist and racist explanation for ‘Abbasid “decline”. Zaidan the novelist, however, deals sympathetically with women and non-Arabs, even to the point of inventing them so as to give them a voice—as we might put it today—in the Islamic history he was helping to create. *The Sons of al-Rashid* goes even further: it seems genuinely interested in rethinking the lives of women, non-Arabs, slaves, and gay men during this period. For example, the chronicler who provides occasional voiceovers is a woman, ‘Aziza (played by Nadya ‘Awda), who is secretly writing a biography of al-Ma’mun (Iyad Nassar).[20] Al-Ma’mun himself is heard to complain of the prejudice against Persians (his own mother is a Persian slave).[21] And al-Amin (Mundhir Rayahina), who is

20 No works written by women have survived from this period.

21 The historical Marājil died shortly after bearing al-Ma’mūn, but her counterpart in the series is given a longer life.

condemned as a libertine even in medieval sources, is here depicted as a misunderstood gay man who would never have interfered with the succession if his mother had not forced him to marry and have children.

Unsurprisingly, this disruption of the moral shorthand triggered protests from many viewers. In one protest, a self-proclaimed representative of the 'Abbasid family denounced the depiction of al-Rashid (Rashid 'Assaf) as a drinker and music lover, explaining that the historical al-Rashid was a famously pious caliph and a zealous upholder of the pilgrimage and the *jihad*.[22] In another, Twelver Shiite viewers complained that 'Ali ibn Musa al-Rida (Ghassan Mas'ud), their eighth imam, is shown attending a drinking party.[23] The sincerity of these protests is indicative of the extent to which viewers have come to consider the so-called *musalsalat diniyya* (*sic!*)[24] as responsible for presenting the real past—a point to which we will return.

The most striking innovation—to me, anyway—on display in *The Sons of al-Rashid* is its treatment of religious controversy. Far from being depicted as defending or corrupting some genuine Islam, the characters are shown working out what Islam *should* be, and in the process creating—for better or worse—the religious traditions we are familiar with today. In this respect, the series genuinely goes beyond the timid precedent set by Sunni historiography and popular fiction alike. In the series, the caliph al-Ma'mun, for example, struggles to reconcile the Sunni and Shiite positions on the imamate; his friend Qusayy (Muhammad al-Majali) takes the rationalist view of scriptural interpretation; and the Ḥadith-scholar Ibn Hanbal (Ghazwan al-Safadi)

---

22 "Muwāṭinūn Sa'ūdiyyūn yaḥtajjūn 'alā Musalsal Abnā' al-Rashīd al-Amīn wa'l-Ma'mūn," *Al-Riyāḍ*. Online at: http://www.alriyadh.com/2006/10/11/article193390.html.

23 "Tabāyun fī'l-ārā' ḥawla Musalsal Abnā' al-Rashīd al-Amīn wa'l-Ma'mūn," *Dīwān al-'Arab*. Online at: http://www.diwanalarab.com/spip.php?article6478.

24 Apparently because audiences imagine the past as a time when people spoke Standard Arabic (as the characters do) and practiced true Islam—the two being presumptively concomitant.

argues the strictly literalist position. Admittedly, the characters express their opinions in modern terms quite alien to the spirit of the extant sources. No 'Abbasid-period theologian, as far as I know, ever argues—as Qusayy does at one point—that Muslims have no right to assume that their religion is valid for anyone but themselves.[25] Indeed, it is likely that these scenes, in which Ibn Hanbal, a foundational figure for present-day Wahhabi and Salafi Muslims, is depicted as a narrow-minded bigot, are intended to express disapproval of twenty-first century "fundamentalism". Ironically, however, it is precisely this kind of anachronism that permits the series—or forces it—to historicize religion. By depicting ninth-century Muslims as engaged in debating basic questions of belief, and making them sound more or less like present-day figures debating the same issues, the series opens up the possibility that the figures of the "golden age" were no closer (and no farther) from "true Islam" than we are today. "How do we know for certain," says Qusayy at one point, "which Islam it is that God speaks of in the Koran? Is it your Islam, or Abu Hanifa's, or mine? Or some Islam that only the Prophet, his family, and Companions could attain? Or is it all of these?"[26] We are still a long way from real historicity, but the fact that mass entertainment can get this close seems to me extraordinary.

Let us conclude by approaching the problem of historicity from a different direction. In Ramadan 2000, Iranian television broadcast a series called *Velāyat-e Eshgh* or *The Rule of Love*, a historical drama about the life and times of 'Ali al-Rida, the eighth imam of the Twelver Shi'a.[27] The period covered by the series is exactly that of Zaidan's *The Caliph's Heirs*, and almost exactly that covered by *The Sons of*

25 Episode 9 (YouTube), 7:10ff.

26 Ibid. 12:04ff.

27 *Velayat-e 'Eshgh*, written and directed by Fakhimzadeh, Mehdi (Tehran, Sorush Media Productions, 2000). I thank Pari Iranmanesh for bringing this work to my attention, and Mahsa Maleki for helping me with the Persian.

al-Rashid. Though it depicts the same events, *The Rule of Love* has its own story to tell. According to the modern Shiite point of view, neither al-Amin nor al-Ma'mun had any business occupying the throne at all. The series accordingly does its best to make the two caliphs as unappealing as possible. Al-Amin (played by Rambod Javan) spends his screen time issuing absurd commands, beating his servants, or shrieking in infantile frustration. His rival al-Ma'mun (Muhammad Sadeghi) seems at first to be a thoughtful, high-minded ruler who means what he says when he asks al-Rida to succeed him as caliph. But then, as the Shiite view of history requires, he turns out to be a scheming monster who poisons al-Rida when the Imam's superior virtue threatens to undermine his authority.[28]

One might imagine that, with its radically different theological and historical premises, *The Rule of Love* belongs to a different tradition of historical representation than *The Sons of al-Rashid.* In practice, though, the Iranian series is equally dependent on the conventions established by Zaidan. We find the same reduction of historical process to court intrigue, and the same reliance on invented characters—including two women whose dexterity at horseback-riding and hand-to-hand combat suggest the influence of the 1995-2001 US television series *Xena the Warrior Princess.* The Iranian series even reintroduces one tradition that its Arabic counterpart does not: like Zaidan, who prefaced his novels with a brief bibliography and included footnotes within the text, *The Rule of Love* lists several medieval histories in its final credits.[29]

---

28 I deal with this series, and its putative sources, in detail in "Al-Ma'mūn and 'Alī al-Riḍā (Emam Reza) on Iranian Television," in *The Rhetoric of Biography: Studies in Arabic, Persian and Turkish Narratives of Lives* edited by Louise Marlow (Boston, Ilex Foundation; Washington, DC: Center for Hellenic Studies; Cambridge MA, Distributed by Harvard Univ. Press, c2011) pp. 140-64.

29 These include the *Tārīkh al-Rusūl wa'l-Mulūk* of al-Ṭabarī, the *Murūj al-Dhahab* of al-Mas'udī, and the *'Uyūn Akhbār al-Riḍā* of Ibn Bābawayh al-Qumī.

These dependencies of form do not of course imply an identity of manifest content. Equipped, as it is, with an organizing premise—"Truth forever on the scaffold, Wrong forever on the throne," as James Russell Lowell put it, in a different context[30]—*The Rule of Love* has no need of a racialist interpretation of history. This is not necessarily to anyone's credit: the series' creators can hardly have wished to offend the many Shiites who are not Persians. The series can be described as pre-racialist, in the sense as above that it—like the pre-modern sources—assumes no connection between ethnicity and ideology; or post-racialist, in that it represses ethnic difference, as indeed it must do, as an officially sanctioned mass-culture production in a multi-ethnic state. In any event, it stages history in a way that differs markedly from traditional Sunni narrative history, even if it cannot question its own categories in the same way that the Arabic *Sons of al-Rashid* has managed to do.

In a certain sense, Iranian religious series like *The Rule of Love* are not so much realistic as hyper-real. So much is clear from an interview with Shahreyar Bohrani, the director of a series about Mary, the mother of Jesus. Chroniclers, he says, are concerned with glorifying kings, not prophets; it is therefore pointless to commit oneself to a conventional understanding of historical fidelity. The only way to proceed, he says, is to depict the prophets and imams as we know them to have been: that is, in such a way as to highlight their exemplary character. The result may not agree with the history books but it will be more faithful to the truth.[31] In *The Rule of Love*, this hyper-reality is evident in the appearance of the Imam, whose head is obscured by a nimbus of light. Apparently, we are not to suppose that he looked that way to his contemporaries, who in that case would necessarily have accepted him as imam. Rather, "the halo exists only in parallel reality, that is, in that version of the ninth

30 In his poem "The Present Crisis" (1845).

31 http://www.soroush-media.com/en/?action=artists&c=06. I thank Mahsa Maleki for this reference.

century that has been constructed for us with the appropriate labels attached. This parallel reality... is meant to be accepted as a more faithful representation of ultimate reality than the real thing could ever be, especially since the real thing has been distorted beyond recovery by the historians."[32]

Despite this hyper-reality, or because of it, audiences nevertheless insist that television productions are appropriate venues for the depiction of the past as it really was. I have twice watched *The Rule of Love* with an Iranian friend who cried at the Imam's death—even though I had explained, at tedious length, that the Imam was probably not poisoned in the way the series insists he was. Similarly, the protests against *The Sons of al-Rashid* suggest that, if only this or that offending element were removed, the series would give us history *wie es eigentlich gewesen.* What all this tells us is that the conventions established by Zaidan—with greater or lesser dependence on Scott, and doubtless others—have become so well established as to become invisible: that is, no one even thinks of them as conventions any more. Instead, viewers regard what they see on the screen either as unvarnished truth, or as a willfully distorted version of an unvarnished truth that the creators could have provided had they wished to do so.

As far as I know, the only writer to draw attention to these conventions as such—or, in Brechtian language, to de-familiarize them—is the Persian comic novelist Īraj Pezeshkzad. In Pezeshkzad's 1958 novel *Mashalla Khan at the Court of Harun al-Rashid*, a bank clerk becomes so immersed in Zaidan's novels that he actually travels back in time to the court of the 'Abbasid caliph.[33] When he arrives, he encounters many of Zaidan's characters, and amazes them by predicting the future based on his knowledge of what happens in the novels. The whole conceit is

32 Cooperson. "Al-Ma'mūn and 'Alī al-Riḍā," p.161.

33 Pezeshkzād, Iraj. *Mashallah Khan dar Bargah-e Harūn al-Rashīd.* Reprinted (Los Angeles, Nashr-e Kitāb, 1996).

played for laughs, but the point to be drawn from it is a serious one: namely, that Zaidan has given generation after generation of readers and audiences an image of the past that many of them have come to take for the real thing.

The Historical Poetics of Jurjı Zaidan's Andalusian Fictional Cosmos

William Granara

When Jurji Zaidan composed his chapters on contemporary Arabic fiction (both short stories and novels) in his grand compendium *The History of Arab Literature*[1] he listed himself, after Fransis Marash and Salim al-Bustani, as the author of seventeen (plus) historical novels dealing with pivotal moments ranging from the rise of Islam to his own time. He categorized this kind of novel as among the foreign literatures (*al-adab al-dakhila*) he and his contemporaries were appropriating from western writers.[2]

As an assiduous and prolific reader and scholar of Islamic history and literature, Zaidan had most assuredly attained a thorough understanding of Arab historical consciousness as articulated in Arabic writing in its many forms. The oral narratives of tribal heroes and glories of ages past, along with the memorization of thousands of lines of poetry evoking names, places and events passed down from one generation to another by the tribal transmitters (*rawi, pl. ruwat*), and thirdly the meticulous preservation of ethnic/tribal genealogy (*nasab*), so revered by Arabs for centuries and inscribed throughout literary and historical texts and monuments wherever they settled, constitute the articulation of collective memory which helped shape both Arab identity and culture, high and low, well into the "modern" period.

The rise and spread of Islam with all its challenges to traditional Arabian lore built on and expanded Arabian historical consciousness, as Arabic

1 Zaydān, Jūrjī. *Tārīkh Ādāb al-Lugha al-'Arabiyya* in 4 vols. (Beirut, 1980). It was first published in Cairo (Cairo, Maṭba'at al-Hilāl, 1911-1914).

2 Zaydān. *Tārīkh Ādāb*, vol. 4 p. 573.

culture made the highly dramatic and richly significant transition from a predominantly oral to a written culture. The demands for historical fact and accuracy took their place alongside the records of popular myth and tribal beliefs, and eventually elevated themselves through the development of a scholarly, scientific historiography, especially by way of the rigid method of *hadith* transmissions. Moreover, the prophecy of Muhammad allowed the Arabs to look beyond the time/place of the Arabian peninsula and its predominantly Bedouin ethos and to consider the processes of historical development against Jewish, Christian, and Zoroastrian traditions.

The rise of the socio-literary movement of *adab* in the ninth century, and the proliferation of its manuals instructing the refinement of manners in the context of a burgeoning urban way of life, forced the Arabs to rethink, judgmentally, their past and present in new and creative ways. The lessons of history, by way of anecdotes, real or imagined, of the rise and fall of nations, of good and evil rulers, and of successful and failed civilizations, gave the rising Arabic-language readership much to ponder. The discovery of the 'Greek sciences' gave Arab scholars and intellectuals new tools to investigate, interrogate, and replace traditional views, all contributing to a dynamic process of evolving historical consciousness. This ongoing and dynamic process of maturation of classical Arabic historiography, of both universal and local scope, comes into clear view when plotting a trajectory from al-Tabari to Ibn al-Athir, and culminating, in the view of many, in the work of Ibn Khaldun,[3] a line of progression which attests to the Arabs' ability not only to embrace change but to understand it, explicate it, and record it with scholarly sophistication. Finally, the later medieval phenomenon of Sufism, not only as a religious-spiritual movement but one of widespread popular culture, itself generated significant changes in the ways Arabs and Muslims saw themselves in the context of their own local and recent pasts. The veneration of holy men in the construction of shrines is a

3 Al-Ṭabarī (d. 923), Universal historian and Koran commentator, Ibn al-Athīr (d. 1233), Ibn Khaldūn (1332-1406) universal historian.

powerful marker of collective memory. Another manifestation of this changing self-perception was a shift in personal narrative writing, from the biographical to the autobiographical, whereby the individual sought to understand and explain his own existence against the bigger forces of history. This shift constitutes one of the most significant bridges in Arabic writing from the pre-modern to modern eras.[4]

As a prominent figure and pioneer in the Arabic literary revival, Nahda, that sprouted in the late nineteenth and early twentieth centuries, a movement not unlike the *adab* movement a millennium earlier, Jurji Zaidan was faced with the challenge of how to negotiate between a long and well developed *indigenous* tradition of writing history and the conscious decision to embrace the *foreign* modern *European* novel as a literary site to launch a modern Arabic national literature. The ways in which he does so informs the first constituent part to what I call here the "historical poetics" of Zaidan's novelistic project.

During the period of the Nahda, that is, the span of Zaidan's professional life, the Arab world witnessed a staggering series of disruptions against persistent continuities on many fronts. Politically, the Ottoman Empire was well in its stage of decline and Turkish nationalism was spearheading a radical transformation of the traditional "Middle East". As sectarian violence erupted from time to time throughout Greater Syria, both the French and British waged their colonialist interventions and takeovers of local governments from Algiers to Baghdad, arousing increasing outbursts of popular resentment against European imperialism. The steady flow of rural Arabs into the urban centers, the migration of Arab and non-Arab communities from one country or province to another, and the spread of modern technology, education, and literacy all contributed to the changing face of the modern Arab world,

4 For a recent in-depth study of the rise of the Moroccan Arabic novel see Head, Gretchen. *Moroccan Autobiography: the Rhetorical Construction of the Self and the Development of Modern Arabic Narrative in al-Maghrib al-Aqsa.* Unpublished Ph.D.Thesis, University of Pennsylvania, 2011.

especially in the urban centers. On the linguistic and cultural fronts, the reformist movements of the nineteenth century, initiated by religious and legal scholars, infiltrated the literary terrain, and the emergence of the Arab Nahda united a significant number of Arab intellectuals, predominantly from Syria, Egypt, and Tunisia, in a common cause: to craft a modern Arabic national literature, by (i) reviving the Arabic literary heritage (*al-turath*) and (ii) adopting western forms of literary expression (theatre, short story, and novel, in particular). The ambiguous position of embracing western culture and resisting western colonial rule is the second constituent part of the "historical poetics" of Zaidan's novelistic project.

These two components of Zaidan's "historical poetics", of recovering and continuing Arab historical consciousness and embracing the modern European novel on the one hand, and contesting western imperial hegemony while accepting western models to forge a modern Arab nationalist literature, combine both the *global* and *local* dimensions of his novelistic project. I read the *global* less in the surface transportation of the historical novel from Europe to the Arab world but more in the many ways Zaidan's adaptation, interpretation, and manipulation of the art form establishes a literary connectedness to the European text and critical studies, as represented, for example, in the way his literary output bears affinities with that of Walter Scott, and resonates with the seminal ideas of Alessandro Manzoni and Gyorgy Lukacs. I read the *local* in the very ideology of pan-Arabic discourse that binds the politics of reform, national unity, and resistance to western imperialism to the aesthetics of social justice, freedom of expression, and artistic creativity. I read the powerful force of this very pan-Arabist discourse as the third constituent part of Zaidan's "historical poetics".

The Historical Novel between Politics and Poetics

The historical novel in the modern sense of the term, emerged, as conventional literary history tells us, in Europe during the early to middle decades of the nineteenth century, with Sir Walter Scott (1771-1832) earning and maintaining the distinction of being its most prominent pioneer and influential practitioner. By the time it made its way to the shores of the modern Arab world in general, and in Jurji Zaidan's novels in particular, the historical novel had already fallen victim to a "rise and decline" cycle, especially from the point of view of the European literary and cultural elite. In his own words, Scott himself understood all too well its popular appeal:

> I am sensible that if there is anything good about my poetry, or prose either, it is a hurried frankness of composition which pleases soldiers, sailors, and young people of bold and active disposition.[5]

Despite the belatedness of the Arabic historical novel in relation to its European forebear, both socio-political conditions and aesthetic values and inclinations draw the two into credible comparability. Moreover, the mid-twentieth century interest in re-examining historical fiction, as most notably exemplified in Hungarian Marxist critic Georg Lukacs' *The Historical Novel* (1885-1971),[6] has allowed for expanded cross-cultural and trans-historical approaches to studying Zaidan's historical novels. Being both an Arab nationalist and student of what we now call *comparative* or *global* literature, Zaidan, like several of his Arab literary peers, was highly cognizant of both the social and political benefits of historical fiction.

Lukacs' study of the historical novel with his special emphasis on Walter Scott is a most effective lens through which we can define and situate Zaidan's historical poetics on a global scale: Lukacs identifies salient features that resonate loudly and are reflected clearly in Zaidan's historical fiction: the nineteenth century European historical novel constructs "the individuality of characters from the historical peculiarity of their age";

5 Green, Martin. *Dreams of Adventure, Deeds of Empire* (New York, Basic Books, 1979) p.109.

6 Lukacs, Georg. *The Historical Novel* (Lincoln, Nebraska Univ. Press, 1983).

the lessons of history provide the principles for transforming an "unreasonable" (past) feudal society into a "reasonable" (present) society; the new historical novel includes "a broad delineation of manners and circumstances attendant upon events, the dramatic character of action, and the new and important role of dialogue in the novel"; Scott's greatness lies in his capacity to give living human embodiment to historical social types:

> The great historical personality is the representative of an important and significant movement embracing large segments of the people ... whose personal passion and aim coincides with the movement because he concentrates within himself its positive and negative sides, because he gives these popular strivings their clearest expression, because he is the standard bearer in good and evil; [and thus] we see no evolution in character: each is presented as a complete personality appearing to fulfill his mission; not the retelling of an historical event but the poetic awakening of the people who figured in those events; and finally that we "re-experience" the social and human motives which led men to think, feel and act just as they did in historical reality.[7]

The work of the earlier Italian novelist and literary scholar, Alessandro Manzoni, may very well hold richer significance for constructing a Zaidanian "historical poetics". On a broader historical (read: political) level, nineteenth century Italy was closer to Syria than the more politically and linguistically stable England of the same time. Italy was in the pre-modern nation phase, politically divided and linguistically disconnected. The tug of war between traditional values and modern technology complicated the development of a unified national historical consciousness that is instrumental to the success of both the modern nation-state and the formation of a national literature. The project of writing a historical novel in both Italy and Syria aimed beyond the project to provide the masses with an entertaining albeit instructive novel, what Scott purportedly referred to

7 Ibid. pp.19-42.

as "a mere elegance, a luxury contrived for the amusement of polished life and the gratification of that half-love of literature …" [8]

Above all, Manzoni's ongoing obsession with the contradictions inherent in any historical novel, that is, the tension between the [real] facts of history and [unreal] fictional invention, and his insistence on the difference between history's "what happened" and literature's "what may or could happen" allow for a study of the genre—in all its strictures and conventions—against a complex of historical specificities and local politics. While Jurji Zaidan's historical novels may be read, intertextually, with those of Sir Walter Scott by way of reading Lukacs, these same novels may be read contextually against Arabic literary history and contemporary Arab politics when reading Manzoni. It is the politically charged sense of connection to both a pan-Arab past and a pan-Arab present which Zaidan's novels enable, situating their "historical poetics" at a medial point between [classical] Arabic and [modern] European literatures.[9]

Jurji Zaidan and Arab-Nationalism

Beyond the literary and stylistic features the Zaidanian historical novels came to share with their European counterparts, a reflection of what we may consider as a positive result of cross-cultural fertilization and influence emanating from contact with Europe, lies what I would call the politics of history that lurk at the subtext of each of his novels. The importation and imitation (imitation being the highest form of flattery) of the European historical novel, or any other type of novel for that matter, does not, however, include the importation of European history or European interpretations of history. It is precisely here where pan-Arabic discourse, or at least the early (read: abstract, romanticized) articulations

8 Manzoni, Alessandro. *On the Historical Novel.* Translated with an Introduction by Sandra Bermann (Lincoln, Nebraska Univ. Press, 1984) p.12.

9 "… the historiography of the historical novel is that it enables a sense of connection which is deeply politicized …" See De Groot, Jerome. *The Historical Novel* (London, Routledge, 2010) p.28.

of the idea of pan-Arab unity allowed the Arabic historical novel to break away from, and at times subvert the conventions of, its European forbear.

As a Levantine Christian Arab intellectual, Zaidan, like many Arabs of his own ilk, embraced European languages, education, technology and other facets of its culture while remaining ever mindful of the deleterious effects European cultural hegemony held over Arab identity. At the same time he and his peers, from Tunis to Damascus, were equally mindful and weary of the recidivist forces within their own societies, past and present, and the dangers lurking behind pan-Islamist and territorial nationalist tendencies that rivaled pan-Arabism. The politics of the Zaidanian historical novel was thus built on the project to create and promote a modern, authentic Arab identity to counter the offensive of the European onslaught, and its most powerful weapon, we now all know, was history.

The fact that Jurji Zaidan composed three novels on the early history of the Arabs in Spain (al-Andalus) is highly significant. Given the state of affairs of his own time, European colonialism, cross-cultural conflict and fertilization, religious rivalries, ethnic tensions, cultural creativity, and the expansion of new physical and intellectual frontiers, the history of Muslim Spain bore rich significance for the Zaidanian novelist project. The eight centuries of Arab-Islamic civilization north of the Mediterranean, well into Christian European territory, provide a massive archive from which the modern Arab could draw examples of its earlier encounters with and ascendancy over his European counterpart. In the particular time-place of Arab history in Spain is neatly folded a universe of facts and figures that collectively constitute a discreet chapter in Arab history replete with "rise and fall" narratives, the lessons of which provided the historical novelist with expansive fertile ground to expound and educate an eagerly receptive audience.

Zaidan's Andalusian trilogy, as I like to call them, deal with momentous historical events: *The Conquest of Andalusia* deals with the Arab defeat of the Visigoths and their conquest of the Iberian Peninsula in 711 CE; *The Battle of Poitiers* narrates the events leading up to and including the Arab defeat by the army of Charles Martel in 732 CE, putting an effective end to Islam's advance in Europe; and *'Abd al-Rahman, the Victor*[10] delves into the court intrigues and ethnic rivalries that ultimately lead to the demise of the Ummayad caliphate in Cordoba at the end of the tenth century. Generically, all three fit into the familiar pattern of the Zaidanian novel and exhibit most of the salient features of historical fiction identified by Manzoni and Lukacs. Thematically they read closely to the specificities of Arab Muslim history in Spain, drawing on real names, places and events. Most significantly, their geographical setting beyond the borders of Islamdom and their plots which include the ongoing rivalries with the Europeans undoubtedly resonated with pan-Arabist rejection of western imperial hegemony.

I see particularly meaningful in reading Zaidan's Andalusian trilogy less the mixing of historical fact with artistic invention but rather an evolution of the historical consciousness they display. Read in the chronological order of the histories they seek to retell, all three may be read as representations of Giambattista Vico's cycle of ages: the age of *gods*, the age of *heroes*, and the age of *men*. The "historicalness" of this trilogy has both literary and political implications.

The Conquest of Andalusia (Spain) takes as its premise the expansion of the Islamic wars of conquest of the seventh and eight century, extending from the Arabian peninsula to the northern shores of the western Mediterranean. In its epic mode, it posits a clash of civilizations in which the forces of good and evil, represented by the Arab army and the Visigoth government of Iberia, come face to face. Aside from the incorporation of details from the historical archive and the romantic relationship between two characters from different political camps, recurring motifs in all Zaidanian novels, the novel evolves around a contest

10 Titles in sequence: *Fatḥ al-Andalus, Sharl wa 'Abd al-Raḥmān and 'Abd al-Raḥmān al-Nāṣir.*

between the noble, just, tolerant and merciful message of a unified Islam against an unjust, corrupt and divided Christian world. The heavy use of dialogue, a dominant feature of the historical novel in general, situates the characters well within the overarching good/evil binary.

The Battle of Poitiers takes the Andalusian trilogy away from the purely epic mode of writing and into a more philosophically and politically laced romanticism. The relationship between Commander 'Abd al-Rahman and his senior officer, Hani, and the romantic relationship between Hani and the mysterious and ethnically ambiguous Maryam, insert stronger individual voices in this novel as opposed to the one-dimensional and overdetermined cast of characters of its precedent. The theme of the novel, the defeat of the Muslim army in central France by the forces of Charles Martel, brings the novel onto complicated political terrain on which the Arab defeat must be considered and explained. While *The Conquest of Andalusia* glorifies Arab military, religious (moral), and historical ascendancy over "Europe", *The Battle of Poitiers* draws attention to divisiveness, weakness, and the limitations of power. These novels, written and read during the period of European colonial rule through much of the late nineteenth and early twentieth century Arab world, offer up the lessons of history with which, as I have argued elsewhere, Arabs could understand their past, view their present, and aspire for a better future.[11]

The third Andalusian novel, *'Abd al-Rahman the Victor*, takes the historical novel into further realistic modes of writing and well within the outskirts of the modern novel. The good vs. evil binary and the world of gods and heroes are replaced by men in all their free will and agency. The Arab vs. non-Arab, or good Muslim vs bad Christian, is backgrounded, allowing the bifurcated Arab, politically, socially, and

11 Granara, William. "Nostalgia, Arab Nationalism and the Andalusian *Chronontope* in the Evolution of the Modern Arabic Novel," *Journal of Arabic Literature* 36 (2005) pp. 57-73; and "*Extensio animae*: The Artful Ways of Remembering al-Andalus," *Journal of Social Affairs* (Sharjah, UAE) 19 (Fall 2002) pp. 45-70.

intellectually divided and hostile, to take center stage. The caliph 'Abd al-Rahman al-Nasir's murder of his own son on suspicion of plotting against his father for being replaced by a younger brother in the line of succession provides the skeleton to the plot of the novel, and the cast of characters who jockey for positions or join the various opposition groups provide the flesh. The Cordoba of the late tenth century is the modern metropolis where political and professional ambitions prompt men and women to do bad things. Once again the lessons of history are retold, with much flesh on the skeleton, as Manzoni would say, to illustrate, educate and guide the modern reader toward the path of unity and progress.

Conclusions

In his astute observation that "it is the reawakening of past national greatness which gives strength to hopes of national rebirth", Lukacs was speaking as much about the modern Arabic novel as he was about German nationalism.[12] In the composition of his historical fiction in general, and in the Andalusian trilogy in particular, Zaidan maintained an equal focus on the past and present. By incorporating the many specifics of Andalusian history, bringing it alive in all its richness and complexity, its rises and declines, he recreated a fictional cosmos in which, the many indulgences of "invention" aside, he remained faithful to the real lessons of Andalusian history: that is, that it was a dynamic process in which men and women came to define their lives and determine their own fates. Zaidan's progression in the literary modes of his own creative writing in his novelistic project, from the epic, to the romantic, to the realistic, reflects a historical consciousness he himself developed as a novelist, historian, and thinker. His commitment to the facts of history, wherever they may lead, and to the lessons that may be drawn from them, along with his passion to awaken his fellow Arabs to the glories of Arab civilization and achievement and guide them, by way of fashioning a modern Arabic

12 Lukacs. op.cit. pp. 22-23.

national literature, to unity, tolerance and progress as they face the challenges of modernity, and, finally, his staunch loyalty to pan-Arab ideals of self-determination, justice and equality, all in combination comprise an "historical poetics" he bequeathed to future generations.

Part IV

Jurji Zaidan—The Man

Jurji Zaidan—The Cultural Entrepreneur: His Values, Beliefs and Attributes[1]

George C Zaidan

What were the values and characteristics, personal and professional, that made Jurji Zaidan so successful and influential in so many areas? Jurji Zaidan was my grandfather but he died in 1914 some twenty five years before I was born. I therefore came to know his personal and professional qualities indirectly: (a) first and foremost through the family reminiscences of his children[2]. The value system and principles he instilled in them guided their private lives and enabled his sons to build Dar-al-Hilal into one of the biggest publishing houses for periodicals in the Middle East; (b) his autobiography, cut short by his untimely death and covering only the first twenty years of his life; (c) some personal reminiscences by his literary and journalistic peers who knew him well; and (d) his own writings, mostly in articles in his journal *al-Hilal* describing his beliefs, the attributes of successful people and the progress of nations.

---

1 I am grateful to Thomas Philipp, Hada and George Zaidan Jr for comments on earlier drafts of this paper. None is responsible for any remaining errors. Selected articles by Jurji Zaidan in *al-Hilāl* quoted in this paper were translated by Paul Starkey, Hilary Kilpatrick, Kamran Rastegar and myself. The articles translated by Paul Starkey and Hilary Kilpatrick will appear in the Anthology of Thomas Philipp's book on *Jurji Zaidan and the Foundations of Arab Nationalism* (New York, Syracuse University Press, 2014). Those translated by Kamran Rastegar and myself appear at the end of this volume.

2 For example his eldest son, Emile, had a favorite saying "Lā Yaṣiḥ illā al-Ṣaḥīḥ" which was inscribed on a plaque on his desk. This is also the title of one of Jurji Zaidan's articles in *al-Hilāl* 20 (May 1912) pp. 476-480 translated by Paul Starkey as "Only the Fittest Can Survive or Truth Will Prevail in the End". The article conveys the importance of truth and honesty in personal and business relationships as elaborated in the section on Entrepreneurship below.

Zaidan's professional life and career may be best understood through the nexus of politics and literature which became the hallmark of his legacy. In the political sphere, he is considered a pioneer and leader of the Nahda—a revival of the Arab cultural heritage in the late nineteenth and early twentieth century that spawned the birth of Arab nationalism. On the literary scene, Zaidan is best remembered as the author of twenty two historical novels set in the context of Arabo-Islamic historical events from pre-Islamic times to the nineteenth century. These novels, very popular to this day and regularly reprinted in the Arab world, were instrumental in fashioning an Arab consciousness in much of the Arab world. In addition to the novels, his prodigious output included scholarly books on Islamic history, the history and development of languages and other topics; as well as articles on political, social, educational, and ethical issues. He published the latter in *al-Hilal,* the magazine he founded in 1892 and which is now in its one hundredth and twentieth year of operation.

It has been said that Zaidan was "many men in one man". Others are much better able to assess his contributions as a journalist, historian, linguist, social and educational reformer, political scientist and more. But whatever one may think about his professional contributions, Zaidan remains popular to this day in the Arab world and beyond as one of the leaders of the Nahda. Taha Husayn put it succinctly when assessing *al-Hilal's* contribution to modern (Arab) literature as follows: "The critics may say what they want but about one thing there is no doubt: the historical novels that Zaidan published had the most important impact which enabled the Nahda to bear fruit that readers of today still enjoy."[3] The Egyptian Government commemorated the hundredth anniversary of the establishment of *al-Hilal* in

3 In *Al-Hilāl al-Kitāb al-Dhahabī 1892-1942* (Cairo, Dār al-Hilāl, 1942) pp. 133-137. Other prominent Egyptian and Arab literary scholars, poets and journalists paid tribute to his work at his memorial services, in special issues of *al-Hilāl* to commemorate the fiftieth, one hundredth and, in 2012, the one hundred and twentieth anniversary of the founding of his magazine. For example, the *Al-Hilāl al-Kitāb al-Dhahabī* includes the tributes, both professional and personal, of the most prominent poets, journalists and literary figures of Egypt. More recently in January 2012 *al-Hilal* published a

1992 and commissioned an Opera[4] about his life attended by the President of the Republic, government officials and prominent Egyptian and Arab personalities. The government also issued a commemorative *al-Hilal* stamp and minted a one-pound silver coin with his portrait. More recently the Library of Alexandria documented his legacy as part of its project on the Memory of Modern Egypt.[5] Finally, his reach outside the Arab world is evident. There have been more than one hundred translations of his twenty two historical novels into more than ten languages[6] and studies in various western universities continue to assess his work.

His Values and Character:[7] Early Influences

Two books influenced Zaidan greatly. The first was Samuel Smiles's *Self-Help* translated by Ya'qub Sarruf as *The Secret of Success*[8] when

special issue to commemorate the one hundredth and fiftieth anniversary of his birth which included updated tributes of his work.

4 The Opera as well as speeches by eminent literary scholars and journalists preceding the Opera can be viewed on the Zaidan Foundation's website at www.zaidanfoundation.org

5 In January 2012 the Library of Alexandria's Dār al-Hilāl Documentation Project was completed on the occasion of the one hundredth and fiftieth anniversary of the birth of Jurji Zaidan. The first phase digitized the whole collection of *al-Hilāl* issues and compiled them on DVDs. In the second phase, *Dār al-Hilāl: Madrasat al-Tanwīr* (*Dār al-Hilāl: A School of Enlightenment*) was published within the Memory of Modern Egypt Series. The third phase digitized the photo archive of the publishing house.

6 Also *The History of Islamic Civilization* was translated into Urdu, Turkish, English (one volume) and Persian.

7 Character can be defined as the aggregate of features and traits, positive or negative, that form the nature or personality of an individual. Or, more specifically it can denote honor, moral fiber, integrity and rectitude. In Smiles' book and in this paper "character" is used in the latter sense. Attributes, traits and qualities are variously used to denote the broader meaning of character.

8 Smiles, Samuel. *Self-Help with Illustrations of Conduct and Perseverance,* 1st edition (London, John Murray, 1859). Translated by Ṣarrūf as *Sirr al Najāḥ (The Secret of Success)* in 1880.

the young Zaidan was growing up. The second was E. Demolin's book *A Quoi Tient la Supériorité des Anglo-Saxons*[9] also translated into Arabic. Before reviewing how these books influenced him, it is instructive to see how Zaidan rose above the class in which he was born into a "third class" that emulated the Victorian values of the European middle classes. In his autobiography he says:

> At that time the people of Beirut consisted of two classes, *Tabaqatan*: the lower class, *al-'amma*, which means the riff-raff, the artisans, all the other people with menial occupations, and the small merchants. The people of the government and the rich constituted the upper class, *al-khassa.* But the social norms were basically one and the same. Obscene expressions were predominant in the speech of the rich as well as in that of the poor.
>
> ... after the unrest of the sixties, there developed a third class amongst the people of Beirut educated in the Christian missionary schools. This third social group was determined to change the social norms from what they were to what they became, so that the contemporary morals of Beirut became comparable with the most advanced habits and customs of the Europeans. It was my good fortune that during the phase of imitation I did not succeed in emulating my first friends in their vices. I began to form my own opinions and to express independent views. The credit for this goes to the natural and mathematical sciences: they condition the mind to correct judgment based on coherent reasons. When I met Shawul and his friends *[members of the third class]* I found myself able to follow

9 Demolin, Edmond. *A Quoi Tient la Supériorité des Anglo-Saxons*, 1st edition (Paris, 1897). Translated by Aḥmad Fatḥī Zaghlūl as *Sirr Taqaddum al-Inkilīz al-Saksūnīyīn* (Cairo, Maktabat al-Tarraqī, 1899).

> them, and I imitated them successfully in their virtuous ways.[10]

Further on in his autobiography Zaidan vividly describes how much Samuel Smiles' book *Self-Help* influenced him:

> I had read parts of the book which Dr. Sarruf had translated into Arabic. Vigor and zeal sprang up in me. Too great was the enthusiastic impact it had upon me to read about the lives of men who became highly successful by their own diligence and efforts and self-reliance. Amongst them, barbers and shoemakers, servants, artisans and maids who rose through their eagerness and vigilance to the station of great people. If I read a few pages I would become so agitated that I could not sleep any longer or be calm. So I would put the book aside and till today I have not finished reading it.[11]

In many Victorian homes Samuel Smiles' book *Self-Help* published in 1859 had a status second only to the Bible and was considered a classic display of Victorian values. Smiles gave the world a work that still inspires: its ethos is individualism, personal responsibility and will-power. The self-help ethic comes alive through biography. Smiles packed his book with remarkable people to show the vast range of possible models of success. But common to all these success stories is a philosophy of freedom of thought and action that makes every individual responsible for developing the common traits required for success by himself (self-help). These traits were internalized by Zaidan and recur frequently in his writings as will be described below. The most important of them are:

a. *Will Power and Hard Work***.** Smiles wrote: "It is not eminent talent that is required to ensure success in any pursuit, so much as

10 See the translation of Jurji Zaidan's Autobiography in Philipp, Thomas. *Ǧurǧī Zaidān: His Life and Thought,* Beiruter Texte und Studien. vol. 3 (Beirut, Franz Steiner Verlag, 1979) pp.147-149.

11 Ibid. p.164.

purpose—not merely the power to achieve, but the will to labor energetically and perseveringly." Patience, ordering of the mind, and absorption in the task at hand, are the key elements he cites in all our great advances.

b. *Character.* As Smiles warned, education, wealth, or noble family do not come close to replacing character. He asserted that "*Character is power, more than knowledge is power.*"
c. *Trust***.** In the nineteenth century, business was not seen as it tends to be seen today: the arena for the brightest, most creative minds; yet Smiles was able to see that it would become so. He wasted no time in stripping business to its core element: integrity of word and deed. Since trust is the glue that holds free societies together, it follows that lasting success will be attracted to those who can be trusted.

Individual development can most successfully thrive in a political and social environment of freedom of speech and action, best captured in the philosophy of the British Liberal party of the late nineteenth century—a party that reflected the values and represented the interests of the middle classes. J.S. Mill's principle of political liberty and Adam Smith's economic *laissez faire* provided the enabling environment for personal growth, but it was the ethos of self-help that allowed the individual to realize his full potential. Zaidan's nation-building efforts focused on educating the middle classes—getting them to "graduate" from the *al-'amma*, into which he was born into the "third class" which he joined and whose values he adopted. Zaidan believed this class was the main engine of progress for the nation. As he said: "The teaching of the elite alone, which is the situation with most nations, is not enough. The aim is the teaching, educating and training of the common people, because they constitute the public at large of the nation. No nation will succeed in its plans as long as its common people are ignorant." He saw in the trajectory of his own growth and development the possibility, indeed the desirability, that the progress of nations would mirror his own personal experience.

Zaidan like Smiles studied and analyzed the success stories of the most prominent people in a wide variety of fields. His book on the builders of the Nahda reviews the life of eighteen prominent members of the Nahda[12]—leaders and politicians; reformers; scientists and educators; and literary figures and artists. More extensively he reviewed in *al-Hilal* the success stories of as many as seventy one famous persons in the Middle East and beyond.[13]

A second book that influenced Zaidan much later in his life was E. Demolin's book *A Quoi Tient la Superiorité des Anglo Saxons* written almost forty years after Smiley's book. It argued a similar point: the superiority of the value system of the British middle classes of liberalism and entrepreneurship. A few weeks after its publication Zaidan wrote an article in *al-Hilal* called "The Eastern Youth"[14] in which he followed Demolin's argument about the difference between the French *fonctionnaire* and the British entrepreneur as well as the superiority of the latter. In another article on "The Syrians in Egypt"[15] Zaidan admonished them to seek careers in agriculture and industry rather than Government services in their own pecuniary interest as well as for the benefit of the country.

12 *Bunāt al-Nahḍa al-'Arabbiya* (Cairo, Dār al-Hilāl, 1957). It covers 18 prominent members of the Nahda as follows: leaders and politicians (4); reformers (4); scientists and educators (4); and literary figures and artists (6).

13 These famous people were taken from: *Tarājim Mashāhīr al-Sharq fī'l-Qarn al-tāsi' 'ashar*, 3rd printing in 2 vols. (Cairo, Maṭba'at al-Hilāl, 1922). There were writers (17); journalists (9); other literary and scientific figures (31); and poets (14).

14 "Al-Shabāb al-sharkī fī awākhir al-Qarn al-tāsi' 'ashar," *al-Hilāl* 4 (Jan. 1898) pp. 333-340.

15 "Al-Suriyyūn fī Miṣr," *al-Hilāl* 1 (April 1893) pp. 271-275. Translated by Hilary Kilpatrick. The term "Syrians" does not mean here the citizens of the modern state of Syria but the inhabitants of greater Syria in one of the provinces of the Ottoman Empire consisting at the time of the three Ottoman provinces of Aleppo, Beirut and Damascus.

His Personal Qualities

In a memorial article about Zaidan, Khalil Mutran encapsulates well many of Zaidan's most important personal qualities:

> I have not known a man that combined two such antithetical attributes—greatness and modesty. Nor did I see or hear him ever complain about his fate to anyone or wish any ill towards someone with a word or as much as a hint. I never witnessed once from him a desire to avenge himself from a critic of his work that was the source of his income and the fulcrum of his fame because of his belief in the honor of his mission and the purity of his work. As for his literary work he balanced it and dressed it up so that it would appeal to a prince, draw a friend closer and stimulate the admiration of strangers with no affectation or pretense whatsoever and with the utmost simplicity.

This portrayal, corroborated and supplemented by how his children and others who knew him well described him, was used to select from his own writings those articles that best applied to him. They are grouped under five headings:

A. The Development of Character
B. Honesty in Words and Deed
C. Hard Work and Time Consciousness
D. Entrepreneurship
E. Modesty, Shyness and Moral Courage

A. The Development of Character

Like Smiles, Zaidan accepted the primacy of will, motivation and perseverance in developing character through self-help over education, knowledge or heritage in achieving success. In his autobiography Zaidan wrote: "Though I do not deny the impact education has upon the rectification and improvement of character, I do not believe that it changes the essence."[16] He believed that adversity was one of the main "trigger points" for developing the character needed for success.

During Zaidan's only year at university, he was greatly influenced by the theory of evolution. It affected the way in which he interpreted social phenomena as can be seen in his article on "Overcoming Adversity Brings Forth Latent Strengths":[17]

> It is demonstrable ... that natural forces are latent in matter, and that these may be brought to light by pressure or resistance. This is also the case in the moral, or ethical, field. A man may be endowed with intelligence, sharpness of intellect, courage and boldness, but without the adversity that creates pressure and resistance, these powers will remain latent in him, so that you would think him stupid and lethargic. Then, when some obstacles stand in his way...his talents become apparent, and the man emerges as a genius, carrying out remarkable deeds. We have the clearest evidence in the form of the biographies of famous men and the histories of nations and societies.

Further on he observed, however, that people differ in their reactions to adversity:

> People are not all the same: there are some people who will cringe or cower if you pressure them or subject them to stress and adversity...How he deals with adversity is what

16 Philipp. *Zaidān*, p.169.

17 "Bi'l-Ḍaghṭ wa'l-Muqāwama ṭaẓhar al-Qūwa al-kāmina," *al-Hilāl* 7 (Dec.1898) pp.171-175. Translated by Paul Starkey. The Arabic title of this article can be given either a scientific meaning or one related to human character as reflected in the two possible alternative English translations "Through Pressure and Resistance, Hidden Forces Appear" or "Overcoming Adversity Brings Forth Latent Strengths". The play on words in the Arabic title conveys the central theme of this article—namely the link between the two that Zaidan tries to establish.

> distinguishes one man from another. It makes the strong stronger and the weak weaker, like the friction that heats the iron but smashes the china.

B. Honesty in Words and Deed

Using once more the analogy with the theory of evolution, Zaidan firmly believed that truth in human affairs eventually prevails even if it takes a longer and more circuitous route than for the fittest to survive in the natural world. Focusing on issues, factually and succinctly, in speech and writing were hallmarks of advanced nations; whereas flowery, unfocused and unnecessarily long speeches were characteristics of backward nations in which talk and argument were a substitute for deeds. On honesty, he believed that integrity in conduct and honesty in speech were marks of superior character that typified advanced nations. The following elaborates with selections from three articles.

In the first article entitled "Only the Fittest Can Survive or Truth Prevails in the End"[18] he says:

> The survival of the fittest is one of the natural laws that is inherent in the Law of Evolution. It is a general principle that applies to everything, whether it be matters of nature, or of ethics and morality. In the same way…it also requires the disappearance of views, laws or customs that do not suit the social structure, and be replaced by others that are more appropriate. My present purpose is to demonstrate another law which is obviously applicable to society or to morality..

18 "Lā Yaṣiḥḥ illā al-Ṣaḥīḥ," *al-Hilāl*, 20 (May 1912) pp. 476-480. Translated by Paul Starkey. The title implies both a scientific and an ethical or moral connotation. The term *al-aṣaḥḥ* (superlative of *al-ṣaḥīḥ*) is used in the sense of "the fittest" and has both a scientific and an ethical or moral connotation. Here as in the essay "Through Pressure and Resistance Hidden Forces Appear" Zaidan aims at establishing the link between natural science and ethical or moral social behavior.

> namely the saying that says 'Only the truth (or what is right) prevails...'
>
> If we turn to spiritual and ethical interactions in society, we see that this law is less obvious and slower with regard to results, because it depends on forces that are more confused and mingled. I mean intellectual forces, and other forces that either oppose them, or attach themselves to them, or depend on them, such as intellectual passions like the love of fame, envy, love of self, revenge, etc, which may impede the appearance of the truth so that it is slow to emerge, though it must emerge sooner or later....
>
> Then again, consider the above in the light of other things that admit of exaggeration or distortion, such as commercial or industrial achievements... Someone may announce that he is a skilled doctor, a graduate of the greatest schools, and enumerate all he knows of science or diseases he has specialized in. The announcement attracts attention so that he is consulted by the sick. If what he says is true, he will become established and his services will be in demand, but if not, he will be thrown out and sidelined....

In the second article entitled "Reality and Illusions or The Essence of Things and Appearances"[19] Zaidan observes disparities between different peoples:

> For the English, as an example, are of the nations that are most inclined towards focusing on the essence of things. An example of this that is well known these days is the amusing story about the English soldier who purchased a donkey in the center of Cairo to ride to *al-'Abbasiyya*. It happened

19 From *al-Hilāl* 20 (June 1912) pp. 530-536. Translated by Kamran Rastegar.

> that the donkey-seller gave him a beast, but as he sold the donkey he began to curse the rider, thinking that he did not know Arabic. On the street, a passerby heard him and went to the Englishman and stopped him, asking, 'Do you understand Arabic?' 'Absolutely not,' he said, 'The donkey-seller was cursing you and laughing at you.' 'And can his cursing prevent me from reaching *al-'Abbasiyya*?' 'No.' 'So let him curse as he likes, as I only want to go to *al-'Abbasiyya*.' So, in addition to being amusing, this story is an example how the English focus on the substance of a matter...Perhaps Eastern peoples are most inclined ... to focus on trivialities and extraneous matters ignoring what is important.

In the third article entitled "Honesty in Speech as a Form of Superior Conduct"[20] Zaidan elaborates on the traits marking superior character asserting that the most important of these are honesty in speech and courage in expression. He contrasts the tendency in the East to tailor one's opinions to what the listener would like to hear out of exaggerated "politeness" with the practice in the West to voice opinions honestly even if these displease the questioner. He elaborates:

> In the East, courteousness expressed among ourselves exceeds politeness and becomes obsequiousness, which only attracts problems, and is an evil gnawing at the body of civilization. For it misleads people and makes interactions difficult—for no person will depend upon advice or place confidence in opinions offered.
>
> The error of 'courteousness' extends to what is expressed to journalists and intellectuals by way of criticism or praise for their publications or articles, for most fear that criticizing them will lead to anger. So the first thing a writer who

20 From *al-Hilāl* 20 (April 1912) pp. 414-419. Translated by Kamran Ratsegar.

> reviews a book or an article or a poem does is to praise it, and to flatter the author—this is exaltation. And this is done in the name of 'offering encouragement'. This is a noble aim but if criticism is offered to improve style and to raise standards, it contributes to intellect and is of the greatest use to writing and reading. If the author is new to writing and only hears praise and flattery, he will be duped and become conceited. It is a grave error if a person only is allowed to hear praise and flattery for his works and his views, for nothing of human endeavor may truly approach perfection.
>
> ..If you were to hear what your friends say about you in your absence, it would change your view of your standing, and would change their standing in your view. Your conceit would end. And the happiest person is he who knows that what his companions say about him in his absence is the same as what they say to him when he is there, for he benefits from their criticism. And the point of what one reports to him about his standing relative to the ideal of perfection, is that he should see himself as others see him.

Regarding honesty in interactions, Zaidan continues in the same article:

> A person...should not make a contract or promise to do something unless he is certain that he will be able to do so. This is rare among us, for we may observe that a feature of courteousness is that one does not reply to a request made other than by wanting to please, and if we are unable to do what has been requested of us, we still feel we should reply to the request positively. But when an intelligent European is asked to do something, if he is unable to do so—or if he does not want to—he will say to you that he cannot, or he does not want to do that. And perhaps his response will seem rude or brusque, but it is better than the Eastern responses of 'command me'

> and 'I would sacrifice my eye' and 'by my head', which are often said even when there is no intention of carrying out the request. Also related to this is the matter of appointments. A person may promise to meet you at a particular hour in such-and-such a place, without any intention to fulfill the promise. Is this not a form of cheating and deception?

In analyzing the success of famous people, Zaidan elaborates on the importance of integrity in word and deed in the case of Salim Sednaoui,[21] the founder and owner of one of the biggest department stores in Cairo, as follows:

> It is a widespread delusion that 'wealth cannot be acquired honestly', that 'trustworthy, honest men are poor during their lifetime and die destitute', and that 'only dishonest, hypocritical tricksters get rich'. But this is the excuse of those who fail in their undertakings despite their desire to work, their vigilance and their uprightness. They attribute their failure to their honesty and good intentions, whereas it is due to their lacking some of the prerequisites for success, such as intelligence, knowledge, perseverance and the like. For honesty alone is not enough even if it is accompanied by efforts and vigilance.

C. Hard Work and Time Consciousness

Zaidan's phenomenal output was nothing less than astounding. He edited and wrote in *al-Hilal* for almost twenty two years (1892-1914) and at the same time wrote a large number of books,[22] articles and correspondence. In particular:

---

21 "Salīm Ṣīdnāwī." First published in *al-Hilāl* 16 (May 1908) pp. 471-478; then published in *Tarājim Mashāhīr al-Sharq.* op.cit. vol 1, pp. 302-309 and reprinted in *Bunāt al-Nahḍa al-'Arabiyya.* op.cit. Sednaoui so spelt his name in French and English. Translated by Hilary Kilpatrick.

22 See the complete list in the Bibliography at the end of this volume.

- The History of Islamic Civilization in five volumes,
- The History of the Arabs before Islam as well as five other books on history, mostly national (Greek, Roman, Egyptian, Ottoman, etc.).
- The History of Arab Literature and Culture in four volumes
- Two books on the history and philosophy of the Arabic language.
- Twenty two novels, all but one historical.
- An autobiography plus other works on a variety of subjects.
- An intensive correspondence with many scholars and friends.

He did all this in the span of some twenty two years. As Bishara Takla the founder of the newspaper *al-Ahram* wrote in his newspaper: "Truly if the age of authors were measured by their output, we would have thought that the owner of *al-Hilal* died at the age of one hundred whereas he left us at barely the age of fifty."

All this he did virtually by himself. Sometime during the year 1891 Zaidan came out with his first historical novel, *The Fugitive Mamluk*, which met with so much success that he felt encouraged to quit his job as a teacher. From that time on he remained an independent writer, working as a journalist, novelist, linguist and historian, but always on his own. Ahmed Hafez Awad elaborates:

> I do not believe anyone in the Arab world in the last century has produced a quantity of serious literary and scientific work comparable to that produced by the founder of *al-Hilal.* His novels, the volumes of *al-Hilal*, his books on history, language, and literary works represent in their totality a huge output. And if we, as his contemporaries did not know with certainty that our departed friend and colleague wrote with his own pen all these works, organized their structure, thought of their subject-

> matter, and supervised himself the way they were edited and published—all alone without the ability to call on hired writers, or rely on contributions from literary figures—had we not known with certainty all of this, then we would have had very serious doubts that he was able to accomplish all this by himself. Because the quantity of his work is so monumental as to defy being the product of just one individual.[23]

How was he able to accomplish all this? Zaidan learnt from his youngest age to put in long hours of work as he would study late into the night after helping his father to manage his restaurant from sunrise to sundown. Throughout his life he retained this habit of starting his working day very early at dawn. He learnt to organize his time effectively by putting a high premium on punctuality and "not delaying until to-morrow anything that could be done today as it might never get done".[24] As a researcher he developed effective methods of building his knowledge as an inspection of his "working books", now preserved at the American University of Beirut Library, clearly shows. These books were divided into very neat and clearly handwritten "chapters" each one covering a specific theme or subject matter with the information that different sources provided on that particular topic. This way he could quickly find in one place all the information needed to cover that topic.[25]

Finally, and most importantly, Zaidan was most efficient in the use of his time not wasting a single minute—literally—by what we would call today "multi-tasking". He described in his autobiography how he learnt this quality from his teacher:

23 Reprinted in *Al-Hilāl Al-Kitāb al-Dhahabī 1892-1942* (1942).

24 These last two features were comments that his eldest son Emile made and lived by, frequently quoting his father.

25 One of Albert Hourani's students at Oxford once described how he would teach his students to do research in exactly that same way. Zaidan must have taught himself a similar approach.

> I learned from him to be conscientious about time, *muhafaza 'ala 'l-waqt*....his economizing attitude towards time amazed me. We would study some lesson, and if he left me to do some experimental work by myself, which would take two minutes, he used to turn to a book which he was in the process of translating and would occupy himself with it. He would translate two lines, or three, or a page, rather than sit idly while I was finishing my work. I acquired this virtue from him and it was of great use to me.[26]

In summary, Zaidan mastered all the elements of time management and credits this quality as a major cause for his success. As he said in his autobiography: "At the root of my success were my consciousness of time and perseverance."[27]

D. Entrepreneurship

Well before business studies became an academic discipline or business schools came into being on the European continent, Zaidan wrote that the most important quality for success was management or entrepreneurship in all its forms, especially marketing. He argued in one article that a "practical problem-solving ability" is the highest form of the mind's attributes;[28] and in a second he analyzed how this applies to the successful writer or journalist.[29]

---

26 Philipp. *Zaidān,* p.168.

27 Philipp. *Zaidān*, p.169.

28 "Ṭabaqāt al-'Uqūl: al-Tadbīr Sayyid al-Qūwa al-'Āqila," *al-Hilāl* 22 (Dec.1913) pp. 189-197. Translated by the author of this paper as "Levels of Mental Capability: Management is The Master of the Mind's Attributes."

29 A third article entitled "Social Sense" makes many of the same points arguing that social or common sense (emotional intelligence in today's parlance) more than knowledge explains success in all walks of life including the success of writers. See "Al-Ḥāssa al-ijtimā'iyya," *al-Hilāl* 21 (April 1913) pp. 404-49. Translated by Kamran Rastegar.

In the first article "Levels of Mental Capability: Management is the Master of the Mind's Attributes"[30] Zaidan argues that worldly success is much more the result of management in all its forms rather than knowledge of facts or abstract intelligence. It is the practical problem-solving abilities to variously plan, design, devise, and contrive "to disentangle and find a way out of difficulties"—the French call a man that has these abilities a "*debrouillard*"—that are at the root of success in life. He described the specific traits needed for success in the case of personal-familial affairs, for professionals, traders, generals and politicians. What is of interest to us here is how he applied these principles to the craft of the writer. On this he says:

> The profession of writers is the scientific profession that requires the greatest management skills because it deals with the feelings of people and touches their literary needs and social beliefs. ...The Arab writer, whether journalist or an author of works for the general public, cannot benefit his readers and profit from his profession without having good marketing skills. It is not sufficient for him to master his subject matter—his writings need to generate a basic trust from his readers. He must therefore know the needs of his readers and their values and present his thoughts in a way that appeals to and benefits them… When two writers are equal in their knowledge of their subjects then the one who prevails is the one who has the superior marketing skills. This includes the selection of the subject matter, the prose that is used and the content of his work.

(i) Subject Matter. In a second article Zaidan applied these principles to his successful career as both a writer and a journalist. Commenting on the success or failure of newspapers, he says:[31]

---

30 See footnote 28.

31 Zaydān. "Ṭabaqāt al-'Uqūl," p. 189.

> The press offers the easiest way to discover readers' likes and writers' choices. In this country hundreds of newspapers and journals have sprung up, but only a few of them have survived. Most of them have closed down with their owners complaining about the decline of the East and attacking the readers for, according to them, not appreciating writers at their true value. If they reflected a little, they would blame no one but themselves, because if readers felt satisfied with what they wrote they would read their articles attentively and enthusiastically... Dozens of patriotic political newspapers have been founded in Egypt but only a few survive because they print what readers need to know or else voice their feelings and are in tune with their desires.
>
> A journal's lack of success, however, is not always a sign of its contributors' incompetence. Some of our newspapers are very well written—yet they have few readers, because circulation does not only depend on an excellent style but it demands a choice of subjects which readers need or enjoy reading about. The same is true of all the printed books in circulation with their various subjects; they are only successful to the extent that their readers derive enjoyment or benefit from the subjects they cover.

The prime example of the latter was Zaidan's use of historical novels. The subject matter appealed to readers all over the Arab world and Zaidan serialized them in *al-Hilal* in a way that would entice readers to buy the next issue. On this he comments:[32]

> Among the most important works of history are historical novels. At first glance, they may seem to be the lowest form of historical works because of the entertaining elements they

32 "Kuttāb al-'Arabiyya wa Qurrā'uha," *al-Hilāl* 5 (March 1897) pp. 489-499. Translated by Hilary Kilpatrick as "The Writers and Readers of Arabic."

> contain. But assuming they conform to the conditions of the genre, they are superior to other historical works and more useful than them, because while they too investigate history, they present historical facts in a more attractive manner. They express them in a pleasant style that encourages reading, so that the reader learns about historical facts while he thinks he is reading an entertaining story. This is a course European writers have followed before us, and they have produced many such books.

(ii) Style. Zaidan maintained that authors should write in the *al-sahl al-mumtan'i* style—that is a style that is "simple but difficult (to replicate)". He criticized those that used flowery words or expressed thoughts in a complicated way to impress their readers:[33]

> As for general literary and historical topics, and other topics of that sort, the writer is required to avoid anything that may impede understanding on the part of either the specialist or the common reader. His expression should be simple, clear, fluent, and free of any complication, so that the meanings may be entirely transparent to the reader, who should not need to stop for a moment or consult dictionaries in order to understand them. If the writer fails to do that, it may be counted a deficiency in the practice of his craft.

(iii) Objectivity. Last but not least, Zaidan strongly believed that "writers should display truth and frankness without inclining to any affiliation or party". Gaining the trust of his readers by always sticking to issues and never attacking persons or questioning intentions was a key ingredient of his success. It is easy today especially in the West to take these principles for granted. But in the East it was not common then or even now, since strong emotions often determine the positions that are taken,

33 From *Al-Alfāẓ al-'Arabiyya wa'l-Falsafa al-Lughawiyya.* (*The Philosophy of Language and the Arabic Vocabulary*) first published in Beirut, Maṭba'at al-Qidīs Jāwrjiyūs in 1886 (Cairo, Maṭba'at al-Hilāl, 1904).

and the messenger is often confused with the message. While he took principled positions, they were always argued on the merits of the case giving equal time (space) on the pages of his newspaper to opposing points of view. His sons adhered closely to all these principles as they built up Dar al-Hilal into what it became today.

E. Modesty, Shyness and Moral Courage

Modesty was a hallmark of Zaidan's personality.[34] He was acutely aware of his own limitations and this made him highly accepting of criticism.[35] In an article entitled "The History of the Arabs before Islam: Its Difficulty and Complexity" he outlines in great detail the difficulties and therefore limitations of writing a history about the Arabs before Islam.[36] This is but one example of his modesty and awareness of the limitations of historical findings. It made him welcome criticism as a means of self improvement and a means for the progress of knowledge as we saw above. He was also reserved and shy by nature, shunning the limelight. But he had a great deal of self-confidence so that neither his modesty nor his shyness prevented him from promoting views that could be highly controversial, showing his enormous moral courage.

Thomas Philipp provides a good description of Zaidan's retiring personality combined with his strong character and moral courage when he found himself in the middle of the disturbances that afflicted the Syrian Protestant College. Zaidan joined a strike when one of his professors

34 This was a characteristic of his personality that his youngest son, Shukri, repeatedly emphasized to me.

35 The title of one of Zaidan's articles on this subject says it all: "Admitting to Error is Right and Accepting One's Limitations is Strength," (Al-'Itirāf bi'l-Khaṭa' Ṣawāb wa'l-iqrār bi'l-'Ajz Qūwwa) *al-Hilāl* 16 (Jan. 1908) pp.108-114. Translated by Kamran Rastegar.

36 "Tārīkh al-'Arab qabla 'l-Islām," *al-Hilāl* 3 (March 1895) pp.534-541. Excerpts translated by Paul Starkey.

was dismissed for teaching the theories of Darwin. Thomas Philipp comments on this episode:[37]

> In the first meeting of the protesting students he was made chairman of the meeting. However, Zaidan hastened to explain this was only for one meeting and the only reason he was chosen was that he was on friendly terms with all students, thanks to his conciliatory nature. This was certainly partially true, but it implies somewhat of an understatement of his own role. He was strongly enough involved as to emerge as one of two students of his class that never gave in to the demands of the faculty and left the Syrian Protestant College for good...After the strike at the Syrian Protestant College had come to its unfortunate conclusion, Zaidan refused to accept the conditions the College had set up for the re-entry of the striking students and preferred to look elsewhere for an opportunity to continue his studies.

Regarding his shyness and non-confrontational nature Zaidan writes in his autobiography: "I like to avoid the cause of enmity—from my childhood I noticed this natural disposition in me—therefore, I would avoid anything that would infuriate the teacher or would cause him to rebuke me or beat me." He never became a political activist, refusing to publish a daily newspaper partly because of this nature; partly because of his belief that writers should "display truth and frankness without inclining towards any affiliation or party"; and also because of the sensitivity of his position as a Christian of Syrian origin. This was a position his sons never deviated from even as they built *Dar-al-Hilal* into one of the biggest publishing houses for periodicals in the Middle East with the launching of seven new weekly magazines[38] in addition to *al-Hilal*.

37 Philipp. *Zaidān,* pp. 210 - 21.

38 An illustrated magazine (*Al-Muṣawwar*), a magazine appealing to the young (*Al-Ithnayn wa'l-Dunyā*), a magazine for women (*Hawa'*), for the movies (*al-Kawākib*), two magazines for children (*Micky* and *Samīr*) and a French weekly (*Images*).

As noted, modesty and shyness masked an inner strength born from self-confidence that explains the great moral and intellectual courage Zaidan showed in his writings. The two most telling examples of this are his views on the evolution of the Arabic language and the richness of the pre-Islamic history of the Arabs. Arguing that the Arabic language was a "living being" that needed to evolve and modernize, once again by analogy with the theory of evolution, he clearly questioned the premise of religious scholars that the Koran represented an ideal static model for that language. And contrary to the then-prevailing view by Muslim historians, his book on *The History of the Arabs Before Islam*[39] gave the Arabs a history and civilization that predated the birth of Islam. Thomas Philipp makes this point well:

> Muslim historians had talked about the Arabs immediately preceding the appearance of the Prophet. Emphasizing the negative aspects of that period made the impact of the revelation much more pronounced. Zaidan took an opposing stance. He expanded the history of the *jahiliyya* by more than two thousand years, and included ancient high civilizations in the history of the Arabs before Islam. With one stroke he had established a glorious history of the Arab nation long before the rise of Islam, the impact of which he was keenly aware of. By distinguishing between the history of the Arabs and Islamic history, he not only interpreted the former in a secular, cultural fashion, he also separated it from the fate of Islamic civilization...[40]

39 *Al-'Arab qabla 'l-Islām* (Cairo, Maṭba'at al-Hilāl, 1907).

40 Philipp. *Jurji Zaidan and the Foundation.* op.cit.The book also provides details of the criticisms leveled at Zaidan and his works.

Throughout his life Zaidan was attacked for these revolutionary views—sometimes rationally in measured tones but also viciously by religious dogmatists, as much because of who he was as because of what he said.

Conclusions

Zaidan was born into the lower classes of Beirut and adopted the values and norms of a new westernized class that emulated the values of the Victorian middle classes. He believed self-realization and personal growth were the responsibility of the individual and that character—will-power, integrity and rectitude—was more important than knowledge, education or heritage for worldly success. His life's work can be read as giving the Arabs a sense of community through their shared history and a unique language. By providing them with knowledge and education, he would help them, especially the middle classes, replicate his own personal trajectory of growth and development. He credited his success above all to hard work, time consciousness and perseverance. Entrepreneurship and management, especially marketing, were the most important attributes for success—for writers this meant the ability to select interesting subjects and write objectively in a simple style. His honesty in word and deed won him the following and trust of a wide readership as well as the trust of many friends. Modesty only added to the esteem in which he was held. Finally his shyness masked an inner strength of character that gave him great self-confidence and moral courage. But his non-confrontational nature; his belief that writers should be as objective as possible and "display truth and frankness without inclining towards any affiliation or party"; and his Christian-Syrian heritage all kept him in the realm of cultural activists and away from political activism.

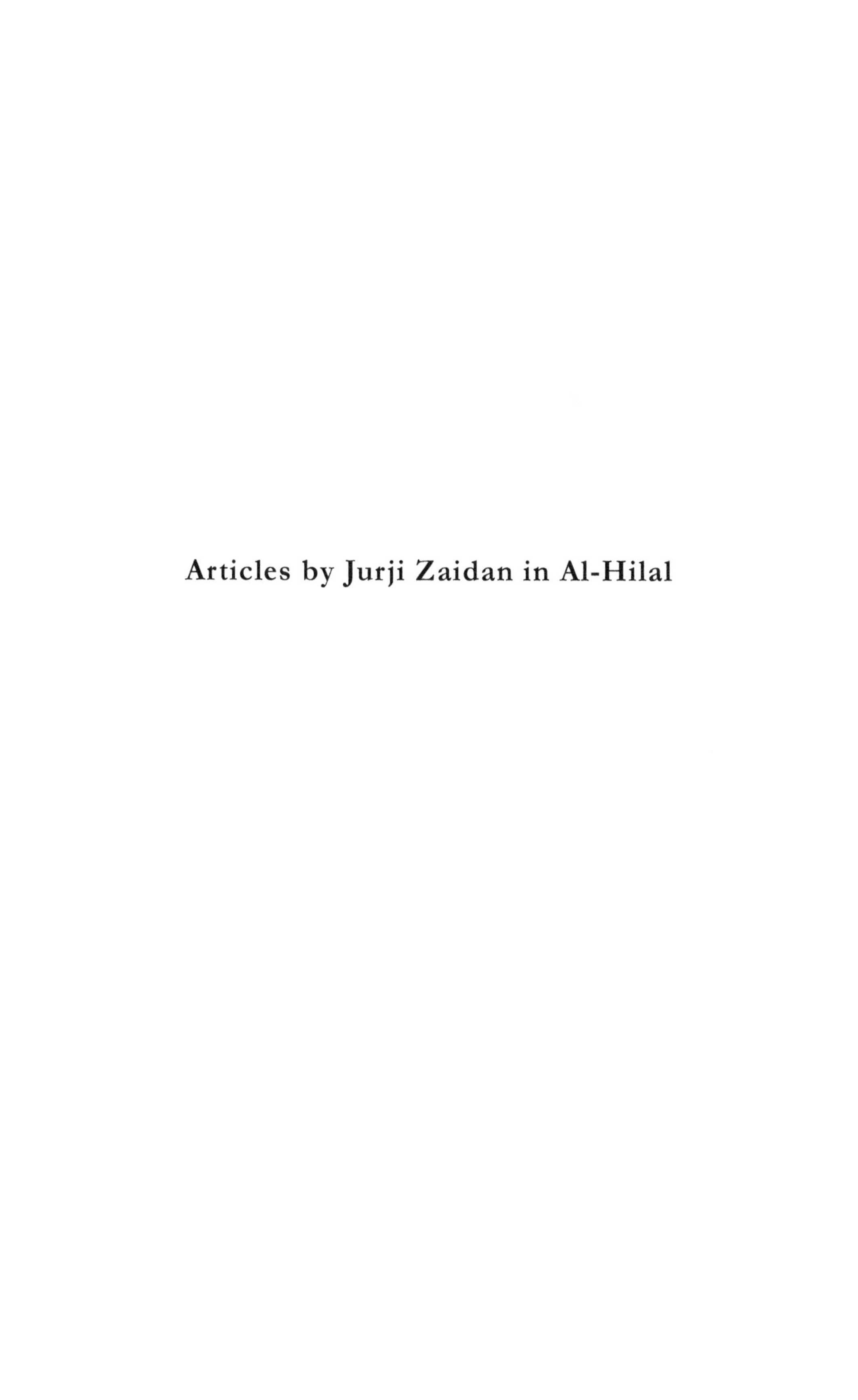

Articles by Jurji Zaidan in Al-Hilal

Reality and Illusions
or
The Essence of Things and Appearances[1]

What we mean by "realities" are matters corroborated by the senses and the rational mind. And these are constituted by natural, social, political, and religious realities, etc. As for "illusions," by these we mean matters whose outward appearance is evident but have no real significance or truth, and which result from imagination, such as superstitions and certain political and social traditions or rituals and beliefs that surround the real essence of things.

Realities have different forms: among these are those things that are certain as a result of the proof of the senses, such as natural laws or mathematical issues, as well as those things that are arrived at by rational judgment based upon experimentation and repeated practice, as with the majority of literary, historical and social realities. For it is said that "materials expand in heat, and contract in cold, and water is composed of hydrogen and oxygen, and that the angles of a triangle equal 180 degrees" are indisputable realities. And it is said that, "the human being is an animal that can talk, or that such-and-such an event occurred in such-and-such a year, or that education strengthens the mind" are social or political realities. And we will limit our discussion to these.

There are varieties of illusions, including those contradicted by knowledge, or which are in opposition to rational judgment, such as belief in demons or speaking to ghosts or other similar superstitions and quackery. There are also those that are peripheral to social and political

---

1 "Al-Ḥaqā'iq wa'l-Awhām: al-Jawāhir wa'l-A'rāḍ," *al-Hilāl* 20 (June 1912) pp. 530-536. Translated by Kamran Rastegar. "Illusions" in this article refers to auxiliary or incidental matters that detract from and dilute the focus on the essence of things. *Translator's Note.*

realities—conventions which in themselves do not reflect realities, such as excessive courteousness, appearances, verbal exaggeration or traditional customs at celebrations and the like. So if a man marries a woman, the reality of this marriage is based on the unification of their hearts in love and the proving of this through a vow based on the Koran. However the illusions that surround this verity are those things that occur alongside the vow which are traditions such as hanging certain decorations and lighting candles and the playing of drums, the consumption of drinks and foods and other matters that require the spending of money in this pursuit.

Likewise, worship is based upon a belief in the existence of God and acting in accordance with his commandments and his wishes; and worship has no meaning without these realities. However, the illusions that permeate it are many, such as what occurs at religious festivals and celebrations.

If a governor were to be appointed to a district, the reality of this act would arise from the Sultan's order announcing his appointment which is announced to a group which acts as a witness to the legitimacy of this appointment. However what surrounds this event, including the wearing of formal or ceremonial robes, the arraying of soldiers with arms or flags, or decorations and the like, are all part of the subsidiary matters that do not affect the validity of the appointment. And even the order itself may contain both its essence and peripheral matters. The essence of the matter would be phrases such as "We appoint so-and-so to this post under such-and-such conditions". But the order can also include phrases of praise and flattery which add no extra meaning to it.

The Origin of Customs

Intellect, if left alone, accepts nothing but manifest truth. However in a primitive state, the human being has an inclination toward fantasy because it gives him pleasure to entertain himself with the wonders that his imagination conjures—this is the reason for the prevalence of illusions in society, although such illusions do not affect the essence of things. Because nature knows nothing and accepts nothing but reality. However social, political and religious matters are tied to human perceptions, feelings and emotions. This opens the door to illusions, which are inherited and grow in the succession of new generations, expanding to the extent that they become rules or common habits that are followed—this itself is the basis for communal traditions and the root of social conventions.

Some of these traditions or conventions, even if they appear to us as illusions, are based on truths from which they originally arose. As we have said, the basis of the appointment of a governor to a district is the declaration of the order certifying this. It was the custom of the Arabs in the early period of their rule that the caliph, when appointing someone as a governor, would do so verbally, or in a short written missive with no honorifics and epithets. If the emir would send a written command to one of his subjects, they would respond in acquiescence, without overstatements. Rarely were they reminded of the conditions for their appointment. But as the bases for succession to high office became increasingly tenuous over time, and as nefarious individuals sought, justly or unjustly, to be appointed as governors to principalities, (and, if successful, they would rule as tyrants even if this was at odds with the wishes of the caliph) it became necessary to note the conditions of their appointment if only to set limits for their governance. With the expansion of urban culture, and the corruption of ethical standards, the granting of governorships and the recognition of their authority began to include a military presence in ceremonies that was embellished with military displays. Perhaps this was originally a rare occurrence, but eventually it came to be customary. So the focus shifted from that of the granting of a governorate and the recognition of a governor to that of the fanfare which accompanied the formations of the soldiers, their dress, their banners and their medals. With the change in emphasis the heart of matter itself changed, and the illusion was created that these ceremonies by themselves constituted the appointment.

Under the same heading fall other aspects of government fanfare, such as the departure of the sultan or emir from an encampment with military escort and flags, or the military formations at the gates of king's palaces, or official protocol in greeting dignitaries as well as celebrations of feasts, alliances, prayers, and the like. This was also the case with marriage ceremonies, funerals, celebrations of birth, and so on. For each tradition has a true origin, which has a specific intention and purpose; the purpose is then lost, and all that is left is the tradition itself.

Choose any human activity, and you will find that it is never free from illusions—be it story-telling, food, drink, marriage, government, politics, or other matters. Each activity has an essence surrounded by subsidiary matters. These are customs that are handed down through the generations. If you studied them, you would find they contain a penny of truth for a pound of illusion.

Degrees of Illusions Between Nations

Peoples differ in their inclinations toward reality or illusion, and we may observe these differences manifestly between nations. Some nations have a higher interest in reality than they do in illusions. For others it is the opposite. The English, as an example, are among the nations that are most inclined towards reality. In work, they make their main concern the adherence to reality and the disabuse of illusion. An example of this that is well known these days is the amusing story about the English soldier who purchased a donkey in the center of Cairo to ride to al-'Abbasiyya. It happened that the donkey-seller gave him a beast, but as he sold the donkey he began to curse the rider, without fear of arousing his anger because he thought he did not understand Arabic. On the street, a passerby heard him and went to the Englishman and stopped him, asking, "Do you understand Arabic?"

"Absolutely not," he said,

"The donkey-seller was cursing you and laughing at you."

"And can his cursing prevent me from reaching al-'Abbasiyya?"

"No."

"So let him curse as he likes, as I only want to go to al-'Abbasiyya."

So, in addition to being amusing, this story is an example of the English focus on the essence of things.

There are nations that tend toward illusion and turn away from reality. Perhaps Eastern peoples are most inclined to this, meaning they focus on trivialities and ignore what is important.

Differences in Tendencies Towards Illusions within a Single Nation

The tendency towards reality or illusion within a single nation depends on its urban composition, and the degree of its civilization. For the Bedouin is closer to the truth than the urban citizen, for urbanism increases the inclination towards illusion just as it broadens civility and increases prosperity. The greatest evidence of this is the transformation of the Arabs and the changes in their customs and their writings. When they were Bedouins, and at the beginning of the Islamic civilization, they limited what they said or wrote to the bare truth, even when addressing their kings and emirs, avoiding exaggerations or honorifics. They would address the caliph by his name, or his title, and then would outline their intentions in terms devoid of flourish and overstatement.

The statements of caliphs and emirs in their own writings and speeches were similar. For not a single word could be eliminated from what they would utter that would not change the meaning of their statements. But then as their civilization developed, their phrases became embellished, extended, prefaced and appended with terms of respect and epithets of veneration which added nothing to the original purpose of the address. These extraneous phrases and epithets at times outnumbered the essential phrases necessary for expressing the purpose of the statement. So much so that these extraneous phrases became at times the purpose of the statement: speaking with a specific purpose came to be replaced by meaningless speech. The general inclination towards honorifics increased as the nation became afflicted with misery and oppression.

Illusions in Speech

The fashion of hollow epithets and repetitious titles common among Arabs in their writing has reached a degree today, in our Nahda, that is beyond rational comprehension. Perhaps these were originally most frequently and widely used among the Persians, for we find sycophantic works from the age of [pre-Islamic] despotism. But then at the outset of Islam, the caliph, when writing to a functionary, would be satisfied with saying, "From so-and-so, servant of God, ruler of the faithful, to so-and-so in Egypt..." and he would go directly to the subject-matter of his letter. But by the time of the Ottoman Sultan of Sultans, letters would be prefaced with a long introduction, recounting his celebrated predecessors, before coming to the heart of the matter, as can be seen in the letter from Sultan Sulayman the Magnificent in his letter to the King of France:

> By the blessings of God who manifests His power and who will remain glorious until eternity, exalting His divine words. And by the blessings of the sun of the skies of prophets, and the star of the tower of guardians, the leader of the army of the pious, Mohammad the pure, may God's peace be upon him. And by the eloquence of the spirit of his four companions, the pure, Abu Bakr and 'Umar and 'Uthman and 'Ali, God's peace be upon them, Shah Sultan Sulayman Khan ibn Sultan Salim Khan al-Ghazi.
>
> I, the Sultan of Sultans, King of Kings, grantor of wreaths to Kings of the world, shadow of God upon the earth, Shah and Sultan of the White and Black Seas, and the lands of Rumeli,

> and Anatolia and Qurmani and Erzerum, and Diyar Bakir, and Kurdistan, and Azerbaijan, and Persia, and Damascus, and Aleppo, and Egypt and Mecca and Medina and Jerusalem the Noble, and the Arab lands, and Yemen, and the various lands that our glorious ancestors, our noble predecessors, opened by the force of victory. As well as the many lands that I, in my royal greatness, conquered with my shining sword. I, the son of Sultan Salim son of Sultan Bayazid Shah, Sultan Sulayman Khan, write to you, O Francis, King of France, who is...

and so on and so forth.

Where once appointees to service were addressed simply, so that the caliph would address his emir by name—"So-and-so whom I appointed as my representative..."—eventually they were addressed with repetitive honorifics, "my vizir Samir al-Ma'ali the director of my subjects' matters, endowed with penetrative intellect and wise judgment..." etc.

As examples of the tendency towards illusion and away from reality in political matters, we find that some countries were content to exercise sovereignty by name rather than by action, which was naturally only carried out by force. The leaders of this civilization invented political phrases to describe this form of sovereignty: "suzeraineté" and "souveraineté".[2]

So with other social matters—during the early period of a government they are closer to reality, while later they begin to tend towards illusion as the government begins to mature. This rule among social rules is reliable in ranking nations as they progress towards urbanization. For any nation where illusion is on the increase, or where one may observe a greater attention to the exterior appearance of matters rather

---

2 In French in the Arabic text. In French the first refers to a partial sovereignty—typically without control over foreign affairs, the second implies complete dominion over a people and /or a state.

than their essence, is undergoing a period of decline. If one observes that the focus on the essence of matters is on the increase and illusions are shunned, one can surmise that they are undergoing a rebirth. This is what compelled me to begin this essay by calling for the renouncement of epithets of honor in statements and speeches, as is practiced by Europeans since they awoke from their slumber and set out upon their modern civilization.

The Consequences of Moving Toward Illusions

The reasons for moving from reality towards illusion is linked to human development and the human inclination towards imagination and what makes up illusions. For reality is the essence in every situation in society, but then illusions increase slowly, until they take the place of truth. This is seen in religions, which are in essence simple and based upon true matters, but then slowly illusions increase, along with the greed of leaders, who exploit the situation when they see that the people themselves are leaning towards illusion and are clinging to the coattails of falsity. We hardly find a religion among the major world religions which is not based in its essence upon the worship of a single God. Even pagan religions such as those in Egypt, Phoenicia, Assyria and others were in essence monotheistic. But then speciousness infiltrates and changes them such that they became idol-worshipping, taken over by rituals and overrun with superstitions that no rational mind can accept.

The essence of the Christian religion is the specific teachings that go back to love and tolerance. But then its adherents began to borrow from pagan rituals which were common earlier, and expanded them. Within a few generations, the most important principles of Christianity were forgotten, and rituals, beliefs and appearances took over, leaving nothing of the original religion. But then Luther called for a return to the gospels and the rejection of extraneous beliefs and the protestant religion was born. Barely was this religion established, before extraneous beliefs infiltrated it again, corrupting some of its truths.

Similarly, when Islam appeared, its basis was monotheism in a simple and sincere form. Within a few generations extraneous elements with no bearing on Islam emerged and became part of it. Reformers then appeared seeking its return to a purer form.

Indications of the Rebirth of Nations

Every reform movement is based upon a return to reality and divestiture from the speciousness of common illusions that obscure its essence. This applies to religions, customs and political dealings, the developments of language and all forms of speeches and transactions. For if you observe a nation avoiding the pervasion of illusion in its affairs, eradicating it or criticizing it in favor of holding on to reality, then you know that that nation is in a period of progress. If you observe it wedded to tradition uncritically and unbendingly, then you may know it is still in need of guidance.

Honesty in Speech as a Form of Superior Conduct[1]

The Socio-political Awakening

In Egypt today a socio-political awakening follows the example of its peers in civilized nations in demanding a constitution and respect for the dignity of the nation in the actions of the government. This is measured in different ways: some attempt to gain this through demands and protests, and others believe that accumulating resources and developing agriculture will insure them of success, while still others see no alternative to using the path of knowledge. The latter of these views is the closest to being the correct one. However, the researcher on the laws of society and the principles of progress will not find in knowledge enough to achieve this end, if it is not coupled with education. Or at least education is the introduction to knowledge. By which we mean education in good conduct; because whatever is improved in terms of the resources of the nation or its knowledge, is without benefit in its calls for a constitution or other aspects of political progress, if it lacks in education or high principles.

There are many components of good behavior, including honesty in interactions, and acting with good intentions, and independence in thinking, and comprehending what is necessary, and restraining the self in worldly matters and refining it with superior conduct. In our opinion, the most important of these is honesty in speech and courage in expression.

---

1 "Al-Ṣarāḥa fī'l Qawl 'Anwān al-Akhlāq al-rāqiyya: al-Nahḍa al-ijtimā'iyya wa'l-siyāsiyya," *al-Hilāl* 20 (April 1912) 414-419. Translated by Kamran Rastegar. The title of this article could be translated either as "Honesty in Speech is a Form of Refined Manners" or "Honesty in Speech is a Form of Superior Conduct." The former may be a more literal translation but the latter better reflects the sense of the article which deals with behaving with integrity and rectitude.

We will discuss the qualities of "honesty in speech" which is a form of courage in expression, which we have already spoken about in the fourth issue of *al-Hilal* earlier in the year.[2] We have chosen to write this article about this particular form of honesty because we find we have the greatest need for this, when we see how burdened we are, generation after generation, by political shackles which humiliate us and weaken our morals. So we have become submissive and compliant, and we wrap this up into the idea of "courtesy" which we enumerate as one of the qualities of Eastern manners. But what is this other than window-dressing for obsequiousness and equivocation? If one of us is asked his thoughts on a particular matter, one would notice that his response would be influenced by the sentiments of the questioner—irrespective of whether it is correct or not. If his view was contrary to that of the questioner, so as to satisfy him, he would pretend to agree with him even if he thought otherwise.

When courtesy is in accordance with honesty in speech, then it is for a good end, but if it surpasses this, it ends with obsequiousness and hypocrisy. Obsequiousness is not a natural and innate quality, as humans speak the truth and are honest by their nature, and if questioned on a matter would respond with the first idea to cross their minds. If one were to note a deviation from the correct path in any matter, he would feel compelled on his own to make clear his beliefs—this is how Bedouin people act, with independence of mind, with no resemblance to the unjust city and its corruptions. In the history of Islam we may observe many examples of the courage of Arabs in their governance, where they would criticize the caliphs and emirs frankly, and without fear of revenge. But this pride dissipated with increasing oppression, especially in the medieval Islamic generations and particularly in Egypt during the Mamluk period. So by the advent of the nineteenth century the populace was driven like cattle, lacking any will or freedom or opinion of its own. Naturally, honesty in speech became rare.

2 "Al-Shajā'a fī'l-Ḥarb wa'l-Jarā'a fī'l-Ra'ī: Tamhīd fī'l-Shajā'a 'ala 'l-Ijmāl," *al-Hilāl* 20 (Jan. 1912) pp. 209-225.

When we consider modern civilizations and begin to enjoy the taste of freedom, and when we see what the modern world offers in terms of a refined education under a constitutional government, and when we see how in these circumstances the public has a voice, and how the doors to a good education are opened to all who work and persevere—when we see this, we are challenged by modern nations to follow in their footsteps in the development of civilization and society, just as they challenge our governments with their constitutional laws. We comprehend many of the reasons for their development, such as science, journalism, printing, economics, etc. We pretend to have reached the heights of civilization—and this is accurate in many ways, but not for "honesty in speech", because we are still lacking in this regard. And this itself has two sides: the first is honesty in opinion and advice, and the second is honesty in transactions.

1. Honesty in opinion and advice

If you were to ask an intelligent European or American his opinion on a particular matter, he would not shirk from disclosing honestly what occurs to him, and what he says may either please you or displease you. This is freedom in speech, and it would not be wrong to say that it is one of the highest benefits of a good education. Should you pose this same question to an Easterner, you would learn some of his beliefs on the subject, but he would refrain from speaking honestly to you about his opinion and he would offer a polite answer honed with excuses to avoid stoking your anger, which he would consider to be a form of good manners. There is nothing wrong with courtesy if that is all it is—if it contributes to the politeness of the interaction, then it is better than free and open rudeness.

But courteousness as we see it expressed among ourselves [i.e. in the East] exceeds politeness and becomes obsequiousness, which only creates problems, and is an evil gnawing at the body of civilization. For it misleads people and makes interactions difficult—for no person will depend upon the advice or trust the opinions offered. This leads to conceit, especially in recent times and in relations between people, as some are duped by praise that is offered for their work. But they are not to blame, since they have not been given honest feedback and all they have ever heard is only flattery and effusive praise.

When we see a friend or a neighbor acting in error, we dare to speak honestly to him about his mistake or guide him towards correcting his actions. But if this same friend were to ask us for guidance or advice, then the first thing we would think of would be to agree with what we think is his opinion, or to approve his actions. This would be considered a form of 'politeness' or courtesy, even if we hold a contrary opinion to his. We do not wish to do our friend harm, or to trick him, but we fear his anger or his ending our friendship; so we agree with him in the name of courtesy or kindness.

This error may be committed by a large part of the public, by ignorance or sentimentality or prejudice, out of a fear of having a negative backlash or adverse consequences. But if the public's leaders or its intellectuals acted as a channel through which frank thoughts were expressed to the public, and advice given, outlining the public's errors within the pages of magazines or from pulpits and podiums, it would serve to correct the public's errors or to guard against dangers. But do our authors or leaders do this consistently and frequently? Of course they do this, but only rarely—rather, most of our intellectuals fix their eyes upon pleasing their readers before everything else, so they write what they presume will satisfy the public's general political, social or religious views. They pluck for them the string of religion, or sex, or other emotive strings, and are satisfied by the tumultuous praise they receive for what they write. But if an author opposed the views of the public, he would be attacked and accused of deficiencies, stoking public anger against him. If this was a result of the critics' convictions, then they would be truthful advocates—and this is an example of honesty in speech as we are describing it. But many only affirm the public's views so as to appease them.

Because our journals rely upon the generosity of their subscribers who are drawn from the public, it is rare to find writers who oppose popular sentiments. They would rather follow the flow of general opinion, considering this to be a service to the public. As for our newspapers, while their writers are drawn from the best intellectuals and rhetoricians some of them are nevertheless deferential to the popular will—which we label as public opinion, following on the practice of advanced nations.

Public opinion in Europe has a high standing, and there are journals there dedicated to articulating it. However, does public opinion exist in Egypt and in other Ottoman nations? I do not know. But if it does exist here, it is different from how it is known in Europe—as different as the conditions of our public is from theirs. There is no doubt that public opinion deserves respect. However it is not necessary for our society to be subservient to it as we are. For our public is still immature in political terms, and so it is necessary to offer them advice and guidance while increasingly helping them to allow their voices to have a practical impact on governance. In this way, if they reach a common agreement or view on a particular matter, the government would be unable to oppose them. But we know from experience that we are still far from this goal.

It is the duty of the free author to speak his mind honestly. We do not deny the difficulty of this for our authors, for our press differs from that found in Europe, just as our public differs from theirs. The East is one of the most difficult places to publish, and for this reason the innovation we most need in this industry is strong, gifted individuals since the most difficult matter for our writers is to satisfy their readers when they are different in most regards: in education, piety, disposition, and objectives. If you add to this the need for the Arab journalist to be true to his conscience, you would justify his shortcoming in comparison to his European colleague. However, one needs to make sacrifices in the service to the public, and this is impossible without honesty in speech and frank expression of views. For the Europeans have suffered a great deal in the line of defending truth, from the tortures of prisons to poverty, before they achieved this level of conduct—they did so in the service of their people and their governments.

The harm of "courteousness" extends also to what is expressed to journalists or intellectuals by way of criticism or praise for their publications or articles, for most fear that criticizing them will lead to anger, for they are not accustomed to hear challenges to what they say. So the first thing that occurs to a writer who is offering information about a book or an article or a poem is to praise it, and to flatter the author—this is exaltation. It is done in the name of "offering encouragement" so as not to undermine the resolve of the author—and this is a noble aim. However, if criticism is done to improve style and to raise standards, it contributes to intellect and is of greatest use to writing and reading. If the author is new to writing and only hears praise and flattery, he will be duped and will be overtaken by conceit. It is a grave error if a person only is allowed to hear praise and flattery for his works and his views, for nothing of human endeavor may truly approach perfection.

Similar to this is the flattery people offer to their friends and their work. You can not find a man who will criticize his friend if the latter were to commit an error in his conduct or interactions—even if he were to know of it, he would endeavor not to make a comment about it. He would justify this to himself by thinking, "it doesn't affect me"—although if his friend were not present he would be critical of him and his opinions. This is why we have said the following in another setting:[3]

> If you claim to know the truth of your standing, then you are on the wrong path and your claim is in error. For the eye cannot discern its own pupil and the palm cannot grasp its own wrist. If currying favor with people places a distance between you and the truth, you will only add to this if you are complacent. If the eye only beholds fog, the owner of the eye can only add to this through his own blindness. So preserve those you

3 Reference to this quotation was not found.

> love from your errors, and only infect your enemies with your flattery and praise. This is what the poet means when he says:
>
> *'My enemies offer me benefits and strength*
> *So may God not distance me from my enemies*
> *For they let me know my errors so I may avoid them*
> *and they compete with me, so I gain excellence'*
>
> And the most intelligent of people is he who sets out for his friends his rationale for criticism with humility and consideration. The most stupid is he who shuts the door of criticism with claims of vigor and perfection.
>
> If you were to hear what your friends say about you in your absence, it would change your view of your standing, and would change their standing in your view. Perhaps you have felt enmity towards people who were your friends, and friendship from some of your enemies, only because some of them claimed to have higher opinions of you than others. What would happen if you discovered the secrets of people, and even could know what was hidden in their hearts?
>
> You would want to apologize to them all together if you were to be fair, and would measure what you conceal from the truth of what you think about them against what they conceal from the truth of what they think of you. Your conceit and persistence would end. The happiest person is he who knows that what his companions say about him in his absence is the same as what they say to him when he is there, for he benefits from their criticism to improve his situation. The highest goal one can hope to achieve on the scale of perfection is that he sees himself as others see him.

What we should do is to refrain from obsequiousness and courteousness, and to rely upon honesty in what we say, as this is a form of superior conduct.

2. Honesty in Interactions

What we mean by this is that a person should be honest in his interactions with another person, and that he should not make a contract or promise to do something unless he is certain that he will be able fulfill it. This is rare among us, for we may observe that a feature of courteousness is that we do not reply to a request made other than by wanting to please, and if we are unable to do what has been requested of us, we still feel we have to reply to the request positively. But when an intelligent European is asked to do something, if he is unable to do it—or if he does not want to—he will say to you that he cannot, or he does not want to do it. Perhaps his response will seem rude or brusque, but it is better than the Eastern responses of "command me" and "I would sacrifice my eye" and "by my head", which are often said even when there is no intention of carrying out the request. One who says this may be asked a second, third and fourth time, and he would invent excuses and create promises, not caring about the time you have wasted waiting for him. Is this not a form of cheating and deception? But still we address him with courtesy and kindness, although there is none.

If a friend were to press you to do something for him, either you should promise and fulfill his request, or you should explain your inability to meet his expectations, and you would leave it to him to decide how to proceed. Also related to this is the matter of appointments, and especially the setting of meetings. A person may promise to meet you at a particular hour in such-and-such a place, without any intention to fulfill the promise, or he may leave the matter to general approximations as if his promise was only made so as not to rebuff you. But we have begun to see a clear improvement in this custom in recent years with the help of increasing knowledge and education, and we may expect it to be abandoned entirely over time.

In a word, we are in need of education in good behavior, for general prosperity depends more upon this than upon wealth or science or other matters relating to the accoutrements of civilization. The success of the individual person depends upon his personal actions and his behavior more than upon his knowledge—and the same goes for society. And the poet put it thus:

> *If a nation's principles no longer remain,*
> *Then those whose values have left them, leave*

The best, most refined, bravest, and most cultured behavior is honesty in speech.

Levels of Mental Capability: Management[1] is the Master of Mental Attributes

Scientists have differed in defining the mind and the components that it includes such as memory, understanding and the like. We do not aim here to examine this matter from a physiological or psychological point of view but rather to address it from a social or ethical point of view—to assess its service to society in fostering beneficial forces; by distinguishing between the mind's different functions and tracing their effects on society. For this reason our classification of the functions of the mind will be simplified to facilitate that analysis and our readers' understanding. We therefore apologize to the scientists of the mind and philosophers for not following their established classifications of the mind and the soul in order to simplify our analysis.

1 "Ṭabaqāt al-'Uqūl: al-Tadbīr Sayyid al-Qūwa al-'Āqila," *al-Hilāl* 22 (Dec. 1913) pp. 189-197. Translated by George C. Zaidan. "*Al-tadbīr*" is most accurately translated into English as "practical problem-solving ability". In this article we have used the term management or, depending on the context, one of its components to designate this ability more simply. In the article "*al-tadbīr*" (noun) and "*dabbara*" (verb) are used in a variety of ways referring to different aspects of management. From the self-management of one's personal affairs, to management of familial affairs; to entrepreneurship in industry and trade where marketability and profitability are emphasized; to marketing in the case of professionals (doctors, lawyers, writers); to administration in the area of public service; to the management of war in the case of generals; and finally to all aspects of managing a country (political, economic, social) in the case of politicians. The unifying theme of all these uses is that Zaidan is talking about something more important than knowledge of facts or abstract intelligence for worldly success: namely the practical problem-solving ability to variously arrange, plan, design, devise, and contrive "to disentangle and find a way out of difficulties"—or what the French call *debrouiller* or a *debrouillard*. Zaidan argues in this article that it is these abilities, more than any other, that are at the root of success in life. *Translator's Note.*

The Classification of the Mind's Functions.

If we take an overall look into the functions of the mind, we will see that those functions can be divided into two groups. The first covers reactive functions that result because the mind reacts to external stimuli such as feeling, imagining and perceiving. All these occur because of the effect of the stimuli that reach the mind from external sources. The second group are the functions that emanate from within the mind itself and appear to initiate the first step such as the mind's awareness of its existence, will power and wisdom. We can divide the first group into two principal forces:

First: Self-consciousness[2] which is the human being's awareness of himself and his surroundings.

Second: Understanding which includes several faculties needed to achieve such understanding. Or putting it differently they are stages that the mind goes through in order to reach this understanding. These are:

1. Sensing which consists of linking external stimuli to the brain through feelings.
2. Imagining which consists of receiving pictures of things or thoughts in the mind.
3. Understanding which is the ability to grasp the issues that are presented to the mind.
4. Memory and Remembering which is to store all these imprints for later use when they are needed.

All these are reactive functions to external events that are presented to the mind which accepts and remembers them. Animals may also share these features which may differ in degree but not in kind from those of humans.

---

2 This exact translation of the Arabic text seems inconsistent with the beginning of that paragraph in which self-awareness is part of the second group of functions emanating from within the mind itself. *Translator's Note.*

Then there are the functions that emanate from within the mind itself [*sui generis*] which are of a higher level than the former and more distinctive of thinking *homo sapiens*. It is these functions that determine the status of human beings in human society. These are:

1. Thinking which is to compare the thoughts and pictures which the mind becomes aware of and to order and clarify them.
2. Judging which is to distinguish between the correct thoughts and the flawed ones to deduce the needed conclusions from this process.
3. Will power which is to decide what needs to be done after judging is completed or what needs to be investigated further and the like.
4. Management or the ability to arrange, plan, design, devise, and contrive in order to disentangle and find a way out of difficulties. This in our view is the most important function since it determines the benefit that the mind can reap from all the other functions by choosing the appropriate course of action on the issues that one confronts in life. Management depends on two important factors:
   a. The ability to innovate, create, devise and contrive using opinions and various methods of synthesis.
   b. Mental flexibility—or shrewdness whereby the mind analyses the different options and prioritizes them in order to achieve the desired objective.

These are the major functions of the mind and I classified them in order to show that they differ dramatically in their importance—some are simple functions that human beings and animals share while others are unique to human beings and these are of different levels with the highest being management and mental flexibility or shrewdness. These are the mental functions that stand above all others and the ability to master them allows one to harness the skills of all the other functions.

Some subjects are learnt through understanding alone; others require thinking and deduction as well as judgment. But mastering one's subject is not beneficial to anyone without the application of management skills to use this knowledge and exploit it. Consider knowledge of industrial pursuits or those in the arts and literature: it is acquired with intelligence and understanding but the person will not benefit from that knowledge unless he is able to use his management skills to exploit it. Conversely a person with limited intelligence but good management skills can benefit from the intelligence of others. These skills and his shrewdness can allow him to employ persons and exploit their intelligence for his benefit.

A common and pervasive error is the admiration that people have for those with superior understanding, intelligence and talent even though they may lack the management skills to exploit their knowledge. Such as poets, painters, writers, artists, handicraft workers and professionals in the sciences who are content to acquire the awareness and understanding of their subject and exploit their natural talent. But rarely do they admire those with management abilities and shrewdness.

The pages of history are replete with the names of poets, literary figures, painters, singers, actors and others who are admired and revered by all. But it is rare for people to do so for those who possess management abilities and among which are politicians, administrators, and traders. Of those, history only mentions those that produce miracles or whose knowledge affects the interests of the nation. As for the poet, one poem is enough to make him famous. One beautiful picture that produces neither benefit nor harm is enough to keep the memory of a painter for several generations. As for the managers they are the ones who control the business of the world—to the extent that the innovations of the former only bear fruit through the intervention of the latter.

Most people are not totally devoid of management abilities but their capacity in this respect differs among people. Every one of us has understanding, will power, management ability and memory—but understanding may be stronger in some and management abilities in others and memory yet stronger in others and so on and so forth. But management is the most important attribute of all because management is able to harness the gains to be obtained from all the other attributes. Such is the case of the general who positions his soldiers in a way that increases their strength towards the enemy several-fold compared to that of the individual soldier.

Management

Management is the prime mental attribute on which depends the condition of the individual, the family, and the nation—much more than intelligence, understanding, or technical talent. This attribute is present in different degrees in eminent as well as in humble people as you will see below.

1. Managing Individual Affairs

The simplest problems an individual faces concerns managing his diet and drink using the simplest means to do so by taking into account his financial means and the benefits of different foods—the quality of his management thereby affecting both his finances and his health.

The solution to this simple problem is extremely important from the point of view of the individual. Because on it depends his health as well as the clarity of his mind both of which affect his future. Some people are unable to adequately address even such a simple problem which makes them subject to avoidable illnesses just because they neglected their diet or their dress.

2. Managing Family Affairs

What we have in mind here is the concern of the individual for his family, putting their affairs in order and planning for the future of each member of the family while paying special attention to the material needs of his wife and children. This is more important than management at the level of the individual because if affects the happiness of a whole family and the future of the children. This is also obviously of importance from the point of view of society which is made up of families. Not to mention the misery that would afflict every member of the family when there is a shortfall in managing its affairs—something which is easy to avoid when the head of the family gives the future of his family his early attention.

We know of some people that have foregone marriage out of excessive caution fearing that their limited financial means would prevent them from providing for the needs of their children and especially the education that they would need. We know others that do not feel any responsibility towards the family such as the man that owns nothing, has no bread in his oven, nor a piaster in his pocket nor do his children have food to eat the next day or clothing to put on their backs in a month. Yet he is as calm as ever as he waits for his situation to change and improve. Therefore you see him repeating all the sayings or proverbs or verses [from the Koran] referring to the need to rely on God, to submit to fate, and that resilience is a bottomless treasure. If not for his poverty and his limitations he would behave in this or that way. Yet he is happy to espouse the values he has as well as to be resigned to his fate. But this happiness is limited to his person and is the cause of the misery of his family that has to rely on outside support to fend for itself. All he cares about is not to be disturbed by the crying of his children as they play. Should he ever feel any responsibility for the state of his marriage, he is quick to lay the blame for the state of affairs of the family on his wife since she is responsible for the family!

Nor is poverty the only source of misery for the family. Indeed we know of well-off families that are unhappy when parents are not concerned with its affairs—the mother being absorbed in social visits while the father spends his time playing games. They may send their children to school but do so without thought or purpose—just out of habit to get rid of the commotion that children often cause at home. This is because they lack any sense of responsibility for the affairs of their family and concern for the future of their children.

At the other extreme you see people that give excessive attention to managing the affairs of the family to the extent that this attention becomes a liability. Such is the case when parents carefully scrutinize and seek to control everything that their children eat and drink—justifying this on health grounds but without real knowledge which can harm their health; or they exaggerate the values and principles they inculcate in their children preventing them from interacting with people or going to public places so that they may not hear an indecent word or a lewd story. Such children grow up with weak loyalties and character as a result of bad management.

3. Management[3] in Industry and Trade

Management of individual and family affairs are examples of this faculty at its simplest level. The next levels of complexity are all related to earning one's living and there are several levels of difficulty here depending on the occupation or profession or trade.

The artisan such as a carpenter, blacksmith or persons in similar professions, does not require many management abilities. His success depends on the precision of his work and the satisfaction he provides his customers. When two individuals produce work of comparable quality in the same craft the one who excels over his competitors is the one who is best able to market his product—i.e. interact well with and satisfy his customers.

The trader is in greater need of management skills as he needs to compete with his neighbors. No product becomes successful without improving its quality, stylishness and attractiveness—and marketing it

---

3 The management that is discussed in this section often refers primarily to marketing and entrepreneurship—managing a group of people, promoting a product and keeping customers happy. *Translator's Note.*

to appeal to people of different classes and tastes catering to a variety of natures, preferences and impulses. The trader also needs to be honest, work hard and select appealing products—the latter being a key managerial ability. If traders promote similar products, then the one who prevails is the one with the superior managerial skills. A group of traders may operate with one commodity in the same market: it will take a few years before differences in their success begins to manifest itself. Some will then forge ahead with the differences increasing year after year. Eventually one or two traders forge ahead of the others and join the club of big traders while some of their colleagues may become their employees. Among the latter may be some who are more intelligent or more knowledgeable—had they competed in school with the former, they would have been the winner in languages, history and poetry. But their weak managerial skills make them unable to compete with the successful traders in a profession that requires them to know the products their customers need and how to sell their products and keep their customers satisfied.

No merchant or artisan is devoid of management skills but their success differs in proportion to the managerial skills they possess. Some spend their life in a shop that they manage by themselves. Their trade does not expand to the extent that they need to hire a helper because their minds do not have a broader perspective. While you see another trader expand his business, hire additional persons, increase the size of his shop, sell more products and double his profits. This expansion does not prevent him from exercising his entrepreneurial skills. When his unsuccessful colleague sees his desire to expand his business and his profits, he convinces himself that his behavior is reckless and that he will soon regret his actions. If he sees him succeeding in expanding his business he will reason that amassing more money and worldly goods are fleeting benefits that are not worth all these efforts. If he hears the successful trader complain of being tired or sick he blames him for bringing this on himself by working beyond what he is able to withstand.

All the foregoing also applies to artisans. The small carpenter may become through his management skills the owner of a large carpentry workshop including tens of workers. He may then expand further and sell his products in a furniture store. He would relate to his fellow carpenters in the same way that the big merchants related to the smaller merchants.

All this is also the case with the professions in the sciences such as medicine, law, education, journalism, writing and similar professions where the degree of success of their practitioners depends primarily on their managerial skills. So many a doctor was the best student in his class and excelled over his fellow students in most subjects but found himself outstripped by a colleague whose knowledge of the subject was average and whose intelligence was inferior to his but whose managerial skills were superior. A doctor needs to have a strong ability to understand his patients and their families and convince them of his proficiency and his superiority over any of his colleagues. The same is the case with lawyers whose marketing skills determine their relative success. Legal studies require a high level of understanding and a lot of persistence but the degree of success is determined by marketing skills. Which is why you see some lawyers spend their life in a narrow circle of work while their colleagues who graduated in the same year from the same law school have offices that resemble a government office because of the large number of workers there.

The Profession of Writers

On the whole the profession of writers is the scientific profession that requires the greatest management skills because it deals with the feelings of people and touches their literary needs and social beliefs. The more so in the East given the greater variety of beliefs, religions, sects, tastes and values than is the case elsewhere. The French or British writer writes for a public that mostly shares his religious and social beliefs and has the same education, customs and values. He therefore knows as he puts pen to paper what will appeal to his readers or be of use to them and he can tailor his articles to their needs and tastes. The writer in the East, on the other hand, will face all kinds of stumbling blocks before he begins to write. However important or trivial the matter he wants to write about is, he cannot gauge its impact on his readers. The more so when he deals with social issues or those that deal with principles and values. If he appeals to Muslims he will not appeal to Christians and if he appeals to both he will not appeal to Jews. If he appeals to Egyptians he may not appeal to those in the Maghreb or Syrians or Iraqis or Indians. If he appeals to the educated younger generation he may offend the older conservatives. He may appeal to the poor but not to the rich. Should he be able to appeal to all these, he may not be satisfied with his product because of his limited ability to fully express his thinking. While foreign writers can deal forthrightly and explicitly with social and moral issues, he has to moderate his views and promote them in a roundabout way to protect himself against criticism that is unjustified on its merits but may be effective in turning off readers if it touches on their sensitivities. If such criticism sows doubts in what they read, then the intended benefits disappear. For the first duty of a writer that wants his words to have an impact is to make his readers trust him—for without such trust all his efforts will come to naught.

The Arab writer whether a journalist or an author of works for the general public cannot benefit his readers and profit from his profession without good management[4] skills. It is not sufficient for him to master his subject matter—he needs to apply his management skills to his writings to generate the essential trust he needs from his readers. He must therefore know the needs of his readers and their values and present his thoughts in a way that appeals to and benefits them. This can only come from applying his management skills. When two writers are equal in their knowledge of their subjects, then the one who prevails is the one

4 In the sense of marketing himself (gaining the trust of) and his writings to his readers. *Translator's Note.*

who has the superior marketing skills. This includes the selection of the subject matter, the prose that is used and the quality of his work. For this reason a select group of the most eminent thinkers have stopped writing for the general public explaining their reluctance to do so in terms of the ignorance of the masses. That may be the case but this only strengthens the need of the general public to have writers educate and write for them in a way that is appealing.

The marketing that writers need differs with the subject matter. The translator from one language to another is the one that least needs these marketing skills. He is followed by the author who summarizes several books into one—with the need for his marketing skills increasing with the number of books he summarizes and the variety of their subjects. He needs those marketing skills in order to optimally relay his thoughts to his readers and satisfy them notwithstanding the variety of their purposes and values.

4. Administrative Management

Here we refer to the administration of the government and organizing its financial, internal and military affairs. This requires the highest of the levels of management covered thus far. Dealing with personal and familial affairs and the management of trade and industry, affects the individual, the family and social groups. But the administration of the government determines the success of the nation, maintaining law and order and protecting individual rights. The levels rise from the mayors of small villages to those of large towns and cities up to the governors of provinces and the ministers in the central government depending on the structure of the government in question.

Many people minimize the difficulty of government administration. Several literary figures have convinced themselves that writing an article or composing a poem requires mental capacities that are far greater than those required to run a province or state. They express their thought in these terms: “What does a governor do other than issuing orders and stamping or signing papers?" They imagine that if they were occupying his position they would be able to better fulfill it than he.

This is an illusion. Because the administration of a small country requires management skills and hard work that is more than sufficient to author a book. Of course we do not mean that a mayor can compose beautiful poems if he has no poetic predispositions. What we mean is that solving a legal case or a small administrative problem requires mental capacities that exceed those needed by a poet to compose his poetry, or a journalist to write his article. The more so for those occupying much higher positions covering a much broader area than those of a town mayor.

Consider what a government administrator or governor needs in terms of management abilities to ensure his orders are implemented in response to ministerial requests to meet the needs of the population. In the process they will not be confident that their subordinates will implement their orders in the manner they wish without diluting them to fulfill their own purposes or interests. Consider all this in the functions of a minister or those that occupy similar positions at the head of governments—these are far more difficult to fulfill than those not in the know would ever suspect. For this reason the Ottoman ministers that assumed governmental responsibilities after the constitution have been increasingly criticized; writers claimed that dozens in the nation could have managed the government's affairs much more efficiently. This is an illusion as the needed management skills vary in accordance with the responsibilities that the occupiers of the various positions require.

5. The Management of War

We refer here to generals in the arena of war who require greater administrative skills than we have considered so far because they are in charge of what is of greatest value to the nation—we have in mind matters that concern life and honor. The proficient military leader has to be an outstanding manager with a broad strategic perspective. As he sits in his tent or office and designs his plan of attack or defense he needs to assess the position of every unit and how to attack it or defend it. He has to assess the different ways in which the enemy might attack or defend itself and the military ploys and traps he may have to face. On the basis of all this he has to organize and position his troops. During the battle he may be faced with unexpected developments he had not anticipated which require immediate reactions to defeat his enemy's schemes with hardly any time for thought or to consider different options. A single word from him may determine the survival or demise of the nation. A one minute delay can lead to failure and the loss of a nation's independence and its aspirations.

So consider the attributes that all this requires: management, knowledge, will-power, and strength. And it is for these qualities that the great generals in history have been known.

6. Management in Politics

This requires the most important management skills of all. This is because the management of politics involves looking into the relationship that countries have with each other. Peace and war depends on the political skills of leaders. The perspectives must be very wide to encompass the interests of their country and its relationship with the interests of other countries—and based on this they need to design a plan that can be followed to protect their country's interests. Their skills are especially needed during negotiations when the characteristics of the players come to the fore and compete with each other: minds confront each other and the winner is the one with the stronger political skills and greater mental agility. How many countries failed on the battlefield because of the weakness of its generals only to recoup their losses at the peace table through the political skills of their representatives! This is what happened with Russia in its war against Japan and the Ottomans in their war in the Balkans.

Conclusions

Managerial abilities require different levels of development from managing one's personal affairs to those of the family; to the management of activities in industry and trade with different levels within these categories; to the administration of Government; to the management of war; and finally to political skills which are the most difficult and demanding. There are limits to the management skills that an individual is able to reach. A person can go beyond managing his personal affairs to managing his family and on to managing his profession and so on. But the norm is for people to stop at a level of management that they cannot go beyond however hard they may try. That is why only a few people can manage both the big and small things.

We also see that some persons who have developed the highest managerial skills are sometimes unable to deal with the simpler ones. As when some people with political skills that run countries or great generals that run wars find themselves unable to manage their personal or family affairs. As if their managerial skills represent a solid doughnut with an empty void in its center. This does not happen often.

Some of the games that measure managerial ability are chess and checkers. To excel in these games requires the ability to consider a large number of possibilities and make many assumptions which is what a general needs in war and a politician during negotiations. This is why most politicians and generals are good at these two games. Every general may be able to win at chess but can every chess player successfully manage a war?

Social Sense[1]

What we mean by "social sense" is similar to what the English mean in their phrase "common sense" or "good sense," which for the French is "bon sens".[2] We have chosen the term "sense" in this phrase to approximate the natural senses with which humans are endowed, so as to comprehend their environment. The senses, as is known from ancient times, are five: feeling, sight, hearing, taste and smell. Since then two further senses have been discovered—the sense of balance, which allows humans to balance their bodies while standing and in walking, and the sense of gravity, by which humans are able to calibrate their muscles in carrying objects in accordance to their weight. Finally, humans have a further kind of feeling or sense to discern the truth of things and their manifest attributes, and the ability to judge others by their actions or their speech, in relation to how they fit their own needs. As the ancients have said, the instrument by which we comprehend the visible is the "sense of sight", and we comprehend the tactile by the "sense of feeling", and so we may call the sense by which we comprehend our social relations with others the "social sense", at least until the time when we may agree on a different label to indicate what is meant by this. We shall now undertake to describe this sense, and its consequences for

1 "Al-Ḥāssa al-ijtimā'iyya aw Salāmat al-Dhawq wa-ḥusn al-Ikhtiyār fi'l-Mu'āmala." ("The Social Sense or the Soundness of Taste and Good Judgement in Social Interaction") *al-Hilāl* 21 (April 1913) pp. 404-409. Translated by Kamran Rastegar. As is clear from the article, Zaidan's "al-ḥāssa al-ijtimā'iyya" is meant to approximate "common sense" but in some ways differs slightly from the English phrase. Here I have chosen to render the phrase as "social sense" which is closer to the literal meaning of the Arabic phrase. However, the reader may wish to consider the link with notions of common sense in this discussion. *Translator's Note.*

2 The three terms are given in their original languages in the Arabic text.

influencing the success of humans in their actions in achieving various goals and aspirations.

The reason for success

The success of humans in their work is based upon the degree to which they are endowed with this sense—more than their capacity for knowledge, or their proficiency in a craft or trade, etc., as a means of earning their living. It is more important in the arena of life than intelligence, although it is less commonly found: less than two or three percent of intelligent people possess it. Mothers give birth to forty intelligent children before one is born who is endowed with social sense. For this reason there are many intelligent people, but very few of them are successful. Because success is not dependent upon intelligence when one has not learned how to use this intelligence, and there is no use for knowledge if it is not used to improve performance.

For the products of intelligence are many, such as knowledge and politics and crafts and other matters that explain the development of civilization. But knowledge does not produce a desirable outcome unless it is tailored to the needs of those who use it. It only produces this outcome when the possessor of the talent [of intelligence] understands the effect that his knowledge will have in the minds of people and their capacity to absorb it or their readiness to understand it. For those results are not achieved other than by the use of social sense. This sense also plays a role in the choices people face in their economic pursuits as it is used in selecting the pursuit which provides the greatest returns. One of the British philosophers has said, "knowledge without this [social] sense is idiocy." [3] If one appraises each aptitude without considering social sense, one will not understand a thing about them. It is as if one were to give seeds to a person who does not understand farming, or arms to one

---

3 Probably Thomas H. Huxley (1825-1895) "Science is nothing but trained and organized common sense." *The Oxford Dictionary of Quotations* (London, Oxford Univ. Press, 1966) p. 266.

who is untrained to use them. For this reason, social sense is the bride of other talents: if we wish to do good, then we must wait for the right time to do so, and to do it in the right place. For the intelligent person knows what to do, but the possessor of this sense knows how and when to do it!

The standing of a person in human society is based upon this sense as well as having other superior attributes. It would be possible for the smart person to master knowledge and a trade or craft with effort and work, but it would be in vain for him to try to gain this sense if he is not born with it, although it is strengthened and improved with education and training. But if one possesses this sense along with only a small amount of intelligence, one can benefit from exploiting the intelligence he has to make its yield much greater. Success in various activities is based more on management than on knowledge, and management is ineffective if it does not possess this sense. Let us outline examples of this in the most important social domains:

The Impact of Social Sense in Politics

Politicians are for the most part intelligent, as a person does not rise to a position of political importance if he is not intelligent and knowledgeable. However they differ in their success on the basis of what they possess in terms of guile, which is one of the products of social sense. A seasoned politician does not utter a word unless he is certain of its impact upon the listener, as if he could peer into the depths of his heart. In this way the effectiveness in reaching his aims is increased. If you were to observe a politician in a conference, and if you had the power to comprehend the secrets of people, you would see [in him] the personification of cunning. You would learn how minds enter combat and what kinds of ambushes, looking posts and traps are arrayed in this war, as well as the strategies that enter into attacking, defending, truce-making, skirmishing and maneuvering. Most politicians are cunning. The most cunning are helped by good fortune. Someone might insist on ten when he is quite content with eight. His shrewdness will require him to refuse when he actually intends only to accept. When he acts in this manner he follows only his subtle perception of the effect his words have on his interlocutors.

The Impact of Social Sense In Trade

The trader has to interact with other people more than most people, especially with sellers in the marketplaces. He will not succeed with them without a precise sense of knowing the impact of his words upon his customers—through sweet talk, courtship, and bargaining. It is not enough for his goods to be of excellent quality on their own. They must be appropriate for the market in which he is active, and he must not exhibit them other than to those who would have a need for them. What is necessary is having a good enough social sense to be able to identify the particular area of trade that is most suitable to his disposition and talents, so as to correctly know which goods to procure to best suit the people who will be purchasing them.

In addition there is a need for this social sense in transactions with his clients so as to discern their satisfaction or agreement, and to comprehend the true nature of his relationship with them, as well as to understand their opinions about his goods and the nature of his standing with them. He must not be taken in by appearances, for any pretense or sense of self-importance would corrupt the link between him and his customer, and would work to his disadvantage. So the qualities of social sense include the ability to comprehend the truth of things and to avoid complacency based on appearances. The sensitive trader knows that his relations with his clients will not succeed unless he acts towards them fairly, inviting their confidence. He must reflect their interests with regard to types of products, and their costs, taking these into account and being considerate of their needs and not just use fine words and statements or abundant advertising. For these by themselves are useless and do not bring in new customers. What is useful in satisfying a customer is to convince him that these goods meet his needs and will result in profits and income—he will not be convinced if the claims are untruthful, or unsupported by his experience. The trader who has a weak social sense is unable to discern this, and imagines that he wins over his customers with sweet talk, embellishment and exaggeration. But the one who is sensitive makes the improvement of his goods his main concern to meet the needs of his customers; for him this replaces the need for smooth talk.

If you study the conditions of traders and the different levels of success among them, you will find that the reasons for failure are generally that they complacently follow appearances and ignore the true nature of things. If they dupe their customers with appearances that are elaborate and embellished, they in fact are duping themselves about their own situation. They may find a great deal of money in their hands; however this money does not belong to them but belongs to those from whom they import their goods. A day will come where they will be asked to pay back what they owe, and they will fall short. They then do not feel the real weight of these debts, due to the weakness of their social sense. They engage in spending without any consideration for their debtors. And when the time comes to settle accounts, and they find they are short, they are suprised and justify their inability to meet their debts by claiming bad luck or a general financial crisis. When in actuality it is because they have not comprehended the reality of their condition. They have not distinguished between their own claims and their obligations to others. The failure or bankruptcy of trading companies, when not due to fraud or embezzlement, is rarely due to causes other than failing to comprehend the truth of things, an error which is not committed by those with social sense.

The Impact of Social Sense on Knowledge and Science

Social sense has an important place in knowledge as well, related to its use in meeting public needs. It does not suffice for the scientist to be knowledgeable about science. It is also necessary for him to know how to use his knowledge and present it to people in a way that is useful for them. The scientist safeguards both the ancient and modern sciences but if he does not feel the reality of the milieu within which he lives, and if he does not relate his writings and publications to the needs of his people, his knowledge is wasted, and his work is in vain. He pays to publish his work from his own pocket and receives nothing in return. Then he complains about the lack of interest among the public in his writing, and accuses the public of ignorance and of denying beauty and not recognizing its value, and of rejecting works that he respects—so he threatens to end his service to the public. But if he had insight and had judged himself objectively he would have recognized that he had not made the best choices in what he wrote, and would see that he is not able to judge the needs of people on this topic, or on others. Or to perfect his style so it corresponds to their preferences. All this, rather than a deficiency in the public's taste and their capacity for appreciating it, is the problem. All of which goes back to his shortcomings in social sense much more than it relates to the pervasiveness of ignorance.

We are in need of knowledge and science, but we have a greater need for truthfully understanding the conditions of the public so as to be able to relate our knowledge to its needs. This correspondence requires social sense in all areas—in every line written by an author on any topic, general or not. It is imperative upon him, while in his office, before applying pen to paper, to visualize his reader fidgeting over each complex passage of writing, cursing insincere phrases, laughing at what permeates the text in terms of shortcomings that the author imagines he has hidden from the reader by placing them within elaborate phrases with religious disguises or sexual innuendo. He needs to know first and foremost that the reader, as a customer, will judge the material and literary value of his writings without considering these convoluted phrases. Should he focus upon these flowery phrases, then he will not focus on the truths that may be found therein. If the truths absorb his attention, he will not be distracted by other aspects—so it is imperative for the intelligent author to concentrate on them.

In our recent Nahda we have seen hundreds of authors and thinkers appear in Egypt and Syria and elsewhere, but only a small number of these have made useful public contributions. We have seen hundreds of newspapers and magazines appear as well, while only a few tens of these have lasted. Of these only about ten have found true success. In this Nahda hundreds of books have appeared offering diverse studies, but only a few have been read widely. If you were to account for the differences between the successes of some of these and the failure of the vast majority of them, you will discern that they do not result from differences in the quality of knowledge therein, but in differences in how social sense is applied to determine the public's need and in understanding how to present that knowledge in a style that best meets those needs. Newspapers or popular books do not reflect the superior knowledge of their authors, but rather their superior management and wise choices both of which are fruits of social sense—in addition to hard work and diligence. This cannot be achieved through experience. It is not enough for one to simply increase one's efforts and work, unless his efforts are directed towards the correct path—otherwise he will simply continue to err.

The Impact of Social Sense on Social Relations

The effects of this sense upon social relations is immense. Social relations are the key to social interaction. Suppose you were to meet a person by chance whom you had not seen before, and you considered it a possibly promising encounter. Perhaps you would follow this with trade or financial relations, or family relations such as a marriage, or the like. But perhaps you would want to shun him, and you would feel the urge to reject his friendship, with this feeling increasing over time. Should you consider the difference between these two conditions, you may say that the first is characterized by amity and good feeling, while the second is characterized by antagonism. But if you analyzed this further, you would find that it relates in fact to social sense, as the presence of social sense is characterized by friendliness, and the lack of this sense results in hostility.

Suppose there is a person who is employed by you, and who does not speak to you on subjects other than those relating to his work, and he is careful that every word he says is one that meets with your approval. Suppose also that he is sensitive about what would offend you and never speaks out of turn. If visiting with you, he knows when to leave and does not insist on overstaying his welcome. But suppose there is another who visits you when you are busy with matters that do not concern him. Our Eastern customs dictate that you cannot refuse to accept his visit. He pays no attention to the fact that you are busy, and has no consideration for your time. He speaks to you and most of his talk is about himself or his family and what they eat or drink and what his father or grandfather or he himself gained through their brilliant work. He then begins to insult people in general and blames the difficult times as he meanders from topic to topic, none of which is of interest to you or of others who are present. But he cannot perceive any of this because of his lack of social sense. You should not hold out hopes that he will change, as he is oblivious to his surroundings. It is possible that he is very knowledgeable in some important areas that depend upon great intellectual capacity—he may persevere in these areas, and even prevail over his competitors. But he is unable to overcome the lack of social sense within himself. If he were to contrive to reform himself and try to act in a light-spirited manner, people would see through his act and find him even more obnoxious.

For good taste, wise choices, and acute sensitivity in social relations, not to mention the ability to distinguish the truth of things and set them in their proper perspective, all relate to the "social sense" of which we have been speaking. Human society depends upon this sense even more than it depends upon knowledge and intelligence. Therefore it is incumbent upon those who are educating the youth to comprehend the meaning of this sense and to instruct them about its merits, just as they instruct them about the values of good morals, and the defects of vice, because their standing in the world will depend upon this knowledge. Achieving this would result in guiding them to follow the best path, without any need for the advice of the wise.

Admitting to Error is Right
and
Accepting One's Limitations is Strength[1]

The inability to admit to error, when it occurs, is among the illnesses of our society. Some of us go so far in our obstinacy that we would even harm ourselves, our families, and our countries to avoid having to say "I erred", even when it is absolutely clear that there is no debate about the mistake. The clinging to views of this sort is due to the lack of a channel for criticism or judgment in our society—so much so that the term "critic" appears to us harsh and a kind of taunt or epithet. Criticism is associated with mockery or insinuation and a provocation to anger. Rare are those able to separate the mistakes they make from the criticism they incur as a result. Such individuals are the tolerant among us, able to control their emotions and consider the matter objectively in a philosophical light. But such persons are rare and for this reason we will begin by offering a few words on the topic of criticism, then we will return to the issue of admitting errors.

A. Judgment or Criticism

This heading includes criticism of ways of thinking, of customs, of actions, and of views. It also relates to the criticism of traditions that have developed over the ages, refined by the minds of many generations, altered by processes of revision and modification until they reach the form in which we now know them. We do not mean to say that these traditions have reached a state of perfection, but criticizing them is not an easy matter, and it is not possible to offer judgment on their faults

1 "Al-'Itirāf bi'l-Khaṭa' Ṣawāb wa'l-iqrār bi'l-'Ajz Qūwwa" *al-Hilāl* 16 (Jan.1908) pp.108-114. Translated by Kamran Rastegar.

or shortcomings simply by saying the first thing that comes to mind. However, what one of us may consider to be their deficiencies may also have occurred to the stewards of law, politics and religion who have come before us. If they did not remove that deficiency, it is because there were greater ones to avoid. We would not want people to accept the perfection of laws and religious traditions as they relate to transactions or governance. However we do not wish for them to simply resort to criticism either—although there is nothing wrong with offering insights into the effect of what we might consider a deficiency for the purpose of understanding and research. The concepts offered by philosophers or prophets, which have been elaborated upon by great men, are not undermined by criticism, and yet some go about critiquing these without a rationale other than a fascination with their own flights of fantasy. They do not comprehend reality other than what they are told by their teachers or what they hear from their fathers. The student sees perfection in both his teacher and his father, for the former seems to have all the knowledge in the world and the latter seems to have the capacity to do anything. But if their knowledge goes beyond the world of grammar, mathematics, logic, astronomy and the natural sciences and reaches the arena of experimentation and controversies, and if they hone their talents in intellectual or administrative or legal activity, they will comprehend the value of those who set out earlier traditions. They would then refrain from criticizing them until they have given the issue serious consideration and thought.

What is strangest in what we observe with regard to criticism is that some critics do not like the norms of existence, so they criticize them and find fault with their Creator (may God forgive them). They object to its rules and organization and may imagine that if they had been charged with setting in place an alternative system they would have based it on stronger or wiser methods. The majority of these revolt against the calamities that afflict them with no rhyme or reason, unable to see in them any wisdom or justice But if they returned to the path of reason, they would know that man may have achieved much in science and philosophy, but he is incapable from comprehending the mystery of creation: whatever increases his knowledge only increases his understanding of this inability. Nothing illustrates better how far he is from increasing this understanding than the idea that he who extends his hand to grasp the sun would be blinded by its light and would lower his eyes, and eventually would become once again indifferent to his surroundings.

Were it easy for someone to criticize religious traditions and norms, then it would be possible for him to criticize other things, for he would be skeptical of all kinds of views and studies. Such a person would reject any claim that he is less than perfect and would be fascinated by his own opinions. Even when he praises something, he would think he is superior to its creator, and so he would rarely be surprised by anything, or believe himself incapable of achieving the same. If he faced the same conditions faced by its creator, he would denigrate them in his criticism and would speak without restraint, intensifying his rejection of its creator. This is what we wished to speak of and to warn about.

1. Criticizing Religions and Traditions

When nations adhere to general traditions and schools of religious or scientific thought and the like, and when societies invest in them, it is not easy to criticize these traditons. One cannot ignore the fact that the nation or the community is rarely formed on the basis of an error. Communities are formed when they have a rational reason, and it is not easy to dismiss or ignore this. For the followers of a particular religion may number in thousands or millions, and it is not reasonable to think that their learning is based on ignorance. While this does not prohibit us from criticizing them, it is imperative to be respectful of this grouping. For they would not have gathered on the basis of the legitimacy of a matter that reached them through their ancestors after the progression of many generations, if they had not had very strong reasons for doing so—reasons which will not be apparent to the critic. If you debated with the adherents of specific religions and listened to their arguments, you would come away impressed by their reasons—even in the case of the less developed religions in our eyes, such as paganism and Zoroastianism. I am not saying that you would be convinced, because debate never convinces one to abandon the religion that he is born into and nurtured within. However you would at least see that they did not adopt that religion foolishly or randomly.

Among these common traditions are modesty in dress in the East, and flamboyance in dress in the West, but each people has reasons that justify their adherence to their customs such as food, drink and dress, and for differing from the customs of others. This does not prohibit one from criticizing them, but one must be respectful of the social acceptance of these traditions. Criticizing them with grace and kindness is better than doing so in a way that offends feelings. Because human beings cling to the dignity of their nations and to their customs just as they cling to the dignity of their religions. For this reason, we may see that in advanced nations debates around religion, or traditions, or ethical principles is avoided.

2. Criticizing Opinions

Criticizing personal opinions is more prevalent and more productive, but is only productive when done with kindness and generosity and fairness. For the holder of a particular view may be dependent upon arguments that the critic is unaware of, and so he should not surprise him with criticism without first hearing his arguments. If, after hearing them, the critic continues to view them as erroneous, he should reason with him over which position is the better one. If he does this and treats him fairly in acknowledging his arguments, it would be easy for the one who is wrong to accept what is shown to him—otherwise he would just cling to his views and insist upon the rightfulness of his errors, so as to defend his dignity.

In this vein, criticizing written works or books that pertain to criticizing personal opinions should be treated as has been explained earlier.

Others pertain to the subject of specific scientific criticism or that of professions, such as medicine or the law. If the author has a specialization as a doctor or a lawyer or an engineer, then this enters the arena of the criticism of professions.[2]

3. Criticizing Professions

By this we mean intellectual or scientific professions, and the profession most exposed to criticism by people is medicine, for its practitioners mix with the public. Additionally the public is dependent upon the work of doctors because it touches upon their health, and their life and death may depend upon it. The doctor is rarely protected from blame or criticism, for people expect from him a cure for every ill—and medicine can do no such thing. In addition, some illnesses at their outset may be similar to other illnesses, and a doctor may prescribe a cure that does not improve the patient's condition—after which they will doubt his proficiency and replace him with another one, or speak disparagingly of him, perhaps intending for him to hear what they say. It would be a great catastrophe if one of his patients died, for they may believe that his death was due to an error by the doctor. And if he were to cure the patient by a particular method through his own personal intervention, they would say that God cured him. But if he dies, they would say the doctor killed him.

Compare this to the criticism of other intellectual professions. Here, we single out authors, which are most exposed to criticism. For the author is not trained in a school, and he does not receive a diploma for writing. Most people imagine that they could be writers if they wanted to with no effort at all. When they look over a book or an article, the first thing that occurs to them is to criticize it. They read a text arrogantly, starting with the idea that mastery of its topics is very easy. If the reader is used

---

2 Here Zaidan uses an Arabic term which would more literally mean "productions", or "industries". However from the context I have rendered the term as "professions" although "trades" (in the sense of a trade union) could also apply. *Translator's Note.*

to writing only for himself without exposing himself to public scrutiny or subjecting his taste in subject-matter to the fires of criticism, he will be quick to find fault with what others write. When he reads an article or book, he is shocked by the errors he finds in it, and imagines that if he had written it he would have avoided this error or that mistake, and that he would have expanded this passage or shortened that one. His arrogance emanates from his lack of experience. It is commendable for the author to be humble in the hands of the public, and to stand firm behind his beliefs. If the author published his writings and listened to the criticism of people, and not just their praise, perhaps he would better understand his true worth.

Criticizing a writer is not a simple matter, for the author does not publish his work unless he has reviewed it and revised it and made corrections to it. So if you were to read a book and find errors within it, you should not rush to criticize it, for the author may be basing his work on citations you are not aware of, or perhaps he has read works you have not read. You should know that criticizing a work is easier than writing one. But if his errors still stand out after you have studied the work, place your criticisms in the form of an analysis within a discussion of the merits of the work, for this makes it easier for him to accept your criticism.

B - Admission of Errors

The ability to admit one's errors is one of the greatest signs of wisdom and honesty, and comes easily to honest people with great souls because the intelligent person knows that humans are weak by nature, and that humans have always erred both in what they say and do, and that perfection is an attribute of God alone. Only the imperiously ignorant are convinced of infallibility in their speech and actions. This is the reason why people tend to gather together to challenge the evil of oppression with their opinions, and why they incline towards consultation with each other, even among prophets and kings. As has been said in praise of consultation:

Compare your opinion with that of another, and consult
For two people together cannot fail to grasp the truth
For a person may see his face with a single mirror
But with two mirrors together he can also see his back

If you hear a criticism of an action you carried out, or an opinion you expressed, do not let this disturb you and do not rush to anger or become obstinate before considering the basis for the criticism and the reasons therein. For the reader of a book is more discerning of its faults than its author. So if you learn of your faults, admit them, and thank those who warn you and correct them for you. For it is rare for you to hear criticism of your work, especially in the East, where excessive courtesy is widespread and where people only praise one another. He who points out your errors has done you a service, so do not respond with anger, for there is no degradation in your standing. If he who discovers faults in others is great, the one who accepts his own faults is even greater.

Some people avoid admitting their errors out of fear of the public's judgment of them, for most people do not comprehend the good that this admission entails. This admission may be detrimental to their interests, especially if their interests are dependent on public approval. But this fear does not protect them from injury and is a product of weakness. For if we allow this fear to govern us, we remain deluded. It is desirable that the intellectuals of a nation, *udaba' al-umma*, work to improve the values of the public, and raise them to their own higher level, rather than stoop down to the level of the riffraff. You may notice that the authors in advanced countries do not criticize the works of writers unless they find them worthy of respect. Hence if a writer were not to critique the works of another, this would be seen as a sign of disrespect and dismissal of that work.

For the only person who refuses to admit his faults is a weak person with little to offer—by which we mean the knowledge that should be offered by authors. If an author expends his maximum efforts and focuses his strengths to marshal all his knowledge and experience into a book only to hear its shortcomings, it is difficult for him to admit his faults. So he debates and argues and insists on defending his literary reputation, for the failure of this book would tarnish his name and his influence. On the other hand, one can write a book or article without resorting to all his abilities and knowledge and publish it while knowing that he could do better. So when he hears criticism of it he is not shocked, and does not insist on it being correct, for this admission does not diminish his standing or affect his other products. Like a trader with many goods—if some produce losses, it does not bother him as he has others to cover his loss. But if he has few goods this same loss hurts him and provokes his anger.

When one hears a critique of his writing usually the first thing to come to his mind is to mistrust the critic, believing that he only intends to hurt his standing. But this presumption causes him harm. He should begin by assuming the good intentions of the critic to the greatest extent so as to be receptive to the criticism; otherwise he will not reap the benefit intended by the criticism. For as [Imam] 'Ali said, "Do not presume evil of something you hear someone say—you will discover some good in it, most likely."

What is strange is what sometimes happens with an author who has written and then publishes a book, knowing it is imperfect, refusing to revisit and improve it. His friends may come to him in a hurry saying, "Did you not read the newspaper published yesterday?"

> "No, why? "
> "Because there is a criticism of your book in it."
> "I'll look at it."
> "But you have to respond to it very strongly." He laughs and says, "Why? Is there a mistake in its critique?"
> "I don't know, but the author is criticizing you out of jealousy, because he is unable to produce a comparable work himself."

> "Just slow down, my friend, until I read the critique. If I find the author has a point, I'll admit to it and will correct my error. If he is wrong, I'll show him what is right."
> "And the insult? Will you not respond to it? So-and-so repaid him in kind."
> "As if I would do something like that. The best response for one who is confident in his position is to always improve his work, for if he does so, that is the most potent response."

The most perfect person is he who acknowledges his lapses and gains from admitting his mistakes or accepting his limitations. There are those poor people who know little of science or literature other than what they make a pretense to know. If asked they answer in the manner of know-it-all, because the phrase "I don't know" is heavy upon their tongues and its meaning is heavy upon their hearts. All that a person achieves in life that expands his knowledge, and increases his experience also increases his realization of how much more there is that he still does not know and will remain occluded from him. He is like a drop of water in a great ocean—as [Imam] 'Ali said, "The leader who does not say 'I don't know' weakens his troops," or as [the caliph] 'Umar said, "If someone asked you something which you do not know, say: 'I don't know and may God have mercy on he who points out my errors'."

The written subjects upon which criticism depends are either truths, which cannot have two sides to them, or are opinions, which may include different views. For absolute truths cannot have more than one aspect, and include historical facts and accepted standards such as natural phenomena or logical rules which are dependent upon established norms. If one shows an error in such a topic to a writer or journalist, it is their duty to say in clear terms "I erred" without equivocation or excuses or elaboration. He need not overstate his apology or conjure flimsy excuses or say it was a typographical or editing error. Nor should he resort to deceptions by confirming what he said and then transform a phrase or rephrase it, for this would insult the intelligence of the reader.

For obstinacy and deviousness cannot correct an error, and will not hide the truth from people, especially when dealing with established truths. And we have no expectation of one who has erred other than for him to respond to what his conscience tells him is the right thing to do. It would be enough for him to follow the guidance of his conscience and to not argue when his pen produces an error in a particular matter. For journalists have filled sheets and wasted time with quarreling and equivocation, even when they know in their hearts that the truth is with their adversaries. But still they cannot bear to admit a mistake, so they vainly waste their time and the time of the reader, because they are too ashamed to accept what is right. The only thing they should be ashamed of is to know the truth, but not to embrace it—for how are we to move towards perfection if we are not willing to correct our errors? And whether or not we correct our errors, and whether or not we admit them, the truth will prevail over us and over our errors. For we depend upon the approval of the truth and how it improves us. This way, obstinacy is another sin that we commit against knowledge and integrity.

The motivation for obstinacy or sophistry is defending one's dignity. For one may imagine that he has been violated by the pithy or satirical phrases of the critic, and so accepting criticism weighs heavily upon him, so he turns to obstinacy. This is an excuse we may expect from the weak, but never from the great. The book that they offer is a gift to the public, for the improvement of the public, and if a critic reveals an error in it then they should accept the truth. If the criticism is painful, one should extract from it what may be useful and cast off the remainder just as you would extract gold from the earth and cast the dirt away.

As for errors of opinion, these may have two sides to them, so it is possible to debate them. There is nothing wrong with debating these because there is merit in discussing both sides of an issue with the exchange of views and scrutiny on what is best. However, it is necessary to limit the discussion to the subject at hand, to avoid diverging into personal insults, which are the weapons of the weak. What is most distressing is that we rarely see these rules observed in discussions between our writers, for they often will leave the discussion of scientific, historical, social or political matters and resort to personal insults stooping to below the standards that our intellectuals should have, as they are supposed to be leaders of thought and models of high principles. But we do not deny that over the past few decades our journalists have reached a point where they are much more rational and farther from hurling insults at each other than was the case before.

Bibliography of Zaidan's Works

Thomas Philipp

Works in each section are ordered by the date of their first appearance (given in [ ]). All Zaidan's novels and many of his other works were published in Arabic several times and translated into many languages. Authors may have used newer editions as indicated in the footnotes of their respective papers. Titles in English follow the Arabic titles.

I. Novels

1. *Al-Mamlūk al-Shārid,* riwāya tārīkhiyya (Cairo, Maṭba'at al-Hilāl, [1891]). *(The Fugitive Mamluk)*

2. *Asīr al-Mutamahdī*, riwāya tārīkhiyya (Cairo, Maṭba'at al-Hilāl, [1892]). *(Prisoner of the Mahdi)*

3. *Istibdād al-Mamālīk*, riwāya tārīkhiyya (Cairo, Maṭba'at al-Hilāl, [1893]). *(Mamluk Tyranny)*

4. *Jihād al-Muḥibbīn* (Cairo, Maṭba'at al-Hilāl, [1893]). *(The Lovers' Struggle)*

5. *Armānūsa al-Miṣriyya,* riwāya tārīkhiyya (Cairo, Maṭba'at al-Hilāl, [1896]). *(Armanusa the Egyptian)*

6. *Fatāt Ghassān,* riwāya tārīkhiyya (Cairo, Maṭba'at al-Hilāl, [1897/98]). *(The Ghassanide Damsel)*

7. *'Adhrā' Quraysh*, riwāya tārīkhiyya (Cairo, Maṭba'at al-Hilāl, [1899]). *(The Virgin of Quraysh)*

8. *Sab'at ashar Ramaḍān*, riwāya tārīkhiyya (Cairo, Maṭba'at al-Hilāl, [1900]). *(The 17th of Ramadan)*

9. *Ghādat Karbalā'*, riwāya tārīkhiyya (Cairo, Maṭba'at al-Hilāl, [1901]).
(*The Young Lady of Karbala*)

10. *Al-Ḥajjāj ibn Yūsuf* (Cairo, Maṭba'at al-Hilāl, [1902]).
(Hajji ibn Yusuf)

11. *Fatḥ al-Andalus, aw Ṭāriq ibn Ziyād,* riwāya tārīkhiyya (Cairo, Maṭba'at al-Hilāl, [1903]).
Translated into English as *The Conquest of Andalusia,* by Roger Allen, published by The Zaidan Foundation, Inc. 2011.

12. *Shārl wa 'Abd al-Raḥmān,* riwāya tārīkhiyya (Cairo, Maṭba'at al-Hilāl, [1904]).
Translated into English as *The Battle of Poitiers, Charles Martel and 'Abd al-Rahman*, by William Granara, published by The Zaidan Foundation, Inc. 2012.

13. *Abū Muslim al-Khurasānī,* riwāya tārīkhiyya (Cairo, Maṭba'at al-Hilāl, [1905]).
(*Abu Muslim of Khurasan)*

14. *Al-'Abbāsa Ukht al-Rashīd aw Nakbat al-Barāmika,* riwāya tārīkhiyya gharāmiyya (Cairo, Maṭba'at al-Hilāl, [1906]).
Translated into English as *The Caliph's Sister: Harun al-Rashid and the Fall of the Persians,* by Issa J. Boullata, published by The Zaidan Foundation, Inc. 2012.

15. *Al-Amīn wa'l-Ma'mūn,* riwāya tārīkhiyya gharāmiyya (Cairo, Maṭba'at al-Hilāl, [1907]).
Translated into English as *The Caliph's Heirs, Brothers at War: the Fall of Baghdad*, by Michael Cooperson, published by The Zaidan Foundation, Inc. 2012.

16. *'Arūs Farghāna***,** riwāya tārīkhiyya (Cairo, Maṭba'at al-Hilāl, [1908]).
(*The Bride of Farghana*)

17. *Aḥmad ibn Ṭūlūn***,** riwāya tārīkhiyya (Cairo, Maṭba'at al-Hilāl, [1909]).
(Ahmad ibn Tulun)

18. *'Abd al-Raḥmān al-Nāṣir***,** riwāya tārīkhiyya (Cairo, Maṭba'at al-Hilāl, [1910]).
(*'Abd al-Rahman, the Victor)*

19. *Al-Inqilāb al-'Uthmānī,* riwāya tārīkhiyya gharāmiyya (Cairo, Maṭba'at al-Hilāl, [1911]).
(*The Young Turk Revolution*)

20. *Fatāt al-Qayrawān,* riwāya tārīkhiyya (Cairo, Maṭba'at al-Hilāl [1912]).
(The Damsel of Kairouan)

21. *Ṣalāḥ al-Dīn al-Ayyūbī,* riwāya tārīkhiyya (Cairo, Maṭba'at al-Hilāl, [1913]).
Translated into English as *Saladin and the Assassins,* by Paul Starkey, published by The Zaidan Foundation, Inc. 2012.

22. *Shajarat al-Durr,* riwāya tārīkhiyya gharāmiyya (Cairo, Maṭba'at al-Hilāl, [1914]).
Translated into English as *The Tree of Pearls* by Samah Selim, published by Syracuse University Press, 2012.

II. Works on History

Tārīkh al-Māsūniyya al-'āmm (Cairo, Maṭba'at al-Maḥrūsa, [1889]).
(*General History of Freemasonry*)

Kitāb Tārīkh Miṣr al-ḥadīth min al-Fatḥ al-Islāmī ilā hādhā 'l-'Aṣr: ma'a Fadhlaka tārīkhiyya fī Tārīkh Miṣr al-qadīm (Cairo, Maṭba'at al-Hilāl, [1889]).
(*The Modern History of Egypt from the Islamic Conquest until this Age*)

Al-Tārīkh al-'āmm mundhu 'l-Khalīqa ilā hādhihi al-Ayyām (Beirut, s.n., [1890]).
(*A General History since Creation until Today*)

Tārīkh al-Yūnān wa'l-Rūmān (Cairo, s.n., [1899]).
(*History of Greece and Rome*)

Tārīkh Inklītirā (Cairo, Maṭba'at al-Hilāl, [1899]).
(*The History of England*)

Tārīkh al-Tamaddun al-Islāmī, 5 vols. (Cairo, Maṭba'at al-Hilāl [1902-06]).
(*The History of Islamic Civilization*)

Al-'Arab qabla 'l-Islām (Cairo, Maṭba'at al-Hilāl, [1907/8]).
(*The Arabs before Islam*)

Ṭabaqāt al-Umam aw al-Salā'il al-Bashariyya (Cairo, Maṭba'at al-Hilāl [1912]).
(The Development of Nations or the Descent of Mankind)

Miṣr al-'Uthmāniyya, editor and commentator, Muḥammad Ḥarb (Cairo, Dār al-Āfāq al-'Arabiyya, [2001/2]).
(*Ottoman Egypt*)

III. Works on Language and Literature

Al-Alfāẓ al-'Arabiyya wa'l-Falsafa al-Lughawiyya (Beirūt, Maṭba'at al-Qidīs Jāwrjiyūs, [1886]).
(*Arab Expressions and the Philosophy of Language*)

Al-Lugha al-'Arabiyya bi-'itbārihā Kā'in ḥayy khādi' li-Nāmūs al-Irtiqā' revised by Murād Kāmil (Cairo, Maṭba'at al-Hilāl, [1904]).
(*The Arabic Language as a Living Organism, subject to the Law of Evolution*)

*Kitāb Tārīkh Ādāb al-Lugha al-'Arabiyy*a (Cairo, Maṭba'at al-Hilāl, [1911-1914]).
(*The History of Arab Literature*)

IV. Other Works

Al-Hilāl (Cairo, periodical founded in 1892, published by Dār al-Hilāl to the present day).

Mukhtaṣr Jughrāfiyyat Miṣr (Cairo, Maṭba'at al-Ta'līf, [1891]).
(*A Summary of Egypt's Geography*)

Kitāb 'Ilm al-Firāsa al- hadīth aw al-Istidlāl 'alā Akhlāq al-Nās (Cairo, Maktabat al-Thaqāfa al-Dīniyya, [1901]).
(*Modern Physiognomy or the Evidence of Character*)

Ansāb al-'Arab al-qudamā' (Cairo, Maṭba'at al-Hilāl, [1906]).
(*Genealogies of the Ancient Arabs*)

Kitāb 'Ajā'ib al-Khalq (Cairo, Maṭba'at al-Hilāl, [1912]).
(*The Wonders of Creation*)

Tarājim Mashāhīr al-Sharq fī'l-Qarn al-tāsi' 'ashar (Cairo, Maṭba'at al-Hilāl, [1907]).
(*Biographies of Renowned Men from The East in the 19th Century*)

Bunāt al-Nahḍa al-'Arabiyya (Cairo, Dār al-Hilāl, [1957]).
(*The Builders of the Arab Nahda*)

V. Autobiographical

Riḥlat Jurjī Zaydān ilā Ūrubbā sanat 1912. (Cairo, publication supervised by Idārat al-Hilāl, [1923]).
(*The Journey of Jurji Zaidan to Europe in 1912*)

Mudhakkirāt Jurjī Zaydān edited by Ṣalāḥ al-Dīn al-Munajjid (Lebanon, Dār al-Kitāb al-Jadīd, [1968]).
(The Autobiography of Jurji Zaidan)

The Autobiography of Jurji Zaidan, including four letters to his son. Translated, edited, and introduced by Thomas Philipp (Washington, D.C., Three Continents Press, 1990). Also to be found in part 2 of Philipp, *Ǧurǧī Zaidān.*

Zaidan's Letters to his Son Emile, unpubl. collection. Copies were made in 1973 by Thomas Philipp in Beirut in the office of Ṣalāḥ al-Dīn al-Munajjid. The copies are with the Zaidan Foundation, Inc. The originals were donated by the Zaidan family to the Library of the American University of Beirut but cannot be located there.

Notes on Contributors

Roger Allen is a noted scholar and teacher of Arab literature and experienced translator of many Arab literary works including the Nobel-prize winning novel by Naguib Mahfouz. Most recently he translated Jurji Zaidan's novel, *The Conquest of Andalusia.* Until July 2012, he was the Sascha Jane Patterson Harvie Professor of Social Thought and Comparative Ethics, School of Arts & Sciences, Professor of Arabic & Comparative Literature, and Chair, Department of Near Eastern Languages and Civilizations, University of Pennsylvania. He served as the President, Middle East Studies Association of North America in 2008-2009.

Zaïneb Ben Lagha is Maître de conférences (Associate Professor) at the University of the Sorbonne Nouvelle in Paris. She is a specialist of modern and contemporary Arab literature. She defended her doctoral thesis in 2006 on *Le personnage historique dans l'Œuvre romanesque de Ǧurǧī Zaydān (1861-1914): Entre figure exemplaire et personnage de roman.* Author of several articles on the Arab historical novel and on the novels of Jurji Zaidan, she is co-author of a volume on *Les Expressions et les Usages de la marginalité en littérature. Orient-Occident*, forthcoming publication of Les Classiques Garnier.

Michael Cooperson is Professor of Arabic in the department of Near Eastern Languages and Cultures at the University of California, Los Angeles. He is a graduate of Harvard University and the American University in Cairo. His publications include *Classical Arabic Biography* (2000) and *Al-Ma'mun* (2005). He has translated Abdelfattah Kilito's *The Author and His Doubles* (2001), Khairy Shalaby's *Time Travels of the Man Who Sold Pickles and Sweets* (2010), and Jurji Zaidan's *The Caliph's Heirs* (2012). He is co-author, with the RRAALL group, of

Interpreting the Self: Autobiography in the Arabic literary tradition (2001); and co-editor, with Shawkat Toorawa, of *The Dictionary of Literary Biography: Arabic Literary Culture, 500-915* (2005). His interests include the cultural history of the ʻAbbasid period, time travel as a literary device, and Maltese language and literature.

Georges Corm is Professor at Saint-Joseph University, Beirut, Institute of Political Sciences and international economic consultant. He is the author of numerous books about Middle Eastern contemporary history, among which are *Fragmentation of the Middle East* (London, Unwyn Hyman, 1985) and *History of the Middle East From Antiquity to the Present Day* (London, Garnett Publishing, 2010). He is also a noted commentator on political and economic affairs in the Arab world who served as Minister of Finance in Lebanon from December 1998 to October 2000 and as Advisor to the Governor of the Lebanese Central Bank from 1980 to 1985, in addition to consulting widely with national, regional and international institutions such as the World Bank, the European Union, ESCWA, ILO, FAO and UNCTAD.

Anne-Laure Dupont is Maître de conférences (Associate Professor) of Modern and Contemporary History at Paris-Sorbonne University. Her interests lie in the cultural history of the Arab world and Middle East in the nineteenth and twentieth centuries. She published an intellectual biography of Jurji Zaidan, *Ǧurǧī Zaydān 1861–1914: Écrivain réformiste et témoin de la Renaissance arabe* (Damas, Institut français du Proche-Orient, 2006) and published a number of articles on him. She edited two review issues: "Débats intellectuels au Moyen-Orient dans l'entre-deux-guerres." (with Catherine Mayeur-Jaouen), *Revue des mondes musulmans et de la Méditerranée* (2002) pp. 95-98; and "Islam et l'éducation au temps des réformes. Systèmes scolaires et enjeux de l'enseignement au Proche-Orient et en Afrique du Nord aux XIXe et XXe siècles," *Cahiers de la Méditerranée* 75 (Dec. 2007). She is now working on the reformist movement in nineteenth-century Tunisia.

Marwa Elshakry, Associate Professor of History at Columbia University, is the author of the forthcoming *Reading Darwin in Arabic* (Univ. of Chicago Press), a reader on *Science, Race and Imperialism,* vol. 6 of Pickering and Chatto's *Victorian Science and Literature* series (Alexandria VA, Alexandria Street Press, 2012) and several articles, including: "When Science became Western: Historiographical Reflections," *Isis* 101 (2010) pp. 98-110; "Knowledge in Motion: The Cultural Politics of Modern Science Translations in Arabic," *Isis* 99 (2008) pp. 701-731; "The Exegesis of Science in Twentieth Century Arabic Interpretations of the Quran" in *Nature and Scripture in the Abrahamic Religions:1700-Present* edited by Jitse M. van der Meer and Scott Mandelbrote (Leiden, E.J.Brill, 2008); and "The Gospel of Science and American Evangelism in Beirut," *Past and Present* 104 (2007) pp. 173-214.

William Granara is Professor of Arabic at the Gordon Gray Endowment at Harvard. He teaches Arabic language and literature and presently directs the Department of Near Eastern Languages and Civilizations' program in modern languages. He studied Arabic at Georgetown University and received his PhD in Arabic and Islamic Studies at the University of Pennsylvania. He writes on cross-cultural encounters between Islam and Christendom throughout the Middle Ages, specializing in the Muslim periods of Sicily and Spain. In addition, he lectures and writes on contemporary Arabic literature and has published numerous translations and critical articles on Egyptian and North African fiction. His work on literary criticism focuses on post-colonialism and cross cultural poetics. Most recently, Professor Granara translated Jurji Zaidan's *The Battle of Poitiers.*

Jens Hanssen is Associate Professor of Middle Eastern and Mediterranean History at the University of Toronto. He received his D.Phil. from Oxford University in 2001. He is the author of several books including *Fin de Siècle Beirut* (Oxford, Clarendon Press; New York, Oxford Univ. Press, 2005) and the co-editor of two volumes: *Arab*

Provincial Capitals in the Late Ottoman Empire, (Würzburg: Ergon in Kommission, 2002); and *History, Space and Social Conflict in Beirut* (Beirut, Orient Institut, 2005). He is also the co-editor of the forthcoming *Oxford Handbook of Contemporary Middle Eastern and North African History.* During his visit to Baghdad in June 2003, he filmed a short documentary (posted on Youtube.com) on academic life in Iraq after the U.S. invasion. He has recently published in *The New Cambridge History of Islam* (2010), in the *International Journal of Middle East Studies* (2011) and *Critical Inquiry.* He is currently conducting research on the intersection between German-Jewish and Arab intellectual histories. He also investigates questions of intellectual history of the Middle East in general and, in particular, the legacy of the nineteenth century Arabic revival and reform movement on contemporary political developments.

Thomas Philipp, Professor (retired) für Politik und Zeitgeschichte des Nahen Ostens am Institut für Politische Wissenschaft at Universität Erlangen-Nürnberg, received his Ph.D. in 1971 from UCLA and graduated from Hebrew University in 1966. He taught at the University of Shiraz/Iran and at Harvard University. He is a leading expert on the life and thought of Jurji Zaidan as well as the development of Arab thought in the nineteenth and early twentieth centuries. His study, *Ǧurǧī Zaidān: His Life and Thought,* was published in 1979, supplemented by various articles on different aspects of Zaidan's work. He edited the English version of *Al-Jabarti's History of Egypt* and authored books on *The Syrians in Egypt, 1725-1975* and on *Acre, The Rise and Fall of a Palestinian City, 1731-1831.* He published the proceedings of several conferences on the "Syrian Land—Bilad al-Sham". His most recent book is *Jurji Zaidan and the Foundations of Arab Nationalism* (New York, Syracuse Univ. Press, 2014).

Ismail Serageldin is the Founding Director of the Library of Alexandria and also chairs the Boards of Directors for the Library of Alexandria's affiliated research institutes and museums. The Memory of Modern Egypt Series was one of the major projects spearheaded by Dr Serageldin at the Library. It documents the history of Egypt in the last two hundred years. As part of this project, the five year Dar al-Hilal Documentation project was completed in January 2012, on the occasion of the one hundredth and fiftieth anniversary of the birth of Jurji Zaidan. The first phase digitized the whole collection of *al-Hilal* Magazine. In the second phase, the Catalogue on *Dār al-Hilāl Madrasat al-Tanwīr* (*Dar al-Hilal: A School of Enlightenment*) was published.

Ismail Serageldin is Professor of the International Chair Savoirs Contre Pauvreté (Knowledge Against Poverty) at the Collège de France, Paris (2010-2011). He has been decorated as Chevalier of the Legion d'Honneur (France) and as Commander of the Order of Arts and Letters (France) and the Order of the Rising Sun (Japan). He serves as Chair and Member of a number of advisory committees for academic research, scientific and international institutions and civil society efforts which includes the American Philosophical Society, The US National Academy of Sciences (PW Medal winner 2011), the American Academy for Arts and Sciences, the Institut d'Egypte (Egyptian Academy of Science), TWAS (Academy of Sciences for the Developing World), the Indian National Academy of Agricultural Sciences and the European Academy of Sciences and Arts. He is former Chairman, Consultative Group on International Agricultural Research (CGIAR, 1994-2000), Founder and former Chairman, the Global Water Partnership (GWP, 1996-2000) and the Consultative Group to Assist the Poorest (CGAP), a microfinance program (1995-2000). He was also Distinguished Professor at Wageningen University in the Netherlands and the American University in Cairo (2000-2001). Dr Serageldin has also served in a number of capacities at the World Bank, including as Vice President for Environmentally and Socially Sustainable Development (1992-1998) and for Special Programs (1998-2000). He has published over sixty books and monographs and over two hundred papers on a variety of topics including biotechnology, rural development, sustainability, and the value of science to society. He holds a Bachelor of Science degree in engineering from Cairo

University and a Master's degree and PhD from Harvard University and has received twenty nine honorary doctorates.

George C Zaidan obtained his PhD from Harvard University in 1967 in Development Economics after doing his undergraduate degree in Law at Cairo University and in International Economics at the London School of Economics. Between 1967 and 1998 he worked at the World Bank in various managerial and professional positions traveling to more than fifty countries where he was involved with programs of development assistance in various intercultural settings. Since retiring from the World Bank he has been actively involved as a consultant to various international and regional organizations such as UNDP, the African Development Bank and the International Fund for Agricultural Development. He grew up in Egypt and his family came originally from Lebanon. His family was centrally involved in the intellectual development of the Arab progressive movement that began in the late nineteenth and twentieth century in the Arab world.

Pictures at the Jurji Zaidan Symposium

held at the

Library of Congress

June 5, 2012

To listen to the oral presentations at the Symposium summarizing the papers included in this volume visit the Zaidan Foundation website at:

www.zaidanfoundation.org

or see the Library of Congress Webcast in two parts:

1. Morning Session at:
http://www.loc.gov/today/cyberlc/feature_wdesc.php?rec=5576

and

2. Afternoon Session at:
http://www.loc.gov/today/cyberlc/feature_wdesc.php?rec=5575

Mary-Jane Deeb, Chief of the African and Middle Eastern Division at the Library of Congress, delivering her Opening Remarks

George C. Zaidan being Interviewed on TV

George C. Zaidan delivering the opening address
with Mary-Jane Deeb looking on

Ambassadors Clovis Maksoud, Mohammad
Al-Hussaini and Hussein Hassouna (R to L)

Hada and George C. Zaidan; Hilary Bowker
and George Shukri Zaidan (L to R)

Jens Hanssen delivers his paper as Anne-Laure Dupont listens intently

Anne-Laure Dupont presents her paper as Marwa Elshakry takes notes and Mary-Jane Deeb listens

Marwa Elshakry delivering her paper with Anne-Laure Dupont and Jens Hanssen listening

Zaïneb Ben Lagha's paper is read by George S. Zaidan with Roger Allen looking on

William Granara discusses Jurji Zaidan's Andalusian novels

Michael Cooperson on the influence of Zaidan's novels on the media

Thomas Philipp wraps it all with an Overview of the Symposium

www.ingramcontent.com/pod-product-compliance
Lightning Source LLC
Chambersburg PA
CBHW060223100726
47907CB00003B/489

9780984843541